WOMEN PREACHING

WOMEN PREACHING

Theology and Practice Through the Ages

EUNJOO MARY KIM

WIPF & STOCK · Eugene, Oregon

To three Korean women —
Kyung Sook Jung, my mother,
who planted a seed of the Christian faith in me;
Reverend Ok Soon Kim,
who watered my faith with her preaching;
Reverend Doctor Sang Chang,
who helped me bear the fruits of my faith.

Wipf and Stock Publishers
199 W 8th Ave, Suite 3
Eugene, OR 97401

Women Preaching
Theology and Practice Through the Ages
By Kim, Eunjoo M.
Copyright©2004 Pilgrim Press
ISBN 13: 978-1-60608-903-3
Publication date 6/18/2009
Previously published by Pilgrim Press, 2004

This limited edition licensed by special permission of The Pilgrim Press.

CONTENTS

Foreword		vii
Preface		xi
One	A Theological Reflection on Preaching from a Woman's Perspective	1
Two	Preaching the Risen Christ: Women Preachers in Scripture and the Early Church	22
Three	Preaching as Subversive Rhetoric: Women Preachers of the Medieval and Postmedieval Church	48
Four	The Authority of Preaching: Women Preachers from the Reformation to the Early Twentieth Century	79
Five	Preaching and the Politics of God: Korean Women Preachers during the Colonial and Postcolonial Eras	118
Conclusion	Partnership in Preaching	157
Sermon 1	Stories after Silence	161
Sermon 2	Could We Sing the Lord's Song?	168
Sermon 3	Have You Ever Imagined...?	174
Notes		183
Index		205

FOREWORD

IN ANY HUMAN GROUP there are those who get all the attention and those who go unnoticed. There are the talkers, and there are the silent ones, the prominent and the ignored, those who command center stage and those on the margin, the chief players and the minor cast. No matter how we characterize the distinction, it inevitably leads to a limited and distorted view of reality. Groups too often believe that the voices they have always heard give a sufficient account of all that really matters.

Sometimes, however, the pattern is broken. A new leader emerges and helps the silenced to speak. Those on the margin find their voice, and then their contribution is honored and treated as significant. Things we had assumed become less self-evident. Things we had never known startle us with their freshness and depth. Reality begins to change.

At this point a great choice confronts everyone: Will the group panic and try to restore its old patterns? Or will it have the courage to strike out in new ways and to rejoice at the rich new possibilities that lie ahead?

The church has been struggling with just such a decision for the last thirty or more years. As the number of women in theological education has surged, as more and more women have been ordained to ministries of Word and Sacrament, and as feminist and womanist theologies have challenged male-centered accounts of Christianity, the church has lurched between resistance and acceptance of women as preachers. Eunjoo Kim speaks to this historic situation with wisdom, grace, and theological acumen.

Through her moving account of women preachers from ancient times until the present day, Eunjoo Kim draws out perspectives and insights that enlarge and enrich our understanding of who God is and what God is doing and what the implications are for preaching now and in the future. By the time I finished reading the book, I knew in deeper ways what I have been learning from women scholars and students during my twenty-five years of teaching homiletics: namely, that the church needs to accept women preachers fully and completely as a matter of justice and as a theological necessity. Their experience, perspective, and witness are essential to the church's proclamation because they reveal how the Spirit is moving through women's lives and thought, through their varied modes of knowing and expression.

The strength of Kim's work lies not only in the substance of what she says, but also in the multiple methods by which she recovers voices of women preachers whose names have either been unknown to us or only vaguely present to our awareness. Kim employs a balanced mixture of close literary readings and historical interpretation, placing the women preachers in their particular social context. Out of her analysis emerges the concept of "subversive rhetoric," a form of ironic expression that women preachers have used to cut through the tangles of patriarchal pretension, especially when using a more confrontational idiom would put the women's very lives at risk.

Along with her rhetorical analysis Kim demonstrates that the homiletic of women preachers expands our definition of preaching. Not limiting herself to sermons from the pulpit, she traces how letters, poems, testimonials, teaching, public actions on behalf of justice, and the witness made while being imprisoned and tortured all constitute the legacy of women's preaching. This much broader, inclusive understanding of preaching complements Kim's insistence on our opening ourselves to a more expansive understanding of God and God's work in the world. A God who is greater than the God of patriarchy requires a homiletic that is greater than men delivering sermons from a pulpit.

Kim's theological wisdom has practical implications for us who preach now, women and men alike. Her history of women's preaching feeds a more expansive homiletic that matches our ever-widening sense of who God is. Kim argues powerfully for a more inclusive, communal, and poetic homiletic that is grounded in the women's history she has recovered and in the God that history reveals.

William James once affirmed the varieties of religious experience and belief as a way of drawing us more closely to "the total human consciousness of the divine." Although James has a great insight, all of his immediate examples are men! By exploring the history of women's preaching, Kim helps us claim more fully the truth that glimmered in James's writing. She leads us toward a homiletic that is more than a catch-all of methods. Kim uses preaching from a woman's perspective to make us fully alive to the Spirit wherever She is moving through the human community. Instead of a church where male voices dominate, we hear as well the voices of women. Listening to them preach, we receive more fully "the total human consciousness of the divine," and we hear more completely the wisdom of the Holy One who is addressing us through all of her creatures.

THOMAS H. TROEGER
Iliff School of Theology

PREFACE

WRITING A BOOK about women's preaching is neither new nor surprising. Since the late twentieth century, several books about women's preaching have been published that have greatly contributed to the field of homiletics. Supported by a variety of scholarly works in the area of feminist theology, most books on women's preaching address how to enhance women's voices in the Christian pulpit, given that their voices have long been marginalized in the church. Moreover, today's historians, particularly female scholars, acknowledge the weaknesses present in the history of Christian preaching when narrated solely through the male voice. They insist that we should no longer be content to identify only androcentric traditions within Christianity. Assuming that there must be an enduring tradition that maintains the equality of women's proclamation, some historians are diligently searching for information about women preachers long forgotten, and the lives of these women have been detailed in recently published homiletical books.

What is lacking in current publications, however, is comprehensive theological reflection on women's preaching traditions. Even the books that introduce women preachers in church history simply collect and disperse stories about them rather than attempting a historical reconstruction of preaching from a woman's perspective and providing directions for the future of homiletics from a woman's point of view. It is crucial to develop a new tradition of preaching through theological and historical reflection on the experiences of women preachers from which a new generation of preachers can learn about preaching from this new perspective.

Considering this weakness in the study of women's preaching, this book makes a very distinct contribution to the development of homiletics because it integrates the history of women preachers with theological reflection. The goals of this book are to provide both a broader and deeper basis for the theology of preaching as well as practical ways in which preachers can improve their own preaching from a woman's perspective. In order to fulfill these goals, *Women Preaching* searches for women's experiences of preaching throughout church history — from the biblical era to the contemporary period — and uses them as primary resources to broaden and deepen our theological understanding of Christian preaching. The research in this book regarding women preachers stretches its dimensions from women of the Western church to women of the Eastern church, as well as to women of Asian and Latin American churches.

Chapter 1 begins by describing a changing situation in contemporary Protestant churches and theological schools, which are leaning toward gender inclusivity, and proposes new theological directions for the future of homiletics from a woman's perspective. Christian preaching should be an ongoing, cross-cultural conversation, contributing to the revelation of the wholeness of God, by helping listeners continuously experience the risen Christ, that is, the transforming power of the life-giving Spirit of God who works in the margins of society.

The next four chapters of this book relate the history of women's preaching to theological issues raised from the experiences of contemporary women preachers. Chapter 2 discusses what it means to preach the risen Christ in our contemporary context, reflecting on the experiences of the first women preachers in the Bible and the early church. Chapter 3 focuses on the issue of inclusive language, tracing women preachers in the medieval and postmedieval Roman Catholic Church who were pioneers in using feminine images of God in their sermons and other theological pieces. Chapter 4 develops theological discourse about authority in preaching based on the experiences of women preachers in the Protestant Church from the Reformation to the early twentieth century. Chapter 5 explores the political nature of Christian preaching in connection to the experiences of women preachers in Asia during the colonial and postcolonial period and reminds readers that the task of preaching is to participate in the politics of God in solidarity with women and other oppressed people in the world.

The integration in these chapters of the history of women's preaching with contemporary theological issues enables readers to experience the distinctive voices and particular messages of influential preachers from a given time. Readers may understand not only how women's preaching has reached its present state but also what may have been lost along the way. Furthermore, the integration of history with theology provides readers with new and creative insights into developing their own preaching from a woman's perspective, because recovering our past from a woman's point of view is the essential step to envisioning the future of Christian preaching.

Chapter 6 proposes that the future of homiletics should be more inclusive and egalitarian by building partnerships with God, the congregation, and the world. Preaching from a woman's perspective envisions an egalitarian structure of the church and a democratic environment of preaching by breaking the walls between the center and margins, between both women and men and between clergy and laity.

Following chapter 6, I have included three of my sermons written from a woman's perspective, as samples through which readers can taste the spiritual food prepared according to one woman's recipe.

This book is the result of collaborative work with my students, colleagues, friends, and family. My students at the Iliff School of Theology, particularly the women students who have taken my course, A History and Practice of Preaching from the Woman's Perspective, have been very willing to share their experiences of preaching in class and to openly discuss their views on my lectures and course readings. My students actually compelled me to write this book from my lectures, sermons, and course materials. I am grateful to the Iliff School of Theology for granting me a research leave for the winter quarter of 2003, which gave me time to organize, expand, and create the materials for this book. I am particularly grateful to my two research assistants, Virginia H. Trabulsi and Sara S. Winn. This project has their distinct imprint on it from beginning to end. I also thank Steven Moore and other D.Min. students for their thorough reading of my manuscript and their feedback.

I wish to thank my colleagues Thomas Troeger and Richard Ward for inspiring me with their creative theological and homiletical insights and for their undying support of this project. I am also grateful to Richard Valantasis, Albert Hernández, and David Maldonado for helping me better understand the Latin and Spanish phrases I encountered in my readings. I would like to express my gratitude to Robert Fukada, who teaches homiletics in Japan, for providing me with the information about Japanese women preachers; his efforts made it possible for me to interview some of them during the summer of 2001.

I am indebted to my friend Judy Schiller for her meticulous and skilled work on the draft of my manuscript, to make it as clear as possible. I am deeply grateful to Merle Marie Troeger for translating Latin material into English for me. I feel profound thanksgiving for my friends Kyung Mi Park and Young Joo Park, and my sister, Myung Hae Kim, who live in Korea. They arranged my interviews with Korean women preachers during my visit to Korea in the summer of 2001 and airmailed books in Korean to me that I desperately needed to read.

I am profoundly appreciative of the joy and love that my husband, Joseph, and my daughter, Dorothy, have given me during this strenuous period of writing. They are truly the biggest blessings in my life! Without their patience and encouragement, I would have never been able to finish this project.

Finally, I wish to express my gratitude to my editor, Ulrike R. M. Guthrie, and to the publisher at the Pilgrim Press, Timothy G. Staveteig, who helped complete the final production of this project by offering wise and knowledgeable advice.

Chapter One

A THEOLOGICAL REFLECTION ON PREACHING FROM A WOMAN'S PERSPECTIVE

THROUGHOUT THE LONG HISTORY of the Christian Church, preaching has been traditionally understood as a "men-only" ministry. Although women contributed significantly to the preaching ministry of the early church, soon thereafter they were officially excluded from the pulpit when the Christian Church was institutionalized based on a patriarchal structure. Powerful women of the Spirit have, however, continued to exercise their spiritual leadership through preaching in spite of the oppression and persecution by misogynist church leaders and the patriarchal systems of the church. As the following chapters of this book demonstrate, the history of Christianity is rich with examples of Spirit-filled women preachers. These women have been pioneers of the liberating movements of humanity. Women preachers from the early church period through the medieval and modern eras to contemporary times have led social and ecclesial reformations and freedom movements in varying sociopolitical, economic, and cultural contexts. We find these women not only in Europe and the United States but also in other parts of the world, including Latin America and Asia.

Women preachers have long been regarded by the traditional patriarchal church as either heretical or unconstitutional. Consequently, church historians have excluded women preachers from their research and marginalized their preaching ministry. The voices of women preachers have long been suppressed in the ecclesial and academic arenas; consequently, only male theologians and preachers have played major roles in the field of homiletics. In the center of the homiletical field, we find such famous male theologians as St. Augustine, Alan of Lille, Martin Luther, John Calvin, Philips Brooks, John Broadus, Karl Barth, and others. The homiletical books written by these male scholars — from their androcentric perspectives — were used as major textbooks for teaching homiletics courses at theological schools around the world until the late twentieth century.

A NEW SITUATION

Contemporary Protestant preaching in the United States, however, is facing a new situation. The Christian pulpit is now relatively egalitarian; it is no longer privileged space for male clergy only. Moreover, the development of homiletical theories is no longer limited to discussions of male scholars but is now gender inclusive. As a result, the field of homiletics must address the issues of preaching based on women's experiences.

This dramatic shift in today's Protestant Church and theological education in the United States is the result of at least three changes. First of all, the number of women seminarians is increasing, spurred by some mainline churches ordaining women to become ministers of the Word and Sacrament. According to a 1992 survey by the Association of Theological Schools, the proportion of women enrolled every year steadily increased from 1972 to 1992, rising from 10.2 percent in 1972 to 31.1 percent in 1992. In 1993, 61 percent of the recipients of the Master of Divinity from the Yale Divinity School were women, and other divinity schools and seminaries such as Princeton and the Iliff School of Theology have more or equal even numbers of male and female students.[1] The 1999–2000 ATS *Fact Book* shows that the number of women enrolled in all degree programs increased 15.7 percent from 1995 to 1999, and that overall, women in 1999 constituted 34.2 percent of the total enrollment. Moreover, while the percentage of male M.Div. students declined from 72.4 percent to 69.5 percent from 1995 to

1999, the percentage of female M.Div. students increased from 27.6 to 30.5 percent during the same time period.[2]

Given this change in the student population at many seminaries, preaching classes have been challenged by the increased number of female students and their demands. These students are looking for female role models to enhance their authentic voices as women when they stand in the pulpit, rather than merely copying the traditional male-centered theologies and masculine styles of preaching. This new gender situation and educational demands have required theological schools to welcome women's perspectives in teaching and learning how to preach.

The demand for women's education is not unique to the United States. When I visited the United Theological College in Bangalore, India, in 1999, I attended a morning chapel service, where, amazingly, a woman student preached the sermon. After the service, I asked an attending female faculty member how she felt about the preaching that morning. She said, "I was unhappy about her preaching. In fact, whenever I hear females preaching in the chapel, I am always upset because they simply copy men's preaching style. They speak like men, gesture like men, and even make their voices sound like men's. It is so sad that our school cannot provide students with a more gender-balanced education and that there are few female role models for women seminarians in India."

The second change in today's Protestant Church and theological education is the increasing number of sermons being published by women clergy, as well as their active participation in the preaching ministry. Nowadays, many mainline Protestant churches have opened their pulpits to women, and the number of female clergy has increased dramatically since 1970.[3] Clergywomen are actively participating in church leadership, serving as chaplains in hospitals, schools, industry, the military, and prisons, and as associate or senior pastors in local churches. We can even find some women who are serving as district superintendents and bishops within church hierarchies. Their preaching in churches and other liturgical contexts, along with their published sermons, enriches Christian pulpits by suggesting that preaching should include women's viewpoints and insights. The particular experiences of women preachers and the unique characteristics of their preaching, which are rooted in their creativity and authenticity, challenge male preachers and homileticians to reappropriate the value of women's preaching and to create new theologies and methodologies for developing homiletics from a woman's perspective.

The third change in the contemporary Protestant Church and theological education is the emergence of women homileticians. The development of feminist theology and women's studies, covering such varied areas as biblical hermeneutics, psychology, communication, church history, and soon, has encouraged some female theologians to find women's voices in the field of homiletics. Since 1989, when Christine Smith first published her book *Weaving the Sermon: Preaching in a Feminist Perspective*, which is based on feminist theology, other female scholars such as Carol M. Norén, Lee McGee, Lucy A. Rose, Mary D. Turner, and Mary L. Hudson have also written homiletical books based on a woman's perspective.[4] Their works have forced homiletical theories to be more gender inclusive by participating in theoretical conversations about preaching as well as teaching preaching from women's perspectives.

In this changing climate of today's church and theological education, one of the urgent tasks in the field of homiletics is to develop homiletical theories and practices from a woman's perspective. Preaching from a woman's perspective includes such specific issues as representing women's particular preaching experiences, unveiling women preachers throughout church history, analyzing women's ways of learning and communicating, developing the concept of authority based on the characteristics of women's leadership and exercising this authority, applying feminist pedagogies for teaching preaching classes, and so forth. The development of preaching from a woman's perspective is crucial for many reasons: first, for the practical reason that we must train women to become better women preachers; second, for the political reason that the Christian pulpit should be egalitarian by sharing the preaching leadership with women; and finally, but most important, for the theological reason that preaching from a woman's perspective is responsible for directing the future of homiletics. The study of preaching from a woman's perspective has comprehensive and profound theological accountability for the future of homiletics in relation to three theological themes: preaching as a voice from the margins, preaching as a cross-cultural conversation, and preaching toward the wholeness of God. The following three sections explore this theological accountability of preaching from a woman's perspective, focusing on each theological theme in turn.

PREACHING AS A VOICE FROM THE MARGINS

Preaching from a woman's perspective is distinct in that the medium for understanding truth is through women's particular experiences, which are marginalized in both sociocultural and historical contexts. Studying female preachers in both the past and present reveals that women preachers often use their own life experiences or other women's particular faith journeys as evidence that God is present and at work in the margins of society in order to transform the communities to which they belong.

Feminist theories and women's studies affirm that women's experiences have a common denominator: "marginality." From the ancient times to the present in most parts of the world, women have lived in the margins of society as victims of misogynist attitudes and patriarchal systems. Patriarchal societies, "where men have controlled the conceptual arena and have determined social values and the structure of institutions,"[5] have created "gender ideology," in which women have been defined as senseless, incompetent, less intelligent, substandard, petty, evil, destructive, and lacking responsibility. Gender ideology has been used to justify women's inferiority and to continue the subordination and suffering of women living in the margins of society.

In the Christian tradition, church fathers and other male theologians indoctrinated gender ideology. Tertullian, St. Jerome, St. John Chrysostom, Martin Luther, and others affirmed women's inferiority based on their misogynist interpretation of biblical passages. They regarded women as dangerous descendants of Eve, who caused all the trouble in the world and instigated misfortunes and disasters (Gen. 2–3). For example, Tertullian blames women as follows:

> You are the devil's gateway... the first deserter of the divine law; you are she who persuaded him whom the devil was not valiant enough to attack. You destroyed so easily God's image, man. On account of your desert — that is, death — even the son of God had to die.[6]

Based on this gender ideology, the church admitted women's subordination and suffering as natural and, therefore, fitting that they should be punished for their deeds. Later ecclesial teachings, such as the doctrine of atonement, tranquilized women into accepting their suffering and pain as the path to transcendence. In other words, present suffering ensures future bliss. Women were taught by the patriarchal church to remain in the margins of society and endure their suffering as a way to reach their personal salvation, that is, going to heaven after death, rather than struggling for their well-being in the mainstream of society.

Women's marginalized experiences in patriarchal, misogynist societies is not simply related to their identity but also to their right to live as social beings. Women have long been denied the right to vote, the right to earn a substantive living commensurate with effort, the right to choose whether or not to bear children, and so on. Even in the United States, that women were not allowed to vote until the 1920s. The passage of the Nineteenth Amendment to the U.S. Constitution (the Woman's Rights Amendment) was the result of the cumulative struggles of such pioneer feminists as Elizabeth Cady Stanton, Susan B. Anthony, Lucretia Mott, and Anna H. Shaw.

The misogynist picture of women is still very much alive in today's media. We readily find distorted images of women in TV stories and commercials, letters to the editor in newspapers, commentaries in books and magazines, political campaign rhetoric, in-group jokes, and unfortunately, even in church sermons.[7] Contemporary women exist on the margins of societies and in hostile environments, experiencing sexism, misogyny, and violence in everyday life, regardless of their class and race. In a multiracial and multicultural society such as that of the United States, minority women experience marginalization more seriously than minority men and suffer more than men because they are regarded as less human than men. Margaret Miles states that in the United States, one of the most developed countries today, a woman is raped once every six minutes and is beaten once every eighteen minutes. She also reports that 20 to 30 percent of girls now twelve years of age and older will be victims of a violent sexual assault sometime in their lives. In Massachusetts, a woman is murdered by her husband or partner every twenty-two days. Unfortunately, this bleak scenario is even more depressing in that the likelihood of women becoming victims of violence and/or sexual crimes is far worse in poor families and in developing countries.[8]

Preaching from a woman's perspective takes seriously women's common experience of marginality and is responsible for representing their marginalized voices in the pulpit. Mary Turner and Mary Hudson say that "the world only perceives half-truth" because the voice of "one half of the human family (the female half)" is repressed.[9] Turner and Hudson explain the significance of representing the voice from the margins in terms of a "theology of voice," which they describe as follows:

> The metaphor of "voice" suggests that the Holy Spirit still speaks, gives voice to ongoing revelation in the lives of many who have been silenced, often in the name of the very God who is thus represented.... A theology of voice for preaching, then, suggests that the preacher must listen carefully to the text and, *also*, to revelations that come to her through her experience in the world. The word is contextualized through her understanding and those of her community. The speaking/listening God continues to be present, bringing new insight, challenging a fraudulent finality of understanding.[10]

Preaching as a voice from the margins represents the silenced voices of women in a twofold manner: On the one hand, it represents the voice of lamentation, the cries of women from the margins, with a commitment to liberating oppressed women from the vicious circle of victimization in a patriarchal society. To achieve this goal of liberation, the priority for preaching from a woman's perspective is to analyze women's oppressed experiences in the margins and to indict brutal and violent misogyny, racism, classism, and homophobia before God and God's people.

On the other hand, preaching from a woman's perspective allows an understanding of the margins where women have lived, constructively as well as negatively. The margins are not merely a condition of passive and self-negating victimization by the dominant center, but the margins also have the potential of creating a new reality. In her book *Feminist Theory: From Margin to Center* bell hooks describes her experience of marginality as an African American woman not merely as negative but also constructive because the margin she and her people belong to is a place where she can experience a new reality.

> To be in the margin is to be part of the whole but outside the main body. As black Americans living in a small Kentucky town, the railroad tracks were a daily reminder of our marginality. Across those tracks were paved streets, stores we could not enter, restaurants we could not eat in, and people we could not look directly in the face. Across those tracks was a world we could work in as maids, as janitors, as prostitutes, as long as it was in a service capacity.... We focused our attention on the center as well as on the margin. We understood both. This mode of seeing reminded us of the existence of a whole universe, a main body made up of both margin and center.... This sense of wholeness, impressed upon our consciousness by the structure of our daily lives, provided us an oppositional world view — a mode of seeing unknown to most of our oppressors, that sustained us, aided us in our struggle to transcend poverty and despair, strengthened our sense of self and our solidarity.... This lived experience may shape our consciousness in such a way that our world view differs from those who have a degree of privilege (however relative within the existing system).... Black women recognize the special vantage point our marginality gives us and make use of this perspective to criticize the dominant racist, classist, sexist hegemony as well as to envision and create a counter-hegemony.[11]

hooks believes that the margins to which African American women and men belong are the loci where "an ethic of communalism, shared responsibility, and mutuality" is practiced collaboratively.[12]

The margins of society are the "creative core,"[13] where we experience the dynamic life-giving power of God. Because the margins are where suffering and pain are severely experienced, those places can also be the places where the Spirit of God is at work in transforming the world. The scriptures attest that God is especially present in the margins, "in the least expected place, in the midst of sinners in the company of the poor, in the deep hiddenness of the cross,"[14] to work together with humanity to transform the world. God's incarnation in Jesus of Nazareth affirms this: Jesus lived in the margin, not as a victim but as a liberated person. He saw and thought of himself as someone from the margin and understood things from the perspective of marginality. For example, with regard to women, who were also marginalized in the society of Jesus's time, Jesus overturned the acceptable boundaries of society and entered into friendship with women in his openness toward women, by calling them to become his disciples (cf. Luke 8:1-3; Matt. 28:1-10; Mark 16:1-8; John 20:1-18, etc.), discussing theological issues with and for them (cf. Matt. 15:21-28; 20:20-28; Luke 7:36-50; 21:1-4; John 4:1-42; 8:1-11; 11:1-44, etc.), and working miracles and signs for them (cf. Matt. 8:14-15; Mark 5:21-43; Luke 7:11-17, etc). Through his life, death, and resurrection, Jesus lived an exemplary life, which has brought reconciliation between the margins and the center by breaking down the walls between these groups. Jesus's marginal life invites everyone, even those who belong to the dominant center of a society, to give up their vested interests and live in the margins, the creative new center, as God's partners in the reconciliation and transformation of the world.

Therefore, preaching from a woman's perspective represents not only the cries of the oppressed from the margins but also the amazing experiences of a new reality created in the margins. The task of a preacher is to discover not only the negative experiences of the marginalized but also the "sources, images, and visions of new ways of being human, of loving, of living, and [finding] God working in these sources, images, and visions to transform the 'main body made up of both margin and center.'"[15] By making these discoveries, the preacher proclaims the *basileia* (dominion) of God as an alternative to the old world order, which is rooted in patriarchal power over economic, racial, and gender realities. Preaching as a voice from the margins gives listeners new ways to listen, new eyes to see, and new possibilities to envision reconciliation between the margins and the center. Preaching from the margins invites listeners to move toward creative new margins, the real center, where the Spirit of God is present and at work, to participate as God's partners in the transforming work of God.

PREACHING AS A CROSS-CULTURAL CONVERSATION

While preaching from a woman's perspective has its theological accountability in the voice from the margins, it does not totalize the experiences of women but instead considers them distinct and concrete. Any experience of one group, such as the group of European American, Christian, middle-class, heterosexual women, cannot represent all women's experiences among those who are living in different social locations. As Sheila Davaney points out, there is no "experience in general." Rather, a woman's experience is contextual because it is "a social product," or "historically circumscribed experience and knowledge" relative to its particular sociopolitical and cultural contexts.[16]

Preaching is a theological act that publicly discusses God based on a particular historical and cultural experience of both the preacher and the listeners. Preaching from a woman's perspective acknowledges the significance of its contextuality. The history of women's preaching, explored in the following chapters of this book, clearly shows that women preachers have dealt with particular theological issues generated in their particular historical and cultural contexts. Their sermons reveal their distinctive experiences based on gender, race, and class in their different historical and social locations. Women preachers have spoken of the truth from their particular experiences and provided alternative visions for the future of their particular communities.

In a similar manner, preaching from a woman's perspective gives a voice to all liberating messages in a concrete context. The preacher is called "to stand and speak in [her] time and place, not with complete knowledge or within a totalized theory, but between the faith of God's community and the grace of being in solidarity with the world in the Word."[17] Thus, preaching from a woman's perspective has its theological accountability in developing a contextual approach to the proclamation of the gospel. What types of contextual theology and methodological approaches are relevant to preaching from a woman's perspective?

In his book *The New Catholicity: Theology between the Global and the Local* Robert Schreiter explains two different approaches to contextual theology based on two different definitions of context. The first approach to contextual theology is based on the definition of context as "the integrated concept of culture."[18] Context as the integrated concept of culture is often construed as local culture or social location, including the local traditions and belief systems. The term "contextual" is identified as local, and contextual theology as "local theology." Contextual theology as local theology presumes "distinctiveness and relative boundedness of culture," and aims to form integrity and generalization of a culture in a particular context.[19]

Contextual theology as local theology is applied in Leonora Tisdale's concept of "contextual preaching." In her book *Preaching as Local Theology and Folk Art*, Tisdale defines context as a particular "subculture" of a congregation, composed of "idiom," that is, "a unique web of signs and symbols" built upon common lifestyles, worldviews, assumptions, and values.[20] Accordingly, contextual preaching is "local theology," which is a "highly contextual act of construing and proclaiming theology within and on behalf of a local community of faith."[21] Contextual preaching "not only aims toward greater 'faithfulness' to the gospel of Jesus Christ, but... also aims toward greater 'fittingness' (in content, form and style) for a particular congregational gathering of hearers."[22] The task of the preacher is to catch the particular characteristics of the subculture of the congregation and preach the gospel, appealing to the cultural experience of the congregation.

While contextual preaching as local theology emphasizes unity and harmony by bringing a sense of coherence among the members of the congregation, this definition of contextual preaching runs the risk of being "static and fixated" because it understands context exclusively within its own locality. Moreover, contextual preaching as local theology risks reducing differences and diversity of the congregation, for this type of preaching tends to "exclude or suppress that which cannot be assimilated and integrated into the whole."[23] This generalizing or "totalizing"[24] approach by reducing diversity of the congregation does not appeal to preaching from a woman's perspective because its concern is to represent diversity of women's oppressed experiences.

A second approach to contextual theology, according to Schreiter, is based on the definition of context as "the globalized concept of culture."[25] In the postmodern world, pluralism and multiculturalism are the catchwords for understanding the concept of culture. Culture is not static or fixated but dynamic and open-ended. Because of the development of complex communication networks and transportation systems and the increase in the number of immigrants from one continent to another, the distinctive symbols and patterns of one particular culture are no longer isolated but are readily circulated throughout various regions of the entire world. In this changing situation, the context of culture becomes global and universal across traditions, cultures, ages, and geographical locations rather than remaining local and parochial. Context connotes the etymological meaning of the Latin verb *contexere*, which means "braid," "weave," or "connect." Culture in the global context is something that is created rather than discovered, for it does not restrict itself only to its own and immediate context but is open to different contexts, accommodating certain cultural niches.

In contextual theology, according to the globalized concept of culture, "[d]iversity is prized, but difference is valued even more highly"[26] because this approach is open to change and accepts something new as normal and natural; identity is always viewed as "fragmentary or multiple, constructed and imagined"[27] because life is experienced as fragmented; and peace and harmony remain ideals because the problem of power is a direct central issue in the cultural equation. Contextual preaching based on the global approach to contextual theology understands the context for preaching as dynamic and open-ended. Just as context is not restricted to its own locality, so is contextual preaching open to the larger context. In other words, contextual preaching is rooted in the context, yet is not reduced to context in a "crude contextualism,"[28] restricting itself only to its own and immediate context. Rather, contextual preaching based on the global approach to context broadens its dimensions beyond its temporal, spatial, and cultural boundaries and expands its understanding of God's liberating work for humanity by inviting into the theological conversation a variety of voices from the margins, either disvalued, muffled, or extinguished. At this point, contextual preaching is a cross-cultural conversation.

Preaching from a woman's perspective uses a cross-cultural conversation as its contextual method. A cross-cultural conversation connects preaching with different human experiences across time and space by inviting listeners who have different life experiences in different social locations to an authentic conversation that includes humble, active, and attentive listening. Preaching as a cross-cultural conversation presupposes that humans have an ability to speak beyond their own contexts and an openness to listen to voices from beyond their boundaries. As Schreiter rightly points out, this "universalizing function" of human speech is "not totalizing, which entails a suppression of difference and a claim to be the sole voice... If the message of what God has done in Christ is indeed Good News for all peoples, then the occurrence of grace in any setting has relevance for the rest of humanity."[29] Fred Craddock stresses the significance of this universalizing function of human speech in the act of preaching as "overhearing" or "indirect communication."[30]

Based on the universalizing function of human speech, preaching as a cross-cultural conversation builds up "affinity," "consensus," and eventually "authentic solidarity" within a congregation. More precisely speaking, a cross-cultural conversation makes it possible for the listeners, who have limited experiences within their personal and local contexts, to listen to diverse experiences of oppressed women and creates affinity among the listeners, "the capacity to see grace under the adverse conditions [they] rarely or never live in."[31] The affinity of the listeners further creates consensus among them. Sharon Welch illustrates how consensus occurs during a cross-cultural conversation:

> Imagine a conversation between Euro-American feminists, African American womanists, African American men, and Euro-American upper-class men. What would consensus mean in such a situation? It would be transformative if the Euro-American men and women could be convinced by the African American men and women of the pervasiveness of racism and become convinced that its costs are intolerable. Similarly, the women involved would want the men to recognize the myriad manifestations of sexual oppression and become actively involved in trying to eradicate this form of injustice. The group identified as the oppressor in each case will work for a recognition of their good intentions and sensitivity to the difficulties entailed in their own transformation.[32]

This type of dynamic interaction toward consensus among listeners can happen during the moment of preaching if the listeners grant sufficient respect to the different experiences of women and other oppressed people and are challenged by these experiences, recognizing that the lives of the various people are so intertwined that each is accountable to the other.

Consensus among listeners is the result of both the preacher's honest speaking and the listeners' attentive, humble listening. If the listeners open themselves to differences and allow themselves the possibility of change, authentic solidarity grows within the congregation. M. Shawn Copeland distinguishes authentic solidarity from "clichéd rhetoric of authenticity." While the latter understands authenticity simply as "cultural, religious, and social conformity" without attempting to investigate the complexities of gender, race, and class tangled in human relationships,[33] the former is the "togetherness" of a community, embracing people of all races and classes in their particular situations. Authentic solidarity as togetherness is "a wrenching task: to stand up for justice in the midst of injustice and domination; to take up simplicity in the midst of affluence and comfort; to embrace integrity in the midst of collusion and co-optation; to contest the gravitational pull of domination."[34]

The goal of preaching from a woman's perspective is to achieve this authentic solidarity within a community of faith. For this purpose, a cross-cultural conversation helps a congregation open itself up and listen to the new actions of the Spirit of God, not only within the particular context of the congregation but also within the larger context of the world. Cross-cultural conversations require a preacher to listen to the other voices, not only within the congregation but also among different communities of faith where the Spirit of God is universally present and continues to work for the inclusive well-being of all humankind.

PREACHING TOWARD THE WHOLENESS OF GOD

The postmodern view on the revelation of God guides us to understand theological accountability of preaching from a woman's perspective in light of the concept of the wholeness of God. According to the postmodern view, our truth-claim is partial, fragmentary, and conditioned in our particular social locations. We perceive the truth selectively from our own points of view within the boundaries of our own unique situations and through our own distinct ways of thinking in our limited languages. Because we humans are finite beings who cannot access what is outside of our reasoning, experiences, and languages, we cannot comprehend the wholeness of truth that is hidden in the mystery of God. The mystery of God is "not something we move closer to, but something that surfaces from the depths of the world from time to time."[35] Narratives of a fragmented and broken history and personal and communal experiences constitute a notion of truth simply as probabilities of truth. Therefore, the postmodern view takes into account the "process of truth-creating as an ongoing conversation," rather than searching for "foundations of truth" within the limits of reason.[36] Our perception of the truth remains in our fragmentary knowledge and limited experiences, and the comprehensive account of the truth as a whole is discovered and created during ongoing conversations with diverse people.

This ongoing process of "truth-creating" is the goal of preaching that represents a variety of voices from the margins. The ultimate goal of preaching from the margins is to reveal the wholeness of God. What, then, is the nature of the wholeness of God? How do women's partial and fragmented experiences of the truth reveal the wholeness of God through preaching?

The relational understanding of Christian theology explores these two theological questions. According to Marjorie Suchocki, the wholeness of God implies a deep reality of the divine, which means "divine harmony," that is, "one of enormous inclusiveness, wherein all the world is integrated into God's own beings."[37] Divine harmony reflects the image of God in many different forms and pushes humankind toward transforming societies into inclusive well-being. The nature of God as a whole is the integration of divine harmony into that which can be expressed by the theological term "peace." Suchocki claims,

> God is peace, an ultimate inclusiveness of all values in a transcending, transforming, and everlasting beauty.... God as peace is also God as creator, for it is the peace of inclusive complexity that functions to draw the world toward more complex forms of order. God as peace is the ultimate form of God as free, for it is the power of God's internal creativity, whereby God is able to receive the whole world through the consequent nature and to incorporate that world transformatively into God's own actualization, which is to say, peace.[38]

The theological concept of peace as the nature of God is identified with the term *shalom* in the Hebrew Bible. Etymologically speaking, the Hebrew word *shalom* comes from a verb meaning to "make something complete, to make something whole or holistic." The noun *shalom* means the condition of "being complete, of fullness, or wholeness."[39] Walter Brueggemann explains that *shalom* in the Hebrew Bible summarizes "the substance of the biblical vision," which has been expressed in such words as joy, well-being, harmony, prosperity, love, loyalty, truth, grace, salvation, justice, blessing, and righteousness.[40] *Shalom*, says Brueggemann, includes not only personal and individual but also cosmic, historical-political, and communal aspects because "the vision of wholeness, which is the supreme will of the biblical God, is the outgrowth of a covenant of shalom (see Ezek. 34:25), in which persons are bound not only to God but to one another in a caring, sharing, rejoicing community with none to make them afraid."[41]

In Isaiah and other prophetic writings of exile and postexilic periods, the reign of *shalom* that was granted to Israel is now extended to all nations. In these writings, *shalom*, which means "the harmonious order initiated by God's grace,"[42] develops into the universal hope that one day all nations would stream to Jerusalem to learn of God's covenantal mercies and judgment and that all people would worship and obey the God who would bring all people into the relationship of covenantal partnership (cf. Zech. 8:23; Isa. 19:24–25; 24–27; 49:6). The reality of *shalom*, which even Gentiles of other nations share with the people of Israel, is portrayed as the Jubilee year, the era of blessing when all people restore the order of *shalom* by healing the broken and releasing the oppressed. By imitating the God of righteousness and compassion, creation is renewed to its divinely intended wholeness (Isa. 61:1–4). In the later chapters of Isaiah, *shalom* is proclaimed as the apocalyptic vision for the future of the world (cf. Isa. 65:17–25). *Shalom* as a new heaven and a new earth is no longer "the community's earthly vocation, but is awaited as a divine act."[43] The completion of the wholeness of God is the eschatological anticipation of leading the world to salvation, beyond the suffering and pain of our present reality.

However, the future-oriented apocalyptic meaning of *shalom* in Third Isaiah undergoes a change in the New Testament into a proleptic vision of salvation. Jesus proclaims to the people, in both words and signs, that peace (*eirene*) is already present. Moreover, Jesus's life and death reveal that the peace of God exists alongside suffering. Peace is a profound oneness with God that can exist even when life is difficult, and human living is not very human. Peace does not mean the absence of struggle but the presence of love in the middle of pain and suffering. On the other hand, the resurrection of Jesus Christ is the symbol of God's ultimate power overcoming evil. Based on the promise of God in the risen Christ, the Christian gospel proclaims a peace that embraces triumphs, fears, joys, and strengths, as a "vision of God's realm."[44] Peace as the final consummation of God's sovereignty will be fulfilled on the last day.

Yet, peace as a vision of God's realm has already existed as a fragmentary foretaste through the life, death, and resurrection of Jesus Christ. Peace contradicts our worldly order, which is dominated by a privileged group of society that is based on gender, race, class, and sexual preference, and has the subversive power of disrupting the old order of this world. Peace as a vision of God's realm demonstrates its transforming power among those who are marginalized in the social formation, for the margins are the loci in which God is working on reconciliation and transformation.

In this proleptic schema of "already/not yet," peace is not created out of nothing in a remote future. Rather, the future reality of *shalom* is already here and now (cf. John 16:33; Matt. 10:11–13; Rom. 5:1–7). Nevertheless, peace as the vision of God's realm has never been fully realized. Instead, it is in a continuous process of actualization, for peace is never exclusively the fruit of human activity; peace is God's own nature revealed to us as a gift of God (cf. Rom. 15:33; 16:20; Phil. 4:9; 1 Thess. 5:23; Heb. 13:20–22). In the act of God's love manifested in Christ Jesus, Christians step toward peace by restoring the relationships not only among various individuals and communities but also between God and humanity. We are invited to a new future and to become "God's co-workers" (1 Cor. 3:9) to participate in achieving peace in the world. Thus, the actualization of peace is in a continuous process through collaborative work between God and humans. The actualization of peace is closely linked to what it means to be human.

The partnership between God and humanity when actualizing peace is rooted in the dynamic activities of the Holy Spirit. God is in essence the Spirit (2 Cor. 3:17–18). In the mode of the Spirit, God dwells in, with, and among us, continuously transforming the world. The Holy Spirit takes diverse actions in various places and times toward actualizing divine harmony or peace. The transforming activities of the Holy Spirit can be seen not only in the past but also in the present and the future. In other words, God's self-disclosures in creation, in the history of the people of Israel, and in the life, death, and resurrection of Jesus Christ are not exclusive events of God's revelation but are parables through which we can discern God's continuing activity of grace in our daily lives. The redeeming work in and through Jesus Christ — while historically unique in its character — is continuous with what happens elsewhere, for incarnation is not a once-and-for-all happening but a continuous process. God's liberating activity in Jesus Christ extends graciously to our present time and provides us with the criteria and norms for evaluating the transforming works of the Holy Spirit "to make and to keep human life human in the world."[45] When we open ourselves to the new, continuing actions of the Holy Spirit, we experience God's revelations as new insights and renewing power to build a new relationship between God and humanity, a new identity, a new life, and a new mission, communally as well as personally.

Peace as the wholeness of God celebrates many different words and songs, woven together into a harmonious whole. The Holy Spirit seeks not to annihilate the different voices of the people but to weave them together into a song of mutual respect to reveal the whole nature of God. The wholeness of God is not limited to an individual experience or reason but is open to the world and is experienced in various ways. As Suchocki indicates, "the God who is present to us is present to others as well. The God who guides us guides others also; the God who cares for us cares also for others. The whole world is touched by God, and therefore the world can mediate God's presence to us."[46] Thus, the diversity of human experiences becomes not an obstacle but a vehicle for actualizing peace.

Preaching from a woman's perspective aims to represent the wholeness of God, for the ultimate concern of women's preaching is the actualization of peace, the vision of God's realm. Preaching from a woman's perspective is open, inclusive, and dynamic because it takes seriously the particular experiences of women and other oppressed people. Their partial and fragmentary experiences reveal the wholeness of God. Through cross-cultural conversations, a preacher is required to read the signs of the times, discern the will of God, and provide listeners with new experiences of God's transforming power — a gift of forgiveness, reconciliation, freedom, and a new life, by weaving the different voices of people together to reveal the wholeness of God. Therefore, preaching from a woman's perspective toward the wholeness of God makes it possible for both the preacher and the listeners to broaden and deepen their experiences, feelings, and recognition of actualizing peace in the world, that is, how God is working in the world to make human life human.

The openness, inclusiveness, and creativity of preaching from a woman's perspective uses the image of the kaleidoscope as a viable metaphor for expressing the connectedness and diversity of women's experiences. As Gloria Schaab explains, "The kaleidoscope (Greek: 'beautiful-form-to see') is a contoured structure that, through the use of mirrors and lenses set a different angles, creates a multiplicity of symmetrical patterns from fragments of various materials, illuminated by a source of light."[47] When it rotates, each element of the kaleidoscope produces beautiful, clear, and various patterns by its interaction with the others and with the light.[48] Moreover, when all of the pieces shift, tones seem somehow different in the altered positions, and we recognize the newness of the pattern. Thus, the kaleidoscope never repeats exactly the same pattern.[49]

The kaleidoscope as a series of changing phases or events represents both the "pluriform shards and fragments of the multiple sources of revelation"[50] and the interrelation of the sources of the wholeness of God across temporal, spatial, and cultural boundaries. The image of a kaleidoscope symbolizes the wholeness of God, a multidimensional vision of peace for the world, based on diverse experiences of women and other oppressed people. Preaching from a woman's perspective envisions the beauty of the kaleidoscope, in which "diversity, pluriformity, and particularity of the mystery of God and of all things in God will be disclosed as 'beautiful forms to see' for the women and men who seek them."[51]

CONCLUSION

Preaching from a woman's perspective is a revelatory act because it is based on the theology of marginality, contextual theology as a cross-cultural conversation, and the revelation of the wholeness of God. Preaching from a woman's perspective reflects upon God's gracious actions in our lives and gives expression to the mysterious reality of the presence of God. By revealing the presence and the work of the Spirit of God through a variety of voices from the margins, preaching from a woman's perspective witnesses the extension of God's incarnation in Christ across temporal, spatial, and cultural boundaries. Learning new ways of listening to others through cross-cultural conversations leads to new ways of listening to God, who encounters humanity everywhere, particularly in the margins of society. Genuine conversation with different people does not keep the listeners within their limited experiences of God's transforming power but moves them toward the wholeness of God.

Thus, preaching from a woman's perspective is in an ongoing process toward the wholeness of God, dynamic and inclusive, moving toward the kaleidoscopic events of God's revelations. Preaching from a woman's perspective is a passionate commitment to the revelation of God's wholeness, or peace. Preaching toward the wholeness of God is a continuing process of God's redemptive work. It continually calls on believers to become agents of reconciliation until the entire world is reconciled or until the wholeness of God is fully revealed to the world. All believers, both women and men and even those who belong to the centrality of dominance, are invited to move toward the creative new margins to participate in the revelation of the wholeness of God, who is present among humankind to transform individuals and their communities toward the divine vision of God's realm.

Therefore, preaching from a woman's perspective is accountable to Christian theology. It suggests alternative visions of God for the world in the margins of our socioeconomic, religious, and cultural reality. Such preaching provides listeners both with new cultural values and visions of what it means to be human, as well as theological insight into how to lead a Christian life for actualizing peace.

Chapter Two

PREACHING THE RISEN CHRIST
WOMEN PREACHERS IN SCRIPTURE AND THE EARLY CHURCH

WHEN I TEACH PREACHING CLASSES or lead preaching workshops, I often ask the question, "Who were the first Christian preachers?" Many say that the first Christian preachers were Peter, Paul, Stephen, John the Baptist, or even Jesus, because some of their preaching is recorded in the New Testament. Interestingly, some people go back to the Hebrew Bible and mention some of the prophets; the names of women are seldom mentioned. Were there women among the first Christian preachers? If so, what and how did they preach?

The question regarding women preachers in scripture and in the early church is crucial when studying the history of preaching because it relates to the original nature and function of Christian preaching. It is not easy, however, to research ancient Christian women preachers because they have long been ignored by the patriarchal systems and mind-sets of the Christian Church. Concerns for women preachers were marginal and minor subjects, apt to arouse little interest in male historians and patriarchal church leaders. As a result, written materials about the first women preachers' biographies, journals, memoirs, and sermon manuscripts have not been well preserved during the last two thousand years.

In spite of these difficulties, this chapter attempts to rediscover women preachers in scripture and in the early church and to reconstruct the history of Christian preaching from a woman's perspective. The margins of scripture and other forms of literature, oral traditions, legends, and works of art are used to trace the evidence of ancient women preachers. The first section of this chapter discusses the origins of Christian preaching by reviewing four different views: the liturgical, the religious, the rhetorical, and the kerygmatic. The second section identifies the first Christian preachers as the women who first witnessed the risen Christ. The third section details the lives of ancient women preachers and their significant roles in the fledgling Christian Church. Legends about Mary Magdalene in Gaul and St. Nina in Georgia help us picture their preaching in different time periods and places. Based on the preaching ministry of the first women preachers, the final section of this chapter explores the nature and functions of preaching in three respects: preaching as the proclamation of God's sovereignty, preaching as testimony, and preaching as missionary work of God.

THE ORIGINS OF CHRISTIAN PREACHING

Just as the concepts of preaching are diverse depending on which theological perspective one follows, so are the origins of preaching. The origins of Christian preaching can be summarized into four different views.

The Liturgical View

One of the most common understandings of the origins of Christian preaching is based on our contemporary experience of Sunday worship. In the liturgical context, preaching is a part of worship, usually following scripture readings. The main task for the preacher is to interpret or explicate the readings so that the congregation can better understand the text.

Preaching as an exposition of scripture hypothesizes that the origins of Christian preaching are in Jewish synagogue sermons during postexilic times. Synagogues may have come into being while the Jews were exiled in Babylon around the sixth century BCE. Synagogues were places to meet regularly to worship, by reading, listening to, and interpreting the Torah.[1] Nehemiah 8:1–8 represents how synagogue worship was conducted: The people gathered, and the scribe and priest Ezra brought the Torah to the platform. He stood up and read it in the sight of all the people, and they responded with "Amen." After the Torah was read, the Levites helped the people understand the reading by offering an interpretation. This biblical scene presents preaching as an explication of scripture, set squarely at the center of communal religious life. The preaching originating in the synagogue was didactic, synonymous with teaching. The preacher was essentially a teacher of the Torah, the divine Law.[2]

In the first century, Judaism profoundly influenced both the formation of worship and the development of preaching as Christianity emerged. Peter, Paul, and other apostles preached in synagogues, and many of the first Christians were Jewish converts who had heard Christian preaching in synagogues. Regarding this situation, Yngve Brilioth claims that the "oldest Christian preaching related itself to the tradition of synagogal worship."[3] In her book *Women in the New Testament* Bonnie Thurston affirms Brilioth's view and points out that women in synagogues in Asia Minor shared leadership with men by preaching and administering sacraments.[4] That is, in the early churches the position of women in synagogues in the Greco-Roman Diaspora was not as inferior as that in Jewish communities in general. Women in synagogues in Asia Minor held positions as heads of synagogues as well as being financial supporters, in contrast to the roles of women who were excluded from studying the Torah and leadership in the Jewish community.[5] Philo's works written in the first century also support the assertion that women preached in synagogues in Asia Minor. According to his historical records, both women and men interpreted scripture and participated in rites and festivals in synagogues in Roman Asia Minor.[6]

The Religious View

While the liturgical view limits the origins of Christian preaching to the postexilic synagogue tradition, the religious view investigates the origins of Christian preaching in a broader sense. This view refers back to the Hebrew Scriptures, involving such diverse literary genres as narratives, prophetic oracles, wisdom literature, poems, and songs between God and humanity. Community leaders such as judges, priests, sages, and prophets were called to be servants of God to reveal the divine will to humanity. Using various literary and speech styles, they declared and celebrated salvation wrought by God to the community. Miriam's song (Exod. 15:21), the farewell address that Joshua delivered in the presence of an assembled congregation (Josh. 24), the triumphant canticle of Deborah and Barak (Judg. 5:1–31), the prophetic oracles pronounced by Elijah, Amos, Hosea, Isaiah, Micah, Jeremiah, and other prophets, the psalms that were used in liturgical celebrations (e.g., Pss. 66, 77, 78, 135, etc.), and so on, are considered primal forms of preaching.[7]

This religious view does not regard preaching exclusively as the exposition of the sacred books but rather inclusively as the delivery of the will of God by using a variety of means of communication. According to this view, preaching is deep reflection on life's issues within a particular historical context. The preacher is not merely the expositor or the teacher of an ancient text but the bearer of the Word of God being given to contemporary listeners. The preacher's own spiritual and religious experiences of theophanies and visions are the primary avenues for perceiving the will of God for the community of faith.

The Rhetorical View

The rhetorical view understands the origins of preaching in terms of the styles and modes of preaching. In his book *Folly of God: The Rise of Christian Preaching*, Ronald E. Osborn considers Greco-Roman rhetorical culture the most influential style in Christian preaching and concludes that Christian preaching is public speaking, originating from the classical art of Greco-Roman rhetoric. Osborn states that early Christian preachers adopted rhetorical forms of speeches, tracts, letters, and other aspects of Hellenistic oratory and culture as models for sermons. In addition, Hellenistic thinkers such as the Stoics and Cynics, who combined spiritual sensitivity with a commitment to serious reflection on a virtuous life, remarkably foreshadowed the role of Christian preachers as rhetoricians. Hellenistic philosophers' ethical concerns for "a good society and enunciated principles of justice and equality based on natural law" also influenced the theological content of Christian preaching.[8]

Since St. Augustine wrote his *De doctrina Christiana*[9] based on Ciceronian rhetoric, most homiletics textbooks used by the Christian Church and academic institutions have employed Greco-Roman rhetorical theories in teaching the substance and style of preaching. In particular, medieval universities developed a point-making thematic style based on Aristotelian logic and techniques of argumentation as the unique mode of Christian preaching. Since then, this rhetorical genre of preaching has become the traditionally accepted style of Christian preaching.

The Kerygmatic View

Regarding the origins of Christian preaching, C. H. Dodd gives special attention to "primitive preaching."[10] According to his analysis, in the New Testament, the term "preaching" is used distinctively from "teaching." While teaching means "the reasoned commendation of Christianity," including ethical instruction and/or the exposition of theological doctrines, delivered to "persons interested but not yet convinced," preaching is

> the public proclamation of Christianity to the non-Christian world. The Greek verb *Keryssein* properly means "to proclaim." A *Keryx* may be a town crier, an auctioneer, a herald, or anyone who lifts up his voice and claims public attention for some definite thing he has to announce.[11]

Primitive preaching during the formation of the church was done by apostles. Their preaching was the "Christian kerygma" — proclaiming Jesus Christ, the crucified and risen one, as the Messiah, through whom God's salvation reaches humanity.[12] According to Acts, after Jesus ascended into heaven, his followers began to preach the good news of the risen Christ by declaring him the Messiah, whom God had raised from the dead. Those who heard the *kerygma* developed new communities of believers, the Christian Church, and their faith in the resurrection of Christ Jesus called the church to continue proclaiming the risen Christ to the world. So began the mission of the church through preaching.

Kerygmatic preaching has not been taken seriously enough by contemporary homileticians because it tends to narrow the nature and function of Christian preaching to christological events. For example, Brilioth says, "By this emphasis [on the proclamation of the risen Christ], however, we have doubtless shortened the perspective and cut the lines of communication between the [Hebrew Scriptures] and the church."[13]

Nevertheless, of the four different views on the origins of Christian preaching, the kerygmatic view deserves to be reevaluated because it reveals the uniqueness of Christian preaching. Generally speaking, the term "preaching" has been used not only in the Christian Church but also in other religious communities such as Judaism, Buddhism, and Islam. Compared to preaching in other religions, Christian preaching is unique in that it is based on faith in the risen Christ. As David Buttrick says,

> The Gospels were written by resurrection faith. If Jesus had not been raised from the dead by the power of God, he would not be remembered except perhaps as a footnote in Jewish history — one more messianic pretender.... Resurrection was nothing less than a sign, a great sign, of God's approval; it was a divine endorsement. Thus, for astonished first Christians, the life of Christ became mightily important, a new living torah: the way, the truth, and the life.[14]

Although the stories of the resurrection appear only five times in scripture — at the end of each of the four Gospels and in 1 Corinthians 15:3–12, the unique character of Christian preaching is rooted in the "Easter surprise," the joyful message of the resurrection of Christ. The resurrection was the key element in early Christian preaching.

When we understand the origins of Christian preaching in relation to the Easter surprise, the first Christian preachers were neither the teachers of the Torah, nor the prophets, nor the rhetoricians, but the witnesses of Jesus's resurrection. Without the first witnesses of Jesus's resurrection, Christian preaching would not exist. Who were, then, the first witnesses of the risen Christ, and what were their testimonies?

THE FIRST CHRISTIAN PREACHERS

If we understand that the first Christian preachers were in fact the first witnesses of the risen Christ, most of us would readily assume that Peter and the other male disciples of Jesus were the first preachers. Paul's writing of 1 Corinthians 15:3-12, the earliest record of the resurrection, says that "he [Jesus] appeared to Cephas, then to the twelve. Then he appeared to more than five hundred brothers and sisters at one time, most of whom are still alive, though some have died. Then he appeared to James, then to all the apostles. Last of all, as to one untimely born, he appeared also to me" (vv. 5-8).

However, whatever tradition Paul took over, the resurrection narratives in the four Gospels are different from Paul's. Although they do not provide a consistent story because of the multifaceted oral traditions of the earliest Christian communities, all four Gospels have one thing in common: The first announcement of the resurrection was given to the women who came to Jesus's tomb. Against all expectations, they became the first witnesses of his rising from the dead. The women who followed Jesus from Galilee and watched his crucifixion on Golgotha were the first to encounter the risen Christ. They were instructed to "go and tell" the resurrection of the crucified Jesus to his male disciples.

Mark 16:1-8, which is considered the original ending of Mark,[15] tells that three women — Mary Magdalene, Mary the mother of James, and Salome — went to Jesus's tomb to anoint his dead body. The women did not expect Jesus's resurrection. Upon entering the tomb, they saw a "young man" — an angel — dressed in a white garment and heard the Easter kerygma: "Do not be alarmed; you are looking for Jesus of Nazareth, who was crucified. He has been raised; he is not here. Look, there is the place they laid him. But go, tell his disciples and Peter that he is going ahead of you to Galilee; there you will see him, just as he told you" (vv. 6-7). This announcement of the good news terrified the women so much that they fled the tomb in terror and amazement. Reaching a crescendo in the closing verse, Mark concludes the Gospel with the final sentence, "... and they said nothing to anyone, for they were afraid" (v. 8). The women who had first heard about the risen Christ were so fearful that they lost their voices. This climactic but somewhat abrupt conclusion leaves the Gospel open-ended. Robert H. Smith is probably correct when he states that Mark did not want his story to be viewed as completed in the past, to be easily set aside. Rather, Mark probably wanted to make his Gospel a never-ending story by challenging readers to supply an ending in their own lives by becoming disciples of Jesus and accomplishing the commission given to the three women.[16]

The resurrection narratives in Matthew and Luke are revised versions of Mark's report with some minor variations.[17] Matthew 28:1–20 states that two women, Mary Magdalene and the other Mary, went to see Jesus's tomb rather than anointing his dead body as Mark reports, and heard the Easter kerygma from the angel, "He is not here; for he has been raised" (v. 6). The angel told them to go and tell the good news to Jesus's disciples. On the way, the women met the risen Christ for the first time, and he asked them to tell his disciples that they would meet the risen Christ in Galilee. Because of the women's announcement of the resurrection, the disciples went to Galilee and met the risen Christ there. The disciples were then told by Jesus to preach his resurrection to the world.

Luke 24:1–11 says that Magdalene, Joanna, Mary the mother of James, and the other women with them went to Jesus's tomb to anoint his dead body. When they found the empty tomb, they were perplexed. Two angel-like men then appeared to them and told them the Easter kerygma, "He is not here, but has risen" (v. 5). They also reminded the women of what Jesus had said about his resurrection. The women went to Jesus's male disciples and told them what they had witnessed, but the disciples regarded the women's story as an "idle tale." Peter ran to Jesus's tomb to confirm the women's witness and found it empty. Later in the chapter, Luke reports that the risen Christ appeared to his disciples to confirm that the resurrection had truly happened (vv. 13–50).

The plot of John's resurrection narrative is somewhat different from those of the synoptic Gospels. John 20:1–18 states that Mary Magdalene went alone to Jesus's tomb and found the stone covering the entrance of the tomb removed. She reported this to Peter and Jesus's beloved disciple. The two male disciples ran to the tomb and returned home after learning that Jesus's dead body was gone. Mary Magdalene, however, who was in sorrow for the loss of Jesus's dead body, bent over to look into the tomb and encountered two angels there. They asked her why she was weeping. When she answered them, she heard a man's voice calling her from behind. She finally realized that he was the risen Christ. Jesus told her about his ascending to God and asked her to tell his male disciples about his ascension. Mary Magdalene went to them and said, "I have seen the Lord" and delivered to them what she had heard from the risen Jesus (v. 18).

Of the various resurrection narratives in the four Gospels, Matthew and John report that women eyewitnessed the risen Christ for the first time and were commissioned directly by him to tell his male disciples of his resurrection. Mark and Luke report that the women did not see the risen Christ face-to-face but witnessed the empty tomb and heard about the resurrection from the angel(s). While the angel in Mark's narrative commissioned the women to announce Jesus's resurrection, the women in Luke's narrative proclaimed it without being commissioned.

Considering that Christian preaching first began with the testimony of the risen Christ, the first Christian preachers were the women who first witnessed Jesus's empty tomb and met with or, at least, were told about the risen Christ. These women first proclaimed the good news of the risen Christ to his male disciples. By stating the following, Osborn supports the belief that the women's proclamation about the risen Christ was the first example of Christian preaching:

> In the secure house where the apostles, all males, still cowered in sorrow and fear, these women were the first Christian preachers. They must have preceded all the others. In a society bound by the presuppositions and customs of patriarchy, who would have invented primacy for them — and why? — unless they had been first with the news?[18]

How could women be the first Christian preachers for the risen Christ? In Jewish and Greco-Roman cultures, women were not accepted as credible witnesses because they were regarded as "weak, insignificant, frivolous, and fickle."[19] In fact, a crucial question for the church fathers, who justified their authority as Peter's successors, was why a fundamental part of the Christian kerygma was based on the witnesses of Mary Magdalene and other women rather than Peter or other male disciples of Jesus. St. Augustine responded in a desperate measure, stating, "Christ first appeared to a woman because the woman was also the first to have brought sin."[20] However, this misogynist justification is laughable. It simply represents the oppressive sexist mentality of the patriarchal society of that time.

The Gospels prove, in fact, that the women followers of Jesus were qualified to become the first Christian preachers because they were his true disciples. The women who first witnessed the resurrection of Christ Jesus were not passive followers of Jesus, simply serving and supporting him, but rather active disciples, well-trained by Jesus to spread the gospel to the world. Jesus educated the women as his disciples in their own right, making them fully capable of receiving unique revelation and worthy of being valid witnesses of his life, death, and resurrection. Luke 8:1-3 is the only passage in the synoptic Gospels that conspicuously brings out the presence of the female followers during the life of Jesus Christ:

> Soon afterwards he went on through cities and villages, proclaiming and bringing the good news of the kingdom of God. The twelve were with him, as well as some women who had been cured of evil spirits and infirmities: Mary, called Magdalene, from whom seven demons had gone out, and Joanna, the wife of Herod's steward Chuza, and Susanna, and many others, who provided for them out of their resources. (Luke 8:1-3)

This passage reveals that there was a group of women who followed Jesus on his travels from the beginning of his public ministry in the land of Galilee. They left their families, their villages, and their everyday lives and stayed with Jesus — listening, learning, and offering their goods and services until he died on the cross. The larger text, Luke 8:1-21, informs us that the women followers were along with the male disciples as they listened to Jesus and learned about the *basileia* (dominion) of God (cf. the parable of the sower [vv. 4–10]; teaching through a lamp under a jar [vv. 16–8]; and the episode of true relatives [vv. 19–21]). Jesus shared with his women followers his special teaching reserved only for his disciples (vv. 10–15). Jesus educated women and men together through the use of parables, sayings, miracles, and signs of the dominion of God. Some of the women were those who experienced miraculous healing by Jesus, while we find no accounts in the Gospels of male disciples whom Jesus cured. Jesus's school was truly co-ed.

Jesus's coeducational teaching was revolutionary during a time when Jewish society treated women as possessions of their fathers and husbands rather than independent human beings.[21] Jesus was not interested in the conventions of his day regarding women. Throughout his ministry, Jesus showed himself as both positive and egalitarian in his attitudes toward women by having them as friends and followers — talking freely and truthfully with them and assigning them roles in his parables and sayings.

The women who were trained in Jesus's co-ed classes were the only ones among all his followers who were also present at the foot of the cross. The Passion Narratives in the synoptic Gospels (Matt. 27:55–61; Mark 15:40–47; Luke 23:49–56) report that the women who had followed Jesus from Galilee watched his crucifixion and burial while all his male disciples abandoned him.[22] These women were then chosen to be the first and privileged witnesses to the ultimate reality of Jesus's resurrection. In a predominantly androcentric environment, the redactors of the Gospels, who probably had little interest in the presence of women in their Gospels, could not help but refer to the women followers in their Passion and Resurrection Narratives because, as Carla Ricci points out, they could find no male witnesses who had stayed close to Jesus during his crucifixion, burial, and resurrection, for they had all fled (Mark 14:50; Matt. 26:56).[23]

MEMORIES OF THE FIRST WOMEN PREACHERS

Unfortunately, the Gospels do not give us any additional information about the women who first witnessed the risen Christ. Mary

Magdalene and the other women who followed Jesus and preached the good news of his resurrection disappear after the conclusion of each of the four Gospels. In contrast, Peter and other male disciples are mentioned repeatedly in the rest of the books in the New Testament. The authors of the books neither indicate women's preaching as a major event of the early church nor preserve any sermons or public speeches given by women. Instead, the authors mention women leaders only in passing while hurrying on to address the ministries of male leaders.

However, some marginal biblical records do give vague descriptions of women preachers and their leadership. For example, Acts 1:14, 8:3, and 22:4 imply that both the female and male disciples who followed Jesus made up the core of the post-Easter community. The female disciples were persecuted and martyred along with male Christians.[24] Acts 16:11-15 reminds us that Lydia in Philippi founded the Philippian church, and it is assumed that she preached in her own church. Acts 18:26, which mentions that Priscilla taught Apollo about Jesus Christ, implies she probably preached in her house church (cf. 1 Cor. 16:19; Rom. 16:5).

We find more evidence of preaching women when we understand that, in the Bible and in the early church, prophetic activities were often identified as preaching.[25] Both in Hebrew Scripture and in the New Testament, prophesying means a charismatic ministry delivering the will of God to rulers and their people (cf. Joel 2:28) rather than ecstatic utterances of future events by soothsayers or fortune-tellers. Prophets in the Bible challenged the people of their communities to examine their actions and beliefs and to live in conformity with the will of God, to live lives of faith, love, and justice. In the early church, both women and men were granted this gift of prophecy.[26] Acts 21:8-9 reports that Philip in Caesarea, a well-known church leader, had four unmarried daughters who had performed this charismatic ministry of prophecy. First Corinthians 11:5 also mentions women's prophetic ministry in the Corinthian church. These prophetic activities of women and men were considered signs of the Spirit at work in the church (Acts 2:17-18).

Romans 16:1–16 also gives evidence of women preachers. Out of ten women appearing as Paul's fellow ministers in this chapter — Phoebe, Prisca, Mary, Junia, Tryphaena, Tryphosa, Persis, Rufus's mother, Julia, and Nereus's sister, Phoebe is described as a significant leader in the early church with three different titles: sister, deacon, and benefactor (vv. 1–2). Her two titles of deacon (*diakonos*), which means minister or missionary, and benefactor (*prostasis*), which means helper or bishop, imply that Phoebe was a preacher. Moreover, Junia is called an apostle (v. 7), which implies that she was a preacher, too, for apostle means "a personal messenger or envoy, commissioned to transmit the message or otherwise carry out the instructions of the commissioning agent."[27]

In addition to these marginal reports in the Bible, some historical records, legends, and works of art attest to women's active leadership in the early church. For example, in his *True Doctrine*, Celsus, a first-century Platonist philosopher, reveals the active leadership of Christian women. He mentions some women's names when discussing the divisions of Christians that existed at that time: "Marcellians who follow Marcellina, and Harpocratians who follow Salome, and others who follow Mariamme [Mary Magdalene], and others who follow Martha."[28] In addition, Karen J. Torjesen presents a convincing case that ancient mosaics, paintings, statuaries, dedicatory inscriptions, and funerary epitaphs disclose numerous pieces of evidence of women's leadership in the early church. In catacomb frescoes alone, more than two hundred depictions exist of the female *orans*, a person praying for the community and presiding over the Eucharist. These paintings of the *orans* present the ministry of women praying, prophesying, and preaching.[29] Furthermore, in a fourth-century basilica excavated in Philippi, inscriptions were discovered that list women as deacons and canonesses.[30] Such historical evidence, ranging from literature to works of art, reveals that the women disciples of Jesus continued their preaching ministries after experiencing the risen Christ and that they had their own followers.

From these biblical and other ancient sources, which reveal a hidden history of women's leadership that has been suppressed by the selective memory of succeeding generations of male historians, we learn that women, along with men, played major roles as preachers during the formation of the early Christian Church.[31] When the first Christians congregated in homes during the first and second centuries, women as well as men were prominent leaders serving in a wide variety of roles such as preachers, apostles, deacons, teachers, prophetesses, and priests. Although by the third century the church was in the process of institutionalizing itself to build an ecclesiastical hierarchy, women deacons survived and continued to preach until the mid-fourth century in the West and even later in the Eastern church.[32]

The lives of two women, Mary Magdalene and St. Nina, call our special attention, for at least two reasons. First, both are prominent female figures who influenced each of the Christian Churches, the Eastern and the Western. Recently, church historians, especially female scholars, have rediscovered the tremendous impact these women have had on the mission of the Christian Church. Second, despite the lack of primary sources from Mary Magdalene and St. Nina, many secondary sources exist that give information about their lives as preachers. Legendary stories, apocryphal writings, paintings, artifacts, and historical records allow us to imagine their preaching lives.

Mary Magdalene, apostolorum apostola (Apostle of the Apostles)

What do we know about Mary Magdalene? Christian stories and movies about Mary Magdalene often identify four different women in the Gospels as Mary Magdalene: the woman who was possessed by seven demons (Luke 8:2), the woman who was caught in adultery (John 8:3–11), the sister of Martha and Lazarus (John 12:1–8), and the sinner who anointed Jesus's feet with perfume (Luke 7:36–50). These combined roles of Mary Magdalene have been admitted by the Christian Church since Pope Gregory the Great (c. 540–604) declared her a penitent sinner, who had once been a prostitute but became a new person after meeting Jesus.[33]

However, the four Gospels present an entirely different character of Mary Magdalene. In the Gospels, her name appears in Luke 8:2 and in the Passion and Resurrection Narratives (Mark 15:40, 47; 16:1, 9; Matt. 27:56, 61; 28:1; Luke 24:10; John 19:25; 20:1,

11, 16, 18). There is no record of how she met Jesus or became his disciple. The only piece of information we have about her identity is from a single verse, Luke 8:2, that she was from the town of Magdalene, located on the west bank of Galilee. The town was a thriving Romanized community, a Jewish-Hellenistic center of trade.[34] Mary Magdalene was once possessed by seven demons and later cured by Jesus. After her recovery, she became Jesus's disciple from the beginning of his ministry in Galilee. She is one of the women named in the Passion and Resurrection Narratives who followed Jesus from Galilee to Golgotha and witnessed his death, burial, and resurrection. John describes Mary Magdalene in great detail as the first and only person who saw and talked with the risen Christ. He movingly narrates the moment when she encountered the risen Christ (John 20:1–18). Because of John's resurrection account, Hippolytus of Rome (170 CE–235 CE) honored Mary Magdalene with the title of *apostolorum apostola*.[35] In the thirteenth century, Robert of Sorbon exhorted his male audience not to disdain women's words because Mary Magdalene was a preacher of the resurrection of Christ.[36]

Although the name Mary Magdalene does not appear in the Bible except in the Gospels, her name is found in fragments of some early-century Gnostic writings, such as the *Pistis Sophia*, discovered in 1773, the *Gospel of Mary*, discovered in 1896, and the *Gospel of Thomas* and the *Gospel of Philip*, both discovered in 1945.[37] These books were written between the late first and fourth centuries against the background of growing institutionalization within the church and the canonization of the Bible. These works describe Mary Magdalene as a disciple of Jesus, who is knowledgeable about scripture and has a good memory of Jesus's teaching. She and Peter are often portrayed in these works as rivals.[38]

Among these Gnostic writings, *The Gospel of Mary* is one of the most important sources for understanding Mary Magdalene as a preacher. The original version of *The Gospel of Mary* is assumed to be written around 150 CE. Fragments of this Gospel are in the *Papyrus Berolinensis*, which was discovered in Egypt in 1896. They were translated into and published in English approximately one hundred years later in 1988.[39] In *The Gospel of Mary*, the author describes Mary Magdalene as a witness and preacher of true faith. She preaches to the male disciples, who are despondent after Jesus's ascension, in order to encourage them to go forth into the world to proclaim the gospel. Her sermon is based on what she learned from Christ Jesus when she encountered him — presumably the risen Christ — in her vision.

Mary Magdalene's life story as a preacher was handed down orally for hundreds of years and later included in both historical and legendary literature in a variety of versions. Among them, two stories in particular are popular. One is by Modestus, the seventh-century patriarch of Jerusalem, who was convinced that Mary Magdalene preached the gospel in Ephesus, where she was eventually martyred.[40] The other story of Mary Magdalene is found in *The Golden Legend*. According to this book, after St. Stephen was martyred in Jerusalem, Mary Magdalene and her companions crossed the Mediterranean in a rudderless boat and disembarked at Marseille, Gaul (France). There, she preached to pagans about the good news of Jesus Christ. She also worked many miracles and signs in the name of Christ Jesus. After some time, Mary Magdalene converted and baptized the prince of Marseille and his wife and, eventually, all of Gaul.[41]

Despite their differences, both these legends present the life of Mary Magdalene as a missionary. She shared what she had learned from Jesus from the time of Galilee, including the love of God manifested in the life, death, and resurrection of Christ Jesus, with those who had never met or heard of him. In many paintings and artifacts of Mary Magdalene created during the early and medieval periods, she is depicted as a preacher holding the traditional preaching gesture of pointing her right index finger upward.[42]

St. Nina, Equal of the Apostles and Enlightener of Georgia

In the Eastern church, St. Nina (?–335 CE) is venerated as the preacher who converted the people of Georgia (ancient Iberia) to Christianity. Information about her life and preaching ministry has come down to us through ancient Greek and Latin historians. The historical writings of Gelasius of Caesarea, Rufinus, Theodoret of Cyrrhus, and others, and some archeological evidence from the fourth and fifth centuries, prove that the eastern kingdom of Georgia was converted to Christianity by a woman preacher named St. Nina. Analyzing historical records in Georgian chronicles and historical narratives, A. I. Natroshvili concludes that "St. Nina appeared in Georgia in 318 or at the beginning of 319. She began openly preaching the Gospel in 323. Queen Nana was baptized in 325, and King Mirian in 326. In this same year Christianity was adopted in Georgia."[43]

Who, then, was St. Nina? Although her own personal writings such as sermons, journals, and autobiographical essays were not preserved, many different narratives of her life and ministry were handed down by oral tradition.[44] The most popular version of her life story is as follows: About seventeen hundred years ago, St. Nina was born in Cappadocia in Asia Minor as the only daughter of pious and noble parents. At the age of twelve, she began to study the rules of the Christian faith and practice under an old female teacher named Nianfora. When Nina was fourteen years old, she received the call of God in a dream to go to Georgia and tell the people the good news of the resurrection of Jesus Christ. The patriarch of Jerusalem, Nina's uncle, gave Nina the official ecclesiastical confirmation of her zeal for mission work with the prayer, "I send her to preach Thy divinity and to spread the good tidings of Thy resurrection, wherever it pleases Thee."[45]

On her journey to Georgia, Nina had another dream in which a man appeared and unrolled a scroll for her to read, on which the following Gospel verses were written:

> Verily, I say unto you, Wheresoever this gospel shall be preached in the whole world, there shall also this, that this woman hath done, be told for a memorial of her. There is neither Jew nor Greek, there is neither bond nor free, there is neither male nor female: for ye are all one in Christ Jesus. Then said Jesus unto them [the women], Be not afraid: go tell my brethren.... He that receiveth you receiveth me, and he that receiveth me receiveth him that sent me. For I will give you a mouth and wisdom, which all your adversaries shall

not be able to gainsay nor resist. And when they bring you unto the synagogues, and unto magistrates, and powers, take ye no thought how or what thing ye shall answer, or what ye shall say: for the Holy Spirit shall teach you in the same hour what ye ought to say. And fear not them which kill the body, but are not able to kill the soul.... Go ye therefore, and teach all nations, baptizing them in the name of the Father, and of the Son, and of the Holy Spirit: Teaching them to observe all things whatsoever I have commanded you: and, lo, I am with you always, even unto the end of the world.[46]

Upon awakening, Nina found the miraculous scroll in her hand. The commissioning words of the scriptures sanctioned her apostleship and encouraged her during the difficult times she encountered in Georgia.

Arriving in Georgia, Nina entered the city of Mtskheta and lived with a royal gardener's family, learning the manners, customs, and the language of the Georgians.[47] When confronted by paganism, she won the followers over by demonstrating the power of "Christ God" by performing numerous miracles and signs. She also preached to the Georgian pagans and Jews the gospel that God in Christ Jesus is one true God. Later, the Georgian Queen Nana, a fervent worshiper of idols, was cured of an incurable disease through Nina's prayer and consequently was converted to Christianity. King Mirian, who was at first against Nina's preaching, also became a Christian after surviving a terrible storm in the mountains when he prayed to Nina's God. The royal couple and others in Georgia learned about the Christian faith from Nina and were baptized by priests sent by the emperor Constantine. The converted royal couple played a major role in destroying pagan cults in Georgia and building the first Christian church, which was consecrated by the Archbishop Eustathius of Antioch. Nina continued preaching the gospel of Christ not only in the city of Mtskheta but also in remote mountain regions, thereby turning thousands of people to Christ.[48]

The ancient Iberian Church recognized Nina as "Equal of the Apostles and the Enlighteners of Iberia" and added her name to the company of saints. The Georgian Orthodox Church established a yearly feast in her honor on January 14, the day of her repose, and has celebrated St. Nina's feast annually by commemorating her missionary work as a preacher. In the prayers celebrating the memory of St. Nina, she is called by many revering titles such as the chosen handmaid of the Word of God, emulator of the feat of the Holy Apostles, our enlightener and intercessor, co-worker of the Holy apostles Paul and Andrew, the wise preacher, beloved servant of Christ, and the Preacher, equal of the Apostles and bearer of Good Tidings. In addition to these titles, St. Nina has also been revered by the church as the one who "wast joined to the choir of the preachers of the Gospel" to deliver the Georgian people "from the darkness of idolatry by her apostolic activity."[49]

It is notable that in present-day Georgia, bishops, priests, monks, nuns, and other religious leaders emphasize even more than in previous centuries the annual feast of St. Nina. Patriarch Ilia II chose St. Nina as the model for renewing Christian preaching in contemporary Georgia after it was freed from the communist regime. In 1989, as a means to awaken the country's dormant faith, the Georgian Orthodox Church began to process along "St. Nina's Way," a missionary pilgrimage retracing St. Nina's path. Every June, following the traditional date of the inception of St. Nina's preaching, pilgrims stop in the villages along the Kura River. They meet with the locals and bring them the message of Christ's resurrection.[50] Bishop Nikoloz explains the significance of the pilgrimage as follows:

> When we are walking on this Way we ask St. Nina to walk and pray with us, and ask that this miracle [the conversion of Georgia] might once again come to pass. We pray like this after a very difficult period in our country — I mean not only the seventy years of the communist regime, but the entire last two hundred years, the most difficult period of our country's history. During that time our people turned away from God. We are now asking St. Nina to intercede once more, to help us to preach in Georgia, so that Georgia will again become a Christian country — not only officially, but truly.[51]

PREACHING THE RISEN CHRIST

The study of the origins of Christian preaching from a woman's perspective reveals that Christian preaching originated from the Easter surprise and that the first preachers were the women who first witnessed the risen Christ. The stories of Mary Magdalene, St. Nina, and other women preachers in scripture and in the early church help us understand the nature and function of Christian preaching in relation to the proclamation of the risen Christ. The nature and function of preaching revealed in early women's preaching can be explained in three ways: preaching as the proclamation of God's sovereignty, preaching as testimony, and preaching as missionary work of God.

Preaching as the Proclamation of God's Sovereignty

Mary Magdalene and the other women who followed Jesus from Galilee and watched his suffering and death were the first witnesses to the risen Christ. Their experiences of encountering the risen Christ were personal but not private mystical experiences or psychological reactions. Rather, their experiences of the risen Christ were cosmic eschatological events through which their personal and communal lives were transformed.

The women who eyewitnessed the life, death, and resurrection of Christ Jesus would interpret his death and resurrection differently from male disciples like Paul the Apostle or early church fathers who did not have direct experiences with Jesus Christ on earth. The women would not beautify or romanticize Jesus's crucifixion as "the sacrifice of atonement" for individual believers, nor did they portray his resurrection as a guarantee of individual salvation or life after death, as later church fathers did.[52] Instead, the women, who followed Jesus as marginalized people of the society at that time, would probably understand the death of Jesus to be a result of vivid evil in the world. For them, Jesus was a victim of the imperial Roman world. The political and religious leaders who had vested interests did not tolerate Jesus's preaching about a new dominion of God. Consequently, they prevented him from spreading such a dangerous message by crucifying him. However, the dominant group in society at that time was not able to stop God's involvement in the human world. By raising Jesus of Nazareth from the dead, God demonstrated God's sovereign power over the evil power in the world. Thus, his resurrection was likely viewed as vindication of God's victory against evil. The power of resurrection was the power of God, breaking the cruel human sinfulness and injustice and raising the innocent victim as the Child of God. The women's testimony of the risen Christ makes it clear that Jesus's suffering and death were divine means of resisting evil. The women disciples nullified the oppressors' efforts to ban Jesus's message of liberation by resuming Jesus's preaching, announcing the end of the old age and the beginning of a new world of God.

The power of the risen Christ manifested itself in the lives of the believers. As we see in Mary Magdalene and St. Nina, the early women preachers showed God's continuing presence and work through preaching. Their preaching had the power to transform their listeners' lives. The old world of idolatry collapsed; the new world of truth in Christ was inaugurated in pagan worlds; and the sovereign power of God was proclaimed through the women's particular rhetoric in their own unique social locations. Early women preached the risen Christ based on their particular experiences of theophanies and created a new life and new hope in Christ among their listeners. Their preaching confirmed God's continuing presence and work in the world.

Preaching the power of the resurrection is an eschatological event because it is the affirmation of God's sovereign power in our world, even in the midst of suffering and pain. Such preaching assists listeners in hearing and seeing a new world completely different from this world and to imagine a future in the promise of God. This kind of preaching is only possible when the preacher stands in the faith that God is the Lord of the world and the source of its transformation.

Preaching as Testimony

The stories of Mary Magdalene and of St. Nina reveal that their personal and communal experiences of the risen Christ laid the foundations for their preaching. They responded with amazement, shock, and joy, to God's initial invitation to a life of resurrection and lived the rest of their lives by sharing their testimonial stories of encountering the living God revealed in Christ Jesus. They preached the risen Christ as personal testimony, based on their concrete experiences of encountering him in their lives.

From early women preachers, we learn that just as the experience of the risen Christ is initiated by the grace of God, so is preaching the risen Christ. Preaching the risen Christ is not based on the preacher's philosophical speculation or scientific knowledge of the Bible, humanity, or the concept of God. Rather, it depends on the grace of God, who reveals Godself to us in our everyday lives. The preacher is convinced of the divine power of the resurrection through her experience of encountering the living God, and with this conviction, she cannot help but preach.

Preaching the risen Christ based on one's testimonial stories, however, is not an easy task. The preacher often takes the risk of falling into the traps of either isolation from the members of the congregation, trivialization of the text, or self-aggrandizing the preacher herself. How, then, can we turn a testimony into a sermon? The process of preparing a testimonial sermon involves three stages: memory, interpretation, and persuasion. First, testimonial preaching begins with the preacher's memory of her personal and communal experiences of encountering the risen Christ. The preacher's personal and communal life is the richest context for experiencing the revelation of God. Yet, not all experiences are valuable for sermons. Thus, the preacher needs to remember when and where she seriously experienced the presence of the living God in her life and select a particular experience by reflecting theologically.

The second stage for preparing a testimonial sermon is the interpretive process. The preacher's personal and communal experiences cannot become a sermon without theological and biblical interpretation. The preacher's restored memory of experiencing the living God only has meaning when it is interpreted from a certain theological and biblical point of view. In other words, when the preacher's experience analogically relates to the listeners' life experiences in view of the will of God, the preacher's testimony serves as a mirror through which the listeners see grace in their own lives.

This interpretive process makes the preacher's personal story a public story, that is, a community's story, beyond the preacher's private ownership. The preacher's story, which now has public accessibility, has the power to help listeners recall their own experiences of the living God in their personal and communal lives and, in turn, be convinced of the promise of God in their future.

The last stage of preparing a testimonial sermon requires certain rhetorical skills to persuade listeners of faith in the risen Christ. If the preacher uses various rhetorical skills to appeal to the listeners' cultural ethos and communication style, her preaching makes it possible to invite her listeners to relate themselves to her testimony and build authentic solidarity between herself and the listeners. Through persuasive performance, testimonial preaching becomes a revelatory act of God that can evoke the presence of the risen Christ among listeners. Therefore, preaching the risen Christ as testimony challenges preachers to continually develop their rhetorical skills of persuasion.

Preaching as Missionary Work of God

The stories of Mary Magdalene and St. Nina show that these women lived their lives as missionaries after experiencing the risen Christ. Their apostolic preaching made the God of Jesus Christ known to people who had never previously heard of him. These women's persuasive speeches about Christ Jesus were imbued with a spirit of urgency, calling their listeners to repentance and a new life in Christ and opened the way to reconciliation between God and their listeners by inviting them to God's future, a vision for a new world.

The fact that Christian preaching was originally missionary preaching pushes us to reassess the significance of the relationship between the Christian mission and preaching. Historically speaking, the Western church has generally understood that salvation means an individual being saved from eternal damnation and going to heaven after death, and that this salvation is only possible through the confession of Christ as the Savior. Based on this exclusive Christocentric view, the Christian mission of the Western church during the colonial period focused heavily on saving people from eternal damnation by converting them to Christianity. Missionaries understood themselves as soldiers of Christ and regarded indigenous religions as the worship of idols or evil spirits that they must destroy in order to save people.

However, in our postcolonial era, this imperialistic view is often criticized by the prophetic voices of third-world theologians and minority-group Christians both in the United States and other Western countries. Moreover, the increase of interfaith dialogue has helped the Western church reevaluate the spirituality of other religions and treat them as equal partners to Christianity. This situation has led mainline Christian churches in the United States to repent the spirit of Western superiority, imperialism, and racism that have so strongly permeated their Christocentric mission strategies. In this light, many mainline churches wonder whether or not missions have a place in today's world. In our postcolonial and postmodern world, the meaning of the Christian mission is often confusing, and its significance is often doubted.

In this changing situation, one thing is certain: The mission of the church must be understood and undertaken in an imaginatively new manner rather than repeating past mistakes. When proposing a new theological perspective for the Christian mission, it is important to consider Christology in relation to pneumatology. The Christocentric view of missions has caused us to ignore the significance of God's mission in and with the Holy Spirit, which has further caused an imbalanced understanding of the nature of God. As Jürgen Moltmann indicates in his book *The Spirit of Life*, it is impossible to talk about Christ without talking at the same time about his experience of God in the Spirit. The Spirit was not something Jesus possessed; rather, it was the power that made him become the Christ as a result of his suffering, death, and resurrection.[53] The Holy Spirit is not something God and Christ possess nor simply an assistant to God or Christ. Rather, God in Jesus Christ is, in essence, the Holy Spirit. In the form of the Spirit, God continuously dwells in, with, and among us, as our companion who shares our present lives in this world.[54]

The experiences of the risen Christ of early women preachers were actually the manifestation of the life-giving power of God the Spirit in individuals and communities. The risen Christ whom these preachers met in their lives was, in essence, the Holy Spirit. Just as the original theological meaning of the word "mission" is *missio Dei*, which means God's sending of the Spirit,[55] so early women's preaching was testimony of the presence and work of the sovereign power of the Holy Spirit. God the Spirit is present and working among us in at least three ways. First, the Holy Spirit is our life-giving energy. It gives us the strength to heal, regenerate, and sanctify our lives. Second, the Holy Spirit is the sustainer of our lives. We are not abandoned or alone in this world because God acts through the Spirit within our lives and helps us during times of weakness and hardship. Finally, the Holy Spirit is the transforming force of the world. God the Spirit works to establish "God's humanizing activity in the world" by guiding and directing our human lives.[56]

Preaching the risen Christ is a participatory practice of the mission of the Spirit by working in the same threefold way as the Spirit does. Just as the mission of the Spirit is to vitalize human life, to sustain life with love, and to transform the world into God's dominion, so preaching as missionary work of God means bringing life-giving energy, sustaining power, and transforming force to the world. Preaching as God's missionary work relies on God's gracious partnership with human beings. God invites preachers to divine missionary activity as God's co-workers and to help people discover themselves as new beings in the grace and compassion of God. Preaching as the missionary work of God calls listeners out of their status quo and fills them with the passion and desire to take responsibility for transforming the world with a new vision, one in which nature and every human being enjoy their restored relationship with God. Through preaching, listeners are invited to live with this vision as living parables.

Mary Magdalene, St. Nina, and other women preachers in the Bible and in the early church remind us that the origin of Christian preaching was not only the women's testimony of the risen Christ but also the transforming power of the Spirit working through their testimonies. The preaching of these women contributes to the understanding of the nature and function of Christian preaching in relation to the proclamation of the risen Christ. Preaching the risen Christ means proclaiming the sovereignty of God over the world in the promise of God through the life, death, and resurrection of Jesus Christ. Preaching the risen Christ begins with the preacher's testimony of experiencing the risen Christ in her daily life and connects it with the diverse experiences of the listeners in their particular social locations. The ultimate goal for preaching the risen Christ is to participate in the mission of the Holy Spirit, the reconciliation and transformation of the world.

Chapter Three

PREACHING AS SUBVERSIVE RHETORIC
WOMEN PREACHERS OF THE MEDIEVAL AND POSTMEDIEVAL CHURCH

A FEMALE STUDENT OF MINE, who was the pastor of a mainline denominational church, shared the following experience in class: In her church, there was a pious couple who were active members, serving the church in numerous ways. One Sunday, she found the husband absent from the worship. The following Sunday, he was absent again. When she asked his wife about his absence, she replied, "Don't you remember that you called God 'our Father and Mother' in worship? My husband was very offended by your naming God the Mother. He was so upset that he has decided not to attend service anymore, but I am okay with calling God the Mother."

This episode represents how deeply the masculine imagery of God has influenced the Christian Church. For some believers, imagining God in feminine terms is considered heresy because the church has traditionally taught about God using masculine images such as Father, Lord, and King on the premise that because female is inferior to male, God cannot be female. Although today liberal theological schools encourage students and pastors to use inclusive and imaginative language to help their congregations understand that God transcends human sexuality and language, many churches continue to use masculine language exclusively in teaching, preaching, and worshiping God.

This masculine-oriented ecclesial culture challenges preachers both theologically and homiletically by raising the following questions: How can preachers preach about God in the masculine-oriented culture of the church and society without distorting the nature of God? What kind of language shall preachers use when naming God? Do any theological and/or homiletical resources exist in the church history regarding the use of theological language when preaching?

The use of masculine language and imagery for naming God is not simply a contemporary homiletical issue. This issue has existed in the Christian Church since its beginning. However, despite the conventional practice of the institutionalized church to use masculine language and imagery, the history of the church reveals that at least a few theologians preached about God using new language with versatility. Especially, the women preachers during the medieval period challenged the patriarchal church and society with their creative use of theological language, including the use of feminine terms and images for God. The way in which these women preachers used language can be considered the counter-rhetoric of gender ideology.

This chapter explores the counter-rhetoric of gender ideology used by medieval women preachers. Their rhetorical strategies give theological and homiletical insight into developing "subversive rhetoric" for preaching in today's societies which many people experience as sexist. The first section of this chapter outlines the process of establishing the gender ideology that became the theological foundation for the institutionalized church which excluded women's leadership. The second section analyzes the characteristics of medieval preaching, in which women preachers were marginalized. The third section reviews medieval women's preaching in general and then concentrates specifically on the lives and works of three women preachers who lived in different times and places: Hildegard of Bingen (1098–1178) of Germany, Julian of Norwich (1342–1416) of England, and Sor Juana Inés de la Cruz (1651–95) of Mexico. Although Sor Juana is not a medieval woman, she is included in this section because her church in seventeenth-century colonial Mexico was under the influence of the medieval patriarchal culture. Based on the analysis of these three women's sermons, the last section proposes subversive rhetoric that can help contemporary preachers better communicate the holistic nature of God in our current sexist environment.

GENDER IDEOLOGY AND THE EXCLUSION OF WOMEN FROM LEADERSHIP

Women preachers were prominent in the early days when the Christian Church was in the private sphere. However, the emerging pattern of institutional life, spurred by such early church fathers as Tertullian, Clement of Alexandria, and Origen, brought the transition of the church from the private sphere to the public sphere. By the third century, the church was in the process of evolving as an ecclesiastical hierarchy, dominated by the male successors of Peter, who held the roles of bishops, deacons, and priests. As a result, the leadership of the church was increasingly masculinized, and the ordained ministry of the institutionalized church became "a male preserve."[1]

In the process of institutionalizing the church, women's leadership in churches was controversial and problematic for the male leaders. They manifested their prejudice against women in their sermons and other writings, thereby developing gender ideology that emphasized women's inferiority and subordination to men. Their gender ideology was supported by the seven strongly anti-women passages of the New Testament (1 Cor. 11:3-10; 14:34-35; 1 Pet. 3:1-7; Col. 3:18-19; Eph. 5:22-23; 1 Tim. 2:8-15; Titus 2:4-5) and the androcentric passages of the Hebrew Scriptures (cf. Gen. 2:18-25; Job 2:9-10; etc.). For example, Origen of Alexandria explicitly states the inferiority of women in his commentary on 1 Corinthians 14:34-35, when he wrote,

> ...let a woman learn from the man who is her own, taking "man" in its generic sense, as the counterpart of woman. For it is improper for a woman to speak in an assembly, no mat-

ter what she says, even if she says admirable things or even saintly things; that is of little consequence since they come from the mouth of a woman. A woman speaking in an assembly — clearly this abuse is denounced as improper, an abuse for which the entire assembly is responsible.[2]

As another example, the *Apostolic Constitutions* — a collection of materials on church order compiled sometime during the closing decades of the fourth century — instructs the church to exclude women from the priesthood as follows:

> Now, as to women's baptizing, ... we do not advise you to it; for it is dangerous, or rather wicked and impious. For if the "man be the head of the woman," and he be the originally ordained for the priesthood, it is not just to abrogate the order of the creation, and leave the principal to come to the extreme part of the body. For the woman is the body of the man, taken from his side, and subject to him, from whom she was separated for the procreation of children.... [I]f in the foregoing constitutions we have not permitted them to teach, how will any one allow them contrary to nature, to perform the office of a priest? For this is one of the ignorant practices of the Gentile atheism, to ordain women priests to the female deities, not one of the constitutions of Christ.[3]

Based on the gender ideology of the early church fathers, the Council of Laodicea (352 CE) forbade women to serve as priests or to preside over churches,[4] and the Council of Carthage (398 CE) officially prohibited women from the ministry of preaching.[5] Later, church fathers continued to stress the Genesis 2 account of woman's creation, in which Eve was created from Adam's rib, as a proof-text of women's inferiority. St. Augustine reinforced gender ideology in his commentary on Genesis by claiming that "[i]f it were not the case that the woman was created to be man's helper specifically for the production of children, then why would she have been created as a 'helper' (Genesis 2:18)?... I cannot think of any reason for woman's being made as man's helper, if we dismiss the reason of procreation."[6]

The gender ideology established by Augustine and other church fathers became a strong theological foundation for the institutionalization of the church. Although a tenth-century letter from Atto, bishop of Vercelli, and other sources during this period provide evidence that devout women were also ordained to preach in churches,[7] the twelfth century became the turning point for excluding women from the leadership of the church. Canonical legislation gradually excluded women from any official role in the church, until finally, in 1140, the author of canon law, Gratian, in his massive work of codification, the *Decretum*, formulated a number of laws that restricted women. Following patristic scriptural evidence,[8] Gratian insisted on female subordination to men by codifying that "[e]ven if a woman is learned and saintly, she still must not presume to baptize or to instruct men in a [congregational] assembly."[9]

It is worth noting that from the end of the twelfth century to the early thirteenth century, the Cathars and Waldensians challenged the established church to reconsider women's right to preach. These groups were wandering preachers who criticized church corruption and who denied the traditional interpretation of the orders in the church. Consequently, Catharism and Waldensianism were the "would-be reform movements" of laity that arose in the South of France, in Italy, in Flanders, and in certain parts of the Rhine Valley. Although canon law only gave clergy, primarily bishops, the right to preach, the Cathars and the Waldensians declared that the right to preach was open to all — laymen and laywomen — and that the qualification of the preacher depended not on the particular training or authorization of the preacher but rather on the apostolic life of poverty the preacher lived. No episcopal ordination was considered necessary to become a preacher. No distinction was made between laypeople and those who happened to be in priests' orders. Women had the same right to preach as men.[10] The influence which preaching had on laywomen and laymen made the Cathar and Waldensian movements especially attractive to those who were dissatisfied with the lack of an institutionally approved way by which laity could gain the authority to preach in the orthodox church. However, the established church felt threatened by the practice of laity preaching and accused the Cathars and Waldensians of heresy. In the late twelfth century, Bernard, the Premonstratensian abbot of Fontcaude, condemned Waldensians in his treatise as "enemies of truth," for they allowed women to preach.[11] In 1234, Pope Gregory IX legally forbade women to preach by inserting an article of prohibition into the Book of *Decretals*.[12]

During the high Middle Ages, male theologians and preachers were still busy justifying the prohibition of women from preaching. Gauthier of Château-Thierry, chancellor of the University of Paris, defined preaching as the privileged office to teach the doctrine based on explanations of the scriptures. He insisted that teaching Christian doctrines be an exclusive right of men who had received their holy orders. Only clerics were allowed to read and interpret the word of God publicly. Gauthier said that Mary Magdalene and a few other women were allowed to preach in the earlier days because men who were capable of preaching were so rare that it was actually a temporary expedient.[13] In his preaching manual, the thirteenth-century preacher Humbert of Romans set the tone for the times as to why women must not be allowed to preach:

> First is lack of judgment, for a woman has less than a man. Second is the condition of servitude that was inflicted on her.... Third, if she were to preach, her appearance would provoke lascivious thoughts.... Fourth, in remembrance of the foolishness of the first woman.... She taught [just] once and subverted the whole world.[14]

In the late medieval era, the ecclesiastical regulations and laws that excluded women from any official function in the church were reinforced, thus bringing to an end the tendency for women to actively participate in ecclesiastical affairs.[15] The new surge in preaching in the thirteenth century and its prevailing definition as the *officium docendi* (ministry of teaching) became the standard position of the late medieval church, thereby depriving women of rights to preach.

CHARACTERISTICS OF MEDIEVAL PREACHING

Medieval preaching is often categorized into two types of sermons: monastic sermons and university sermons. These two types were not separated but influenced each other, formulating particular characteristics of medieval preaching, because many preaching manuals were written by abbots who had received advanced education at universities as well as their local monasteries.[16] Of many preaching manuals written during the Middle Ages, *Ars Praedicandi* (*The Art of Preaching*), written by the twelfth-century Cistercian monk Alan of Lille, is considered a major preaching resource. Alan defines preaching as "an open and public instruction in faith and behavior, whose purpose is the forming of men; it derives from the path of reason and from the fountainhead of the 'authorities.'"[17] Here, the authorities mean the scriptures from which an intellectual point of view should be developed. According to Alan, preaching is counted as the highest of the seven steps to Christian perfection, and preachers are like the angels, ascending and descending Jacob's ladder as in Genesis 28. They ascend when they proclaim heavenly things and descend when they give moral instructions.[18]

The homily, which is considered an ancient style of preaching based on a simple exposition of a text with a view to practical application, was popular from the early Middle Ages until the end of the eleventh century. Later, university education influenced preachers to apply Aristotelian logic and the techniques of scholastic argumentation to their preaching. As a result, the so-called "university style of sermon" emerged. This completely new rhetorical genre of preaching was a point-making thematic approach. It started with a topic about faith and morals rather than with a text and consisted of a threefold or fourfold division of that topic. Each division completed with its own proposition and its own proofs relating to the original theme. Scripture was used to confirm the theological propositions and moral instructions of the preacher. This new thematic sermon mode was the standard form of preaching from the thirteenth century through the post-Reformation period.[19]

The university style of preaching and its emphasis on morality required preachers to attain formal intellectual training. Convent schools, theological colleges, and universities provided educational programs to train preachers. The preacher's role was to bridge the gap "between learned clerical culture and popular lay culture."[20] Women, who were considered intellectually inferior and subordinate to men, were not allowed the opportunity to advance their theological education. In his book *Forma Praedicandi* (*The Form of Preaching*, 1322), Robert of Basevorn defines the qualifications of preachers as follows:

> Three things are necessary for one exercising the act of preaching: the first is purity of life, the second is competent knowledge (at least explicit knowledge of the articles of Faith, the Ten Commandments, and the distinction between sin and non-sin), and the third is authority given by the Church. No lay person or religious, unless permitted by the Bishop or Pope, and no woman, no matter how learned or saintly, ought to preach.[21]

In the subsequent history of the Christian Church, clericalism made preaching a ministry exclusive to men. The medieval church misunderstood the priestly office — including teaching, preaching, and administering sacraments — as a form of rule, an exercise of power, which completely excluded the possibility of an egalitarian community of faith. Panel paintings and frescos during the late medieval era depict women as listeners sitting in the audience rather than preachers. In those artworks, women occupy a separate place in the audience, reflecting the physical separation between the sexes.[22]

MEDIEVAL WOMEN PREACHERS

Despite the rigid prohibition of women's preaching by the institutionalized patriarchal church, the doctrine of virginity and the theology of vision granted some women marginal space to preach. They were allowed the authority to teach and preach to various audiences *ex beneficio* (from grace). More precisely speaking, around

1290, the Paris master Henry of Ghent claimed that women could not be totally excluded from all forms of teaching. He distinguished between teaching *ex officio* (from ecclesiastical approbation) and teaching *ex beneficio*. Women were excluded from the former but included in the latter as long as their teaching was limited to the private sector and was censored and approved by the church's investigation to be of sound doctrine.[23] Franciscan friar Eustache of Arras and other monastic preachers supported this position, stating that virgins were allowed to speak in public when the Holy Spirit inspired them with the special gift of prophecy.[24]

The elevation of virginity and the respect of prophets during the Middle Ages encouraged women who pursued freedom and self-esteem outside the domestic circle to choose monastic lives. In the medieval patriarchal system, the chief route to greater freedom for Christian women was to practice asceticism, namely, to become nuns, anchoresses, and abbesses. Clerics, as well as laity, believed that women who renounced their sexual lives were elevated above their natural abject condition to the degree that they almost constituted a "third sex."

The women who chose to live ascetic lives established their authority as authentic prophets based on their direct communication with the divine through ecstatic visions and auditions. These women did not have equal opportunities to receive formal education like their male counterparts in order to be granted permission to preach. However, they relied on their experiences of divine inspiration to prove their ability to prophesy, which was regarded as a form of both teaching and preaching. Prophesying did not challenge the belief that women were intellectually inferior because their learning was not perceived as originating from a rational process but rather from divine intercession. It is also important to remember that Mary Magdalene's legendary life as a preacher in Gaul was well known during the Middle Ages, and her work influenced laity to respect women preachers and prophets.

Although abbesses and nuns were officially allowed to teach and preach within their convents because this did not violate the seeming biblical injunctions against women teaching men, women preachers such as Hildegard of Bingen, Rose of Viterbo (1233–1252), St. Catherine of Siena (1347–1380), and so on, preached with full authority and sanctity both inside and outside monasteries. They preached not only to women but also to men without rousing opposition or censorship from the clergy, for their preaching had the authority of their mystical experiences of the divine.[25] Among the various women preachers, St. Birgitta (Bridget) of Sweden (1302/3?–1373) was exceptional in the sense that she was not a virgin but a widow. Although she physically was not a virgin like many other medieval preachers, her exclusive devotion to God and ecstatic experience accorded her a privileged status as an authentic prophet and preacher.[26] These women preachers used their prophetic voices to transform the church and society by denouncing moral corruption and exhorting Christians to rekindle their love for God.[27]

While sermons are generally understood as speeches delivered orally in public, Beverly M. Kienzle's research on medieval sermons provides a different view of medieval preaching. According to her research, the sermon in the Middle Ages was a fluid genre, including letters, treatises, and commentaries as well as speeches. In other words, medieval sermons were not only oral discourses but also written texts instructing and exhorting the reader. For example, St. Bernard of Clairvaux wrote commentaries on the Song of Songs in the form of sermons. His sermons were never preached in public but were widely read privately.[28] James Murphy also points out that Guibert of Nogent's *Commentary on Genesis* was actually a series of sermons. His style of writing commentaries was the same as that of his sermons: he applied the fourfold interpretation of the text in both forms of writing.[29] Moreover, in the medieval era, many sermons were written in the form of a letter and sent to individuals or communities to whom the preachers could not deliver their sermons in person. For example, fifty-five of the fifty-six letters of Hildegard, contained in the collection of the Berlin manuscript *Lat. Qu. 674*, were preserved as sermons by the copyist who intentionally omitted their opening salutations in order to make each letter a small treatise or homily.[30]

A broad understanding of medieval sermons allows us to stretch our research area of women's preaching to include commentaries, letters, and other literary works written by female authors. Following this notion, the remainder of this chapter concentrates on three women who used creative ways to participate in the ministry of preaching under the institutionalized patriarchal church. Hildegard of Bingen in the high Middle Ages, Julian of Norwich in the late medieval era, and Sor Juana Inés de la Cruz in the post-Reformation Catholic Church represent how women creatively used their prophetic voices to challenge and reform the rigid and limited male-centered understanding of scripture and Christian doctrines. Their theological works in various literary genres were actually sermons. Through distinctive rhetorical strategies, these three women instructed and exhorted the church and society, which were embedded with misogynist mentality and attitudes.

Hildegard of Bingen

Hildegard was born to a wealthy noble family in Bermersheim (Germany). When she was eight, her parents gave her to an anchoress named Jutta who educated her privately. Jutta taught Hildegard to read the Bible in Latin and to chant the Benedictine office. Although little is known about Hildegard's advanced education, her sermons and other writings — including theological books, visionary tracts, letters, poems, a medical handbook, and Latin hymns — prove that she was thoroughly trained in Western Christian traditions, Neoplatonism, literature, music, and science. After Jutta's death, Hildegard was elected abbess of the small female group that was associated with the male monastic foundation of St. Disibod. Later, she separated her group from the male monastery and established her own Benedictine convent, the Rupertsberg, in Bingen. As the founder and head of the convent, Hildegard demonstrated her political and spiritual leadership. Her leadership was not limited, however, to her own convent. After receiving ecclesiastical approval, she undertook three preaching tours from Mainz to Cologne to preach in monasteries and in public market squares (1158–63). In her sermons, she condemned the continued corruption of the clergy and called the church to become what it was meant to be.

Through preaching, Hildegard proclaimed the beginning of a new age, one in which the church would return to its apostolic purity.[31]

How was Hildegard able to give such a prophetic voice to the institutionalized patriarchal church? What kind of rhetorical strategies made it possible for her, as a woman, to preach a reforming message to male clergy without the prohibition of the church? Concerning these questions, it is worth noting that Hildegard did not stand against the patriarchal hierarchies and traditions of either the church or society in general. More precisely speaking, she acknowledged the ecclesiastical teaching of womanly weakness and submissiveness based on the deutero-Pauline proscription against women's teaching and preaching. Yet, through her visionary rhetoric she did create a space in which she could use her prophetic voice against the patriarchal church. Her rhetoric includes three distinctive elements: a "trope of reversal," a visionary narrative of her personal experience of the divine revelation, and allegorical interpretation. These three rhetorical strategies are always interconnected, thereby bringing authenticity and authority to her preaching.

Hildegard's trope of reversal has as its biblical foundation such scriptural passages as "that stone which was rejected by the builders has become the cornerstone" and "the last shall be made first."[32] According to these passages, the weak are made strong, and the margins become the center of God's salvific activities. Hildegard believes that women, who are "the last" and "the rejected stone," are exalted to be "the first" and "the cornerstone" by which God calls them to preach the gospel. In turn, she uses her marginal position based on her gender as a source of credibility for both her preaching and her qualifications as a preacher.

Hildegard's trope of reversal is often associated with her personal experience of the divine revelation. In her sermons and theological writings, she tells her personal experience of visions as the source of her authority as a preacher and writer. For example, Hildegard begins the sermon she preached in Trier at the feast of Pentecost in 1160 with a trope of reversal based on one of her visions: "I, a poor little figure without health or strength or courage or learning, myself subject to masters, have heard these words addressed to the prelates and clergy of Trier, from the mystical light of the true vision."³³ Another example in which Hildegard uses a trope of reversal can be found on the first page of her book the *Scivias* (*Scito vias Domini* [*Know the Ways of the Lord*]). Here, Hildegard states that it is her visionary experience that gives her the authority to write. She defends herself with the trope of reversal, for she, who is "ashes of ashes, and filth of filth," is exalted by God to be used to deliver God's voice:

> And behold! In the forty-third year of my earthly course, as I was gazing with great fear and trembling attention at a heavenly vision, I saw a great splendor in which resounded a voice from Heaven, saying to me, "O fragile human, ashes of ashes, and filth of filth! Say and write what you see and hear. But since you are timid in speaking, and simple in expounding, and untaught in writing, speak and write these things not by a human mouth, and not by the understanding of human invention, and not by the requirements of human composition, but as you see and hear them on high in the heavenly places in the wonders of God."³⁴

After authorizing her position as a preacher and writer, Hildegard shares heavenly secrets revealed to her in personified forms and interprets them one by one, using allegorical interpretation.³⁵ The use of allegorical rhetoric challenges her audience, who was used to patriarchal teachings, to stretch their ways of thinking about God and the church to include feminine language and imagery. For example, when explaining the concept of the Trinity in Book Two of the *Scivias*, Hildegard focuses on "charity," which is the feminine character of God, as the fundamental nature of the Trinity: "That through this fountain of life came the embrace of God's maternal love, which has nourished us unto life and is our help in perils, and is the deepest and sweetest charity and prepares us for penitence."³⁶

Hildegard also uses allegorical rhetoric to contrast the institutionalized church, which is masculine, with the perfect church, which she describes as feminine. She expresses the perfect church as the "Bride of Christ" and "Mother of the faithful," explaining its nature and function as follows:

> After this, I saw the image of a woman as large as a great city, with a wonderful crown on her head and arms from which a splendor hung like sleeves, shining from heaven to earth.... This designates the Bride of My Son, who always bears her children by regeneration in the Spirit and in water. ... She does not yet have legs or feet, for she has not yet been brought to the full strength of her constancy or the full purity of her fulfillment; for when the son of perdition comes to delude the world she will suffer fiery and bloody anguish in all her members from his cruel wickedness. By this calamity, with bleeding wounds, she will be brought to perfection; then let her run swiftly into the heavenly Jerusalem, where she will sweetly rise anew as a bride in the blood of My Son, entering into life with ardor in the joy of her offspring.... She is always pregnant and procreating children of hers by the true ablution, and offering them devoutly to God by the purest prayers of the saints and the sweet fragrance of chosen virtues both hidden and manifest.[37]

Hildegard's feminine imagery is vivid and imaginative. Through feminine language and imagery, she envisions a desired reality not yet discernible in our mundane lives. Her visionary rhetoric challenges her audience to transform its conventional ways of thinking and living to fit a new visionary world. Through her rhetorical strategies of trope of reversal, allegory, and narration of her visions, Hildegard gives her voice with full authority of the divine from her marginalized position to the center of the male-dominant church and society.

Julian of Norwich

The life of Julian is known only through what she wrote about herself in her book *Showings*, which included the Short and Long Texts. It was written during the fifteenth century and was later published by an English Benedictine, Serenus Cressy, in 1670. While no historical records detail where and when Julian was born or died, we have some clues from her book. In the second chapter of the Long Text, she writes of having received her revelations on May 13, 1373.

In the second chapter of the Short Text and in the third chapter of the Long Text, Julian states that she was thirty-and-a-half years old when she received divine revelations. In addition, the introductory paragraph of the first chapter of the Short Text, which appears to have been written by someone else, describes Julian as "a devout woman,... who is a recluse at Norwich and still alive, A.D. 1413, in which vision are very many words of comfort, greatly moving for all those who desire to be Christ's lovers." Accordingly, what we deduce from this evidence is that Julian was born in the late fourteenth century in England and entered a religious order at a young age.

Julian's book also states she became a visionary because of the visions she received while seriously sick at the age of thirty-and-a-half years old. She lived the solitary, enclosed life of a contemplative, and probably became an anchoress. In the twenty-five chapters of the Short Text, Julian writes about the love of God she felt through sixteen different visions she experienced. Twenty years after writing the Short Text, Julian developed it into the Long Text with eighty-six chapters.[38] Although we do not know anything about her family or religious and educational background, Julian's writing shows that she used the Latin Vulgate text flexibly and had a broad and profound knowledge of the classical spiritual writings that were the foundation of the monastic contemplative traditions of the Western church. Moreover, Julian's writing reveals her highly masterful literary skills. As Edmund Colledge and James Walsh rightly point out, she was "a master of rhetorical art as to merit comparison with Geoffrey Chaucer."[39]

Considering that no historical record exists of Julian's preaching and that all we know is that she was an anchoress and writer who lived in a cell, socially excluded, it may be questionable to regard Julian as a preacher. However, medieval sermons were written not simply for oral delivery in public but also for private reading, using diverse literary genres such as theological treatises, biblical commentaries, letters, poems, and drama. In this regard, Julian's *Showings* calls our special attention to both its form and its content because it is a collection of theological treatises written in a variety of different literary forms. By examining the style and content of the book, it becomes clear why *Showings* should be regarded as a collection of sermons and Julian should be identified as a preacher.

Julian employed many different literary genres in her book. For example, Brad Peters categorizes the thirty-ninth chapter of the Long Text, which covers sin, as a typical style of medieval sermons, involving divisions and subdivisions. According to Peters's analysis, the theme is divided into two parts. First, sin is a scourge, and second, sin is vile. In the first division, Julian's prosecution consists of a series of cause-and-effect relationships along the sin/confession/penance continuum. Her second division exemplifies how the devil tries to turn this continuum toward evil. Her conclusion directs the minds of her readers toward the Incarnate God and God the Father.[40] This university style of medieval preaching is also found in other chapters of the book. For example, in the forty-first chapter of the Long Text, Julian explains prayer in two divisions: rightful prayer and confident trust. In the following chapter, she explains the nature of prayer in three ways and defines prayer as "a right understanding of that fullness of joy which is to come, with true longing and trust." She concludes that chapter with the exhortation that "when we do it [prayer], still it will seem to us that it is nothing. And this is true. But let us do what we can, and meekly ask mercy and grace, and everything which is lacking in us we shall find in him."[41]

Showings includes some parables. The fifty-first chapter of the Long Text, in which Julian describes her vision of the Lord and a servant, is a parable. Julian uses this parable to free the Genesis fall story from the medieval misogynist interpretation. She tells a new version of the Genesis text from the perspective of the divine grace. Just as Jesus often used parables in his preaching to help his audience recognize new dimensions of truth, so did Julian in her writing. *Showings* is also regarded as a collection of allegorical dramas. According to Elizabeth A. Petroff,

> [Julian] "reads" each vision as a kind of allegorical drama in which every detail of the imagery and the dialogue is significant — the color of clothing, the movements and gestures of the characters, the similes that occur to her as she observes her

recollections, which sometimes take the form of static, hieratic images but more often are visualized as scenes dramatizing parables original with her.[42]

Elisabeth K. Koenig affirms Petroff's emphasis on the allegorical nature of the book by analyzing common elements between medieval drama and Julian's book. Koenig assumes that Julian was so influenced by the medieval drama of the time that when she described her divine visions, she used such elements of drama as "the scenery, costumes, and action of the plays" to help her readers experience the visions as vividly and realistically as she did. These dramatic elements are particularly evident in the parable of the Lord and a servant in the fifty-first chapter of the Long Text.[43] In her use of dramatic elements, Julian attempted to re-create her experience of visions so that her readers would experience the same attractive power that drew her into a profound relationship with God.

By using a variety of literary forms and artistic techniques when describing her visions, Julian invited her readers to experience the divine presence as tangibly as she did in her own visions and made it possible for readers to experience the revealing love of God in various ways. What, then, did Julian proclaim in her book? What function did her visions serve in her writings?

One of her major contributions as a woman of the Middle Ages was her articulation of a new vision of Christ in the image of motherhood. The allegory of Jesus as a mother is the most interesting of Julian's speech genres found in *Showings*. God has been traditionally perceived by male theologians and scholars of the church in masculine language and images. However, such language and imagery narrowly limit the understanding of the nature and concept of God to the masculine image and often makes people believe that God is of the male gender. Ultimately, the use of masculine language and imagery for God fails to represent the wholeness of God, which is beyond human sexuality. Julian grasps this and develops the theology of the motherhood of God as a way of overcoming such a limited understanding of God. She explains the motherhood of God in terms of the three persons of the Trinity as follows:

> As to the first, I saw and understood that the high might of the Trinity is our Father, and the deep wisdom of the Trinity is our Mother, and the great love of the Trinity is our Lord; and all these we have in nature and in our substantial creation.... Our great Father, almighty God, who is being, knows us and loved us before time began. Out of this knowledge, in his most wonderful deep love, by the prescient eternal counsel of all the blessed Trinity, he wanted the second person to become our Mother, ... And so Jesus is our true Mother.[44]

Julian compares the motherhood of God with earthly mothering, involving childbearing, nourishing, caring, comforting, and disciplining. Just as human motherhood belongs to "nature, love, wisdom and knowledge," so does divine motherhood. We go to "our mother Church, who is Christ Jesus" and are fastened and united to God through his motherhood.[45]

Julian's theology of the motherhood of God has homiletical as well as theological significance for at least two reasons. First, Julian's theology, which is based on feminine imagery, nicely complements the Christian doctrine of the Trinity, which is primarily grounded in masculine language and imagery. Julian consciously strives to make the image of a maternal God a necessary part of a cohesive and intricate pattern, one which cannot be detached from the divine nature of God. Through her greater emphasis on a maternal image of God — which is less recognized within her masculine-oriented church and society — Julian brings forth the harmony and equality of God to Christian theology. When preaching is considered a theological task, Julian's image of the motherhood of God challenges contemporary preachers to reorient their theological understanding of God to incorporate the feminine nature of God to help their listeners understand God in a holistic way.

Julian's theology is also significant homiletically because her concept of God's motherhood is linked to her "woman-consciousness" and enhances the feminine nature of women. In fact, Julian's concept of motherhood is not completely new. In the Bible, we find a variety of female imagery referring to God. God is particularly described in maternal terms as the one who carries, heals, leads, comforts, cleanses, clothes, and also disciplines children out of love.[46] The influence of the biblical references on a maternal God is found in the writings of such early church fathers as Clement of Alexandria, John Chrysostom, and Augustine. Furthermore, as far back as the eleventh century, Anselm and other spiritual writers described God as a mother "nursing the soul at her breasts, drying its tears, punishing its petty mischief-making, giving birth to it in agony and travail."[47] Seeing Christ, God, and/or the Holy Spirit as a female later became a medieval devotional tradition. As Caroline W. Bynum rightly indicates, however, great differences remain between male writers and Julian of Norwich in developing and emphasizing the theme of God's feminine aspects. That is, for male writers, the motherhood of God was not a major theological topic. They addressed that topic in the margins of their writings simply to teach and nurture male readers to achieve intimate dependence on God. Although the male writers used feminine and maternal imagery in exploring the nature of God, they did not have a consciousness for women nor show an increased respect for women's femininity.[48] However, Julian's idea of the maternal Christ links her great concern for her own significance as a woman with her concern for the significance of all women.

In her writing, Julian shows an awareness of the sexist teaching of the church and secures her position as a teacher and preacher by appealing to *ex beneficio*.

> God forbid that you should say or assume that I am a teacher, for that is not and never was my intention; for I am a woman, ignorant, weak and frail.... But I know very well that what I am saying I have received by the revelation of him who is the sovereign teacher. But it is truly love which moves me to tell it to you, ... in everything I believe as Holy Church teaches, ... and I never understood anything from it which bewilders me or keeps me from the true doctrine of Holy Church.[49]

After authorizing her position as the teacher and preacher by the divine revelation, Julian states that the role of human motherhood is the best representation of the love of God, writing, "our savior is our true Mother, in whom we are endlessly born and out of whom we shall never come."[50] To Julian, God is never simply "like" a mother. Rather, God is a mother and the most ultimate of mothers.[51] She bestows God with a variety of feminine titles in addition to mother, including daughter, wife, maiden, and lady.[52] By placing feminine images of God in the center of Christian theology, Julian challenged the rigid concepts of God in the medieval church and its theology. Her description of God in such feminine images was truly a subversive voice from the margins, chipping away at the masculine-centered Christianity. In this regard, Julian should be considered a precursor to today's feminist theologians and preachers.

Sor Juana Inés de la Cruz

Sor Juana was born illegitimately to Spanish parents in San Miguel, Nepantla, Mexico, in 1651[53] and died in 1695. In the rigidly patriarchal culture of seventeenth-century New Spain, women were not allowed to pursue higher education. Neither university nor any other formal education was available to women. However, from her childhood, Sor Juana was full of intellectual curiosity. When she was three, she succeeded in persuading her older sister's teacher at a *miga* (a girls' elementary school) to give her lessons. At the age of six or seven, she knew how to read and write. She then asked her mother to send her to university dressed as a man. Disappointed by her mother's refusal, Sor Juana taught herself in her grandfather's library.[54]

In 1661, Sor Juana was sent to Mexico City to live with her mother's sister, the wife of a wealthy merchant. There, her "lively intellect, beauty, and vivacious personality" attracted the attention of court circles and exposed her to the culture of court society. At the age of fourteen, she became a "lady-in-waiting" to the wife of the viceroy and lived at the court until she decided to enter a sisterhood in 1667. During this time in history, there were only two places where women were allowed to pursue an intellectual life: the convent locutory and the palace drawing room. Sor Juana made use of both places to develop her intellectual and aesthetic communication with men and women.[55] In 1669, she entered the convent of St. Paula, of the order of St. Jerome, with a desire to have a life of study and meditation. During her convent life, Sor Juana worked as a semiofficial court and church poet. In the predominantly masculine environment of her century, she gave a woman's voice to the world by writing various pieces of literature. She wrote poetry for the celebration of liturgical feasts in the cathedrals of Mexico City, Oaxaca, and Pueblo and composed the sacred drama, *Divine Narcissus*, and other secular comedies, which were often performed in public. She also wrote lyrical poems and verses for songs and dance tunes on various aspects of human and divine love. Her rigorous theological treatise in the form of a letter, *La Respuesta a Sor Filotea de la Cruz* (*The Response to Sor Filotea de la Cruz*), is regarded as the first piece of feminist writing on the North American continent. Her letter is a response to a letter written by the bishop of Pueblo in which he prohibited her from intellectual and literary activity. In her letter, Sor Juana defended the right of women to study and cultivate their minds. Following the bishop's order, Sor Juana ceased her literary activity until her death from an epidemic, while nursing the sick sisters of her community.[56]

Although Sor Juana lived in the post-Reformation era, her sociocultural environment of colonial Mexico was similar to typical medieval society, in which gender ideology and sexist attitudes dominated the church and society. The religious legends, which held women to be "diabolical, fallen, and agent[s] of the Fall,"[57] were the foundation of the misogynist doctrines and attitudes of the Catholic Church in New Spain. In late seventeenth-century Mexico, the clergy ruled the society not only religiously but also economically and politically. More than half of the land was in the hands of the church. The church had a monopoly on political power and often became the arena for political hegemony among bishops. Many political conflicts were caused by disputes over the interpretation of a passage from the scriptures. Sermons, either written or delivered in the pulpit, were major tools for clergy to use for their power struggles and personal squabbles. Like the medieval sermon, sermons in the seventeenth century were equivalent to theological essays or commentaries. It is notable that Antonio de Vieira, a celebrated Portuguese Jesuit, wrote a sermon that Sor Juana sharply criticized. Ultimately, however, she was trapped by political power and became its victim.[58]

Was Sor Juana a preacher? We find her answer to this question in her own poem, sung at the dedication of a church to St. Bernard in 1690:

> The Church, Bernard and Mary,
> it would be a good occasion
> to bring them into concert
> if I were a preacher.
> But no, no, no, no:
> I'm not cut of such fine cloth.
> But supposing that I were,
> what things would I say
> moving from text to text
> searching for connections?
> But no, no, no, no:
> I'm not cut of such fine cloth.[59]

This poem presents Sor Juana's double answers. On the one hand, Sor Juana says "no" about her identity as a preacher because she is aware of her precarious position as a woman in the church. Women should be silent and must obey this commandment in order not to be punished. On the other hand, reading between the lines of the poem, we find that her real answer is yes. Josefina Ludmer defines this style as a "trick of the weak," a rhetorical technique that combines acceptance of her subordinate position with the trick of "not to say but to know, or saying that one doesn't know but knowing, or saying the opposite of what one knows."[60] Using this form, Sor Juana secures her position as a woman preacher, actually preaching while denying she was doing so. Her three major dramas, more than fifty poems, letters, and other writings — not only sacred but also secular — are actually sermons written based on her profound theological knowledge. Many of them were performed and recited in cathedrals and other public spheres.

Sor Juana did not believe that sacred knowledge should be separated from secular knowledge nor that the study of books should be separated from the experience of reality. For her, studies such as logic, rhetoric, physics, arithmetic, geometry, architecture, history, law, music, astrology, and so on, are all linked to the study of theology. Because the revelation of the divine happens in all areas of human knowledge and experience, theology embraces all types of knowledge. The study of theology is so scientific that it is possible through interdisciplinary studies. Sor Juana considered cooking scientific work and discovered "secretos naturales (natural secrets)" while cooking. After illustrating how helpful cooking was in learning about the secrets of nature, Sor Juana commented, "What is there for us women to know, if not bits of kitchen philosophy? As Lupercio Leonardo said: One can perfectly well philosophize while cooking supper. And I am always saying, when I observe these small details: If Aristotle had been a cook, he would have written much more."[61]

While the trick of the weak is one of the characteristics of Sor Juana's counter-rhetoric of gender ideology, at least three other distinctive rhetorical characteristics are found in her writing: humor and satire, allegory, and argumentation. Her famous poem, "Hombres necios (Foolish Men)," is a good example of her rhetoric using humor and satire:

> Silly, you men—so very adept
> at wrongly faulting womankind,
> not seeing you're alone to blame
> for faults you plant in woman's mind.
> After you've won by urgent plea
> the right to tarnish her good name,
> you still expect her to behave—
> you, that coaxed her into shame.
> You batter her resistance down
> and then, all righteousness, proclaim
> that feminine frivolity,
> not your persistence, is to blame....
> So where does the greater guilt lie
> for a passion that should not be:
> with the man who leads out of baseness
> or the woman debased by this plea?

> Or which is more to be blamed —
> though both will have cause for chagrin:
> the woman who sins for money
> or the man who pays money to sin?
> So why are you men all so stunned
> at the thought you're all guilty alike? ...
> your arrogance is allied
> with the world, the flesh, and the devil!⁶²

This poem was a reply to numerous satires of women written by famous and powerful men and circulating during Sor Juana's time. Octavio Paz praises Sor Juana's poem by saying that "for the first time in the history of our literature a woman is speaking in her own name, defending her sex and with grace and intelligence, using the same weapons as the detractors of her sex, accusing them of the very vices they impute to women."⁶³

Like Hildegard and Julian, Sor Juana often uses allegorical rhetoric creatively, particularly when writing dramas and poetry. For example, her *El Divino Narciso* (*The Divine Narcissus*) is a famous allegorical drama, combining the two stories of Narcissus of Greek mythology and Jesus of the Gospels. In the unfolding drama, Sor Juana presents a radical friendship between God and humanity. Narciso, who represents Jesus, and Human Nature, who is described as female and represents all humanity, mutually search and long for each other, equally anxious and equally confronted with their own limitations and frustrations. In this allegorical drama, Sor Juana uses her imagination and cultural sensitivity to reconstruct the Christian doctrine of equality of all humanity — women and men as well as pagans and Christians.⁶⁴

Sor Juana's formal letter, *La Respuesta* (*The Answer*), is one of the best examples of her rhetoric of argumentation. In the letter, Sor Juana uses simple, direct, and assertive speech rather than the "unctuous rhetoric of subordination" of a conventionalized woman's voice.⁶⁵ She writes in a narrative mode, which is "common to women's religious writing of the sixteenth and seventeenth centuries,"⁶⁶ combined with autobiography, theological essay, biblical commentary, and legal polemic. By pulling these different types of writings together, Sor Juana presents her biblical, historical, and theological knowledge to defend her right to perform intellectual activities as a religious woman. To support her argument, Sor Juana first lists forty-four outstanding female individuals, both from the Bible and the history of the church, who demonstrated their spiritual and intellectual leadership. Then, she discusses various interpretations of biblical texts regarding women's teaching and preaching. She interprets scripture based on her historical knowledge and critical analysis of the text and challenges the conventional patriarchal interpretations:

> The understanding of many passages doubtless requires much study of history, customs, ceremonies, proverb, and even the ways of speaking of the times in which they were written, so as to learn to what certain locutions of Holy Writ are referring and alluding.... All of this requires more study than is thought by some who, not having gone beyond the level of grammar or knowing at most a few terms of formal logic, undertake to interpret the Scriptures and fasten onto *mulieres in Ecclesiis taceant* ["Women should be quiet in church" (1 Cor. 14:34)], with no idea of how it should be interpreted. And, from elsewhere in the Bible, onto: *Mulier in silentio discat* ["Let the woman learn in silence" (1 Tim. 2:11)], even though these words speak more in woman's favor than against them, since they direct them to learn, and it is obvious that while women are learning they must keep silent. And it is also written: *Audi, Israel, et tace* ["Hear, Israel, and hold thy peace"], words which address the whole conglomeration of men and women telling them all to maintain silence, since anyone listening and learning must naturally be attentive and keep silent. If all those interpreters and expositors of Saint Paul think otherwise, I should like them to explain to me how they understand the passage *Mulieres in Ecclesia taceant*.[67]

Such diverse rhetorical characteristics as the trick of the weak, the rhetoric of humor and satire, the rhetoric of allegory, and the rhetoric of argumentation attest to Sor Juana's ability to wield various strategies so that different audiences can hear her voice. By using a variety of rhetorical skills in many different types of writing, filled with poetic imagery, humor, satire, feminine consciousness, keen critical insights, and cultural sensitivity, Sor Juana attempted to subvert the symbolic and social order that upheld the misogynist culture of her time. Her intellect and literary work challenged the sociocultural and religious mores that kept women physically, mentally, and socially confined. For these reasons, Electa Arenal and Amanda Powell declare Sor Juana a precursor of feminism:

> While feminism has its current meanings within a context of twentieth-century women's movements for equality and liberation, a "woman question" debate raged in Europe through the medieval and early modern period. Sor Juana consciously entered this controversy. Because she wrote as a woman aware of her gender status and because she intended her arguments to be applied on behalf of other women *as women,* she is certainly a precursor to worldviews and activities we call feminist.[68]

PREACHING AS SUBVERSIVE RHETORIC

Hildegard of Bingen, Julian of Norwich, and Sor Juana Inés de la Cruz lived their unique lives in their particular historical times and places. The analysis of their sermons manifests their counter-rhetoric of gender ideology, employing such techniques as the trope of reversal; the trick of the weak; the rhetoric of allegory and visionary narrative; the use of feminine language and imagery of God; the rhetoric of humor, satire, and argumentation; and so forth. Through these diverse rhetorical strategies, these three women gave their unique voices to the masculine-oriented church and their respective societies, reflecting their particular feminine experiences. The sermons of these three women subverted the sexist mentality and misogynist attitudes prevailing in their worlds. Their subversive rhetoric had the power to deconstruct the exclusively masculine concept of God and reconstruct new images of God that associate with the matrix of women's experiences. The counter-rhetoric of gender ideology used by Hildegard, Julian, and Sor Juana was the reforming voice of the marginalized, undermining the masculine-centered world.

Unfortunately, there is little difference between medieval and post-Reformation women preachers and preachers today in the sense that our preaching contexts today are still sexist and patriarchal. Women are often treated as inferior to men and oppressed by the masculine power of the church and larger society. Many listeners are still uncomfortable with feminine images of God and prefer to conceptualize God as male. As women preachers have experienced, preaching from a woman's perspective can be "dangerous business," for it often creates hostile reactions from congregations that are used to the patriarchal culture of the church and larger society. This negative situation requires contemporary preaching to be subversive. The goal of preaching is to undermine the symbolic and social order that upholds the sexist culture in order to help our listeners meet the living God in a new way. As the three women showed in their work, subversive rhetoric is not plain speech but involves such rhetorical strategies as tricks, allegories, imaginative language, and creative feminine imagery of God. By using these rhetorical strategies, preaching from a woman's perspective aims to undermine the exclusively masculine-oriented worldviews and attitudes of congregations. In order to tackle gender, sexuality, and other critical issues, preachers need specific rhetorical training to develop their preaching into subversive rhetoric.

Preaching as subversive rhetoric has at least three characteristics. First, theological language is taken seriously. Language is "the systems of signs and structures through which human beings communicate in speech or writing."[69] Although language does not determine how we think, it shapes our thinking and behavior. The way we speak of God shapes and slants our understanding of God. Thus, God-language in preaching and worship forms our concepts of God, beginning in early childhood onward. Untruthful God-language hinders our experience of the divine presence and restricts our knowledge of God, while truthful God-language deepens listeners' experience of God and broadens their understanding of God. If a preacher uses such masculine terms as father, king, and Lord when naming God, the congregation consciously or unconsciously imagines God as male, one who is omnipotent, transcendent, invincible, impassible, and tough. On the other hand, if the preacher describes the nature of God in such feminine terms as mother, wife, maiden, and lover, the congregation imagines God as gentle, patient, humble, immanent, and caring. Furthermore, if the preacher uses prescriptive, propositional, imperative, authoritarian, and judgmental language, which has traditionally been categorized as male language, the congregation is tamed to acknowledge the hierarchy between the pulpit and pews and thereby becomes passive believers. However, if the preacher uses descriptive, imaginative, poetic, inviting, and inspiring language, which has traditionally been categorized as feminine language, the congregation becomes active believers, autonomous in nurturing their faith and understands the church as an egalitarian community. The rhetoric of the three women discussed in this chapter illustrates how powerful feminine language and female images are in communicating the essence of the Christian gospel.

The second characteristic of preaching as subversive rhetoric involves creating new language for naming God based on women's particular experiences. In reality, we live and are formed as social beings in a world where men have predominance over women, and consequently the qualities regarded as feminine are disvalued. The church has supported male dominance by systematically using almost exclusive male God-language. Preaching as subversive rhetoric is aware of this present situation and intentionally uses inclusive language and feminine imagery of God in subtle and heuristic ways to help listeners understand the holistic nature of God and the egalitarian nature which the church should strive for. Using inclusive language and feminine imagery in preaching has the subversive power to deconstruct the patriarchal mentality of a congregation and reconstruct personal and communal faith in a new creative way. As Elizabeth A. Johnson claims, "[I]f God is 'she' as well as 'he,' a new possibility can be envisioned of a way of living together that honors difference but allows women and men to share life in equal measure."[70]

Subversive rhetoric not only discovers unfamiliar feminine images of God included in the scriptures but also creates new feminine images of God from the wealth of women's experiences. Preaching that incorporates new images of God in feminine terms changes the predominantly masculine pulpit language into egalitarian language. To cite Brian Wren's views, changing language cannot be separated from changing actions.

> Language change is an essential part of action. If I cease using racist language I will not thereby end racism. Yet trying out new forms of speech is a necessary part of finding out what I really think. By using nonracist language I also commit myself more deeply than before, even if I can't completely live out my commitment. Language is a public medium. If I use, or abandon, racist or sexist language, or begin to name God anew, I shall open myself to comment and criticism and shall have to explain and defend my usage. It may then be easier than before to act on what I have said.[71]

Changing language for naming God is based on the fact that almost all theological language is metaphoric, not literal. A metaphor is a word or phrase used to express what is beyond literal expressions. A metaphor has a double-character of "is" and "is not." To say "God is Mother" or "God is Father" is not to define God as mother or father in the literal sense but to suggest that we use the term "mother" or "father" to express the partial resemblance with the transcendent reality to which they point.[72] Namely, if we speak of God as mother, we are giving reliable knowledge of God based on our experience of motherhood, rather than pinning down who and what God uniquely is. As such, our metaphors for naming God are not themselves God. Every metaphor we use to describe God has its limits. All of the language about God is technically improper. The language is merely like a finger pointing at the moon, not the moon itself. Despite the limitations of theological language, however, when words and images are used as metaphors, they generate new insights because they move listeners to a deeper level by appealing to their senses and imagination.

The metaphors used in the Bible to name God do not control or restrict contemporary readers for two reasons. First, the metaphors referring to God in the Bible are drawn from the particular historical, linguistic, sociopolitical, and cultural experiences of the authors' communities. The biblical metaphors illuminate the nature and activity of God as experienced by the particular communities of faith of the time. Second, because our experience of God is unique to our own particular context, new metaphors need to be created to express the new qualities of our present experience. We know that God's activity for the world is not limited to biblical times and that God continues to do new things among us to reveal God's nature in our particular time and space. Wren describes this open-ended aspect of theological language as follows:

> In our own century God has shown us that we are coauthors of the script, and that the playwright has placed the remainder of the play in the hands of us, the actors. God's presence is not withdrawn, but remains as always, a questioning and loving presence, not a controlling presence.[73]

The third characteristic of subversive rhetoric is the use of various literary genres both eclectically and contextually. Because creating and using new theological language in feminine terms often takes risks in a masculine-oriented world, preachers must use sensitivity and subtlety when approaching their listeners. The medieval women preachers who were officially prohibited from public speech wrote many of their sermons in a variety of literary forms such as letters, poems, dramas, songs, and visionary narratives. For the medieval women, preaching was not merely positing rigorous arguments surrounding a biblical text or a doctrinal theme but also producing creative literary works which transformed the audiences' ways of thinking by appealing to their intellect, emotion, and intuition.

The visionary rhetoric used by both Hildegard and Julian is a good example of the subtle way in which they could approach their audiences with the authority of the divine revelation through allegorical language. Sor Juana's eclectic use of literary genres in both secular and sacred literature illustrates the high artistic level of preaching. The imaginative, poetic language and creative literary genres used by these three women make their sermons different from typical medieval sermons, which focused on teaching morality in a point-making style. Rather than teaching or giving intellectual and moral lessons, these three women helped their audiences experience epiphanies by leading them to discover the hidden truth in the ambiguity and complexity of human life. In this sense, their preaching can be considered as a performing art.

In fact, contemporary homiletical theories encourage preachers to use narrative and other creative literary forms when crafting sermons rather than using the traditional "three-point-and-a-poem" style. Analyzing the sermons written by these three women reinforces the contemporary homiletical trend to challenge preachers to develop more artistic forms in their sermons. Furthermore, a variety of literary sermon forms makes it easy for the preacher to approach the listeners with the feminine language and imagery of God without raising resisting feelings and, consequently, lead them to affirm the equality of all human beings.

Preaching as subversive rhetoric is sensitive to the use of language and the style of preaching. Because of its artistic style and imaginative and creative language, preaching as subversive rhetoric is a performing art that has the power to appeal to listeners effectively in order to deconstruct the conventional masculine-oriented theological views of the listeners and help them reimagine God using new feminine language and imagery.

Chapter Four

THE AUTHORITY OF PREACHING
WOMEN PREACHERS FROM THE REFORMATION TO THE EARLY TWENTIETH CENTURY

I STILL REMEMBER the moment when I first preached. At that time, I was a student intern at the second-oldest Korean American church in New York City. In its twenty-year history, I was the first woman to stand in their pulpit to preach. When I looked at the seven male elders who were sitting in the first row, I could read from their faces, "This is ridiculous, hearing the Word of God from this little girl!" The remaining three hundred or so congregants seemed to have mixed feelings, between curiosity about my preaching and frustration over my gender and age. As a young female student intern, I seemed to be standing in the wrong place. I felt as if I were standing naked in public. However, as my sermon continued, I realized that the congregation was slowly taking my preaching seriously and ultimately received it as the Word of God. When I finished, I could feel them grant me full authority as their preacher.

That first preaching experience challenged me to seriously consider the issue of authority in preaching. What does authority mean when it relates to preaching? Where does authority come from? What makes preaching authentic? How do preachers, particularly women preachers, understand their authority? What are the sources of their authority as preachers? These questions are covered in this chapter in light of the history of Protestant women's preaching from the Reformation to the nineteenth century. The historical review of women's preaching during this period gives us theological and homiletical insights into developing our understanding of authority in preaching. The first section explores the reformers' doctrines concerning women, which became the theological foundation of Protestant preaching. The second section of the chapter reviews gender issues within the development of American preaching from the colonial period to the nineteenth century. The third section of the chapter traces the life and ministry of American women preachers, concentrating on two American women preachers: Jarena Lee, the first African Methodist Episcopal woman preacher in the first half of the nineteenth century, and Anna Howard Shaw, the first ordained Methodist preacher in the second half of the nineteenth century. Their biographical sketches provide conspicuous examples of how American women preachers understood the authority of preaching in their particular historical contexts. In the last section of the chapter, I discuss the issue of authority in preaching as it relates to women preachers' particular experiences both in the past and present.

REFORMATION THEOLOGY AND WOMEN'S PREACHING

Martin Luther (1483–1546), John Calvin (1509–64), and other sixteenth-century reformers challenged the medieval papal system and tyrannical ecclesial laws by reclaiming the authority of the scriptures and Christian freedom as the foundation of the Christian faith. The reformers, stimulated by Renaissance humanism, emphasized the humanistic skills of interpretation, the knowledge of the original biblical languages, and the revival of the primitive church in the New Testament as the ideal for the Reformed Church. The reformers wanted the Christian Church to return to the practice of the primitive church in which Christian conscience was free from all hierarchical structures. Based on their historical knowledge of the Bible and scientific approach to interpreting the biblical text, the reformers developed new Reformed doctrines and eventually paved the way for women to preach, equal to men, in the Protestant Church.

In particular, the three doctrines of *sola scriptura* (scripture alone), the priesthood of all believers, and the activities of the Holy Spirit both among individual believers and within the community contributed to the egalitarian understanding of preaching. All the reformers attempted to restore the Christian theology based on the Bible by stressing *sola scriptura*, that is, that the Word of God was to be found in the scriptures rather than in the words of the pope. Luther's doctrine of the priesthood of all believers, which meant that all Christians had the freedom to approach God personally and participate in worship equally, resulted from *sola scriptura*. For Luther, scripture must be understood through spiritual interpretation. His hermeneutical principle was based on 2 Corinthians 3:5-6, which reads, "our competence is from God, who has made us competent to be ministers of a new covenant, not of letter but of spirit; for the letter kills, but the Spirit gives life." Luther interpreted these verses to mean that the opposition between the letter and the Spirit was the opposition between the law and the gospel and that the law would be dead and kill humanity if it did not always receive living power from the Spirit. Reading the scriptures in light of the Spirit, said Luther, leads to understanding why Paul said to all Christians, "you may declare the mighty acts of him who called you out of darkness into his marvelous light" (1 Pet. 2:9). Because all Christians are called out of darkness, every Christian is bound to declare the mighty acts of God who has called him or her.[1] Although some Christians should be ordained to preach and administer the sacraments in public ministry, both clergy and the laity — including women and men — have equal responsibilities when it comes to the important duties of prayer and proclamation. In other words, laity has the responsibility of carrying out certain priestly duties just like clergy. Both are obligated to pray to God on behalf of other believers and to speak the gospel to each other.[2]

Calvin also emphasized *sola scriptura* and insisted that the interpretation of the scriptures should be done by the eye of faith in the context of Christian freedom. In his *Institutes of Christian Religion*, Calvin rejected legalistic interpretation of the scriptures by stating that because biblical passages were written in their own particular sociocultural and religious contexts, they cannot function as absolute laws and principles for Christian believers. For example, Paul's teaching regarding the necessity for women to be veiled (1 Cor. 11:5) and his command for women to be silent in the church (1 Cor. 14:34) should not be considered the eternal truth of the Christian gospel or eternal laws of God although the medieval church understood those texts that way and manipulated them to exclude women from the ministry of preaching. Instead, Calvin believed that Paul's teachings should be understood as respected advice in the context of human governance. Based on his analysis of the historical and cultural backgrounds of these two texts, Calvin interprets 1 Corinthians 11:5 as "decorum" that Paul commends to promote reverence in sacred rites and ceremonies, and 1 Corinthians 14:34 as an "order" that Paul gives his readers as discipline to deal with their particular ecclesial situation. Calvin clearly states that these governances which serve the edification of the church during one time period can easily be changed during another time period if they cease to serve the edification. Thus, these governances must be tested to determine whether they are necessary for salvation and whether they fit "the customs of each nation and age" for the upbringing of the church.[3]

In addition to his contextual and functional approach, Calvin's interpretive method always surrounds Reformed theology with the belief that the Christian conscience should be radically freed by the gospel. For example, in his sermon on 1 Timothy 2:11-15, one of the antiwomen passages that has been used to exclude women from preaching, Calvin explains that in his text Paul is not willing to make these instructions binding on people's consciences for the sake of the laws themselves. Rather, God has the freedom to call women to teach or preach or rule by pouring out the Holy Spirit to them. When men do not fulfill their responsibilities and roles, or when the situation is confused by the sinfulness of men, God uses the calling of a woman to teach or rule over men as a means to chastise and punish men's unfaithfulness.[4] In other commentaries and sermons, Calvin quotes Mary Magdalene, Priscilla, Phoebe, the four daughters of Philip, and others to prove how freely the Holy Spirit has broken through the conventional order by calling women to teach and prophesy. God freely chooses, says Calvin, "the weak things of the world to humiliate the loftiness of men."[5]

Although the reformers' theological and biblical perspectives challenged the traditional patriarchal view of the church and prepared theoretical grounds for women's preaching, the actuality of their reform did not give women the freedom to preach and administer the sacraments. In fact, the reformers didn't change the basic principles of the patriarchal system of the church. Despite their relatively generous views of women, they still supported the traditional male-dominant church order and preserved the patriarchal system within the church. In the case of Luther, his position on women was ambiguous. On the one hand, Luther attacked the medieval doctrine of celibacy and women's virginity as a woman's highest calling and stressed the positive sides of marriage. He considered marriage and family life the best means for providing spiritual and moral discipline in the world. Luther's own married life illustrated how positively he felt about women and marriage.[6] In his writing, he praised that "there is nothing better on earth than a woman's love."[7] On the other hand, Luther's emphasis on marriage not only as the "ideal" for women but also as their "natural vocation" reinforced the binding of women in the church's patriarchal structure and in society in general. He basically understood women as "inferior beings" and marriage as a subordinating relation of women to men. Some of his writings show his historically affected misogynous view of women:

> God has created men with broad chests and shoulders, not broad hips, so that men can understand wisdom. But the place where the filth flows out is small. With women it's the other way around. That's why they have lots of filth and little wisdom.... Women are created for no other purpose than to serve men and be their helpers. If women grow weary or even die while bearing children, that doesn't harm anything. Let them bear children to death; they are created for that.... The man has been given so much dominion over the woman, that she must name herself according to him. For that reason, a woman adopts her husband's name and not vice versa. This

has happened because of God's gracious will so that she stays under her husband's rule, because she is too weak to rule herself.[8]

Although Luther insisted that all Christians should have the right and power to preach when the spiritual authority was given to them, his traditional misogynist view prevented him from considering women as equal partners in the ministry of preaching. He generalized all women as inferior to men because they lack "a good voice, good eloquence, a good memory and other natural gifts." Luther prohibited women from preaching, except special cases when no man was available to preach.[9]

Calvin was consistent in claiming that Paul's admonitions for women to be silent in church and to cover their heads were historically conditioned pieces of advice rather than perpetual divine laws that should bind the conscience. In almost every case where he refers to women's subordinate role in society, he clarifies that this is a matter of the "political order of human governance." However, Calvin's attitudes toward women in church and society were excessively "political." According to historian Jane Douglass, Calvin acknowledged the spiritual equality between women and men. Nevertheless, Calvin maintained social inequality between them because he believed that Geneva would be as scandalized by women in public roles of authority in either church or state during his time as Paul had imagined his first-century society would have been. Calvin regarded major social upheaval as a great danger to civilization, and he seemed to be very reluctant to recommend revolutionary social change of women's status either in the church or state. Given his own prejudice and concern for the consciences of his male colleagues who would indeed have been greatly offended by women in authority, Calvin tolerated the traditional misogynist attitudes toward women in both the church and state as a conventional standard approved by the Bible.[10]

The reformers' misogynist attitudes and their church policies toward women later became dominant in the Protestant Church and made it nearly unthinkable that women should be allowed to preach. The seventeenth- and eighteenth-century mainline Protestant churches reinforced the patriarchal hierarchies and kept women from public speech. When the Lutheran and Calvinist churches gained the support of powerful political leaders in parts of Europe and became national churches, women were further removed from the center of organized religious life.[11]

It should be noted, however, that a number of Pietist groups appeared outside the mainstream of the Protestant Church in the sixteenth and seventeenth centuries. They accepted the reformers' doctrine of Christian freedom and their egalitarian view toward women and men. However, they rejected the alliance between the church and the political establishment. Such Pietist groups as the Amish and Mennonites, who emerged on the continent of Europe, and the Quakers and Baptists, who were shaped by English Puritanism, stressed that all regenerated Christians were equal in God's eyes and could, therefore, act as God's representatives on earth regardless of their gender and/or class. They gave little importance to theological education or ordained ministry but rather emphasized the direct inspiration of the Holy Spirit and a personal relationship with God as the major qualifications for being a preacher.

The Pietists' assertion of the Holy Spirit as the source of preaching led to the consideration of female leadership, and consequently, women within the circle of the Pietist movement enjoyed a relatively exceptional measure of equality. The Quakers (or the Society of Friends) especially made the greatest progress toward the realization of sexual equality within the life of a religious community under the direction of George Fox (1624–91). Fox and his followers stoutly defended the ministry of women by reference to such scriptural texts as Acts 2:17–18; 21:9; 1 Corinthians 11:5; and Joel 2:28–29, insisting that the Pauline prohibitions should be understood as "local temporary conditions which have passed away."[12] Under the presupposition of the equality of women and men in spiritual privilege and responsibility, Quaker women engaged in preaching and even received ordination to various ministerial offices. They were encouraged to publicly voice their insights and experiences both in written and oral testimonies. Influenced by the

Quakers, Moravian leader Nikolaus Zinzendorf (1700–1760) also evaluated women's preaching positively:

> To the matrons the teaching is forbidden for the very reason that the husbands do not become jealous if they are ignorant. The Apostle also adds a reason, namely that the women have naturally not the soundness of the men, ... and that it therefore would be good if they kept silence in the congregation. Yet, he would be in the wrong, if he had forbidden it to all. Peter says: I will pour out my Spirit over all flesh, sons and daughters, manservants and maidservants, and the maidens shall have visions. If the women should not teach, this surely would not have come true.[13]

The founder of the Methodist Church, John Wesley (1703–91), is one of the prominent male advocates for women preachers. At the beginning of the Methodist movement, Wesley, who was an ordained Anglican priest, did not allow women to preach because the Anglican Church did not permit it. However, the positive influence of his mother, his friendship with the Moravians, and the legacy of the Reformed tradition later changed Wesley's attitudes toward women's leadership. For Wesley, the Bible was not simply a compilation of laws, regulations, and moral instructions for a Christian life but rather the "living Word," which had the power to renew believers' lives. Through the intervention of the Holy Spirit, believers could transform their lives "with immediate effect and lasting influence."[14] Based on his conviction of the power of the Holy Spirit, Wesley emphasized the experience of personal conversion as the power to transform both the individual and society at large; consequently, he developed a Methodist movement, which included evangelical revivals. Because of the influence of the evangelical revivals, Wesley came to view the church as more and more functional rather than institutional, and charismatic rather than authoritarian.

From the beginning of the Methodist movement in the eighteenth century, women were pioneers in the establishment and expansion of Methodism. They helped vitalize the Wesleyan revivals by teaching the Bible and publicly sharing their conversion experiences. Some women took the initiative in the actual formation of Methodist society with no other authority than their own determination, resulting from the divine calling. They defended their rights to preach and speak publicly by appealing to theological, biblical, and pragmatic reason. First of all, they claimed that they had received a call from God to speak out. Second, they insisted that certain biblical passages support women's preaching. Last, they proved their successful ministry by reminding church leaders that women preachers produced a great number of converts through the presence and activities of the Holy Spirit in their preaching. Women actively promoted their authority as leaders of the Methodist movement and challenged Wesley to reconsider women's preaching as a legitimate practice. For example, Mary Bosanquet wrote Wesley a letter in which she argued against literalists' interpretation of St. Paul's admonition against women speaking publicly. Wesley responded to her letter by saying that he had been persuaded to admit God's call of women to preach.[15]

The increased necessity for pastoral oversight and the contribution of women leaders to the expansion of the Methodist movement led Wesley to accept lay preachers during the early stage of the revivals, and eventually Wesley carefully allowed "exceptional" women to preach. Among the "exceptional" women were Sarah Crosby, Cross Hall, Ann Ford, and Bosanquet. Wesley's endorsement of women's public speech in his movement and the testimony of many witnesses to the abundant fruit of women's labor drove the Methodist Conferences to officially recognize a number of exceptional female preachers. In 1787, the Manchester Conference sanctioned for the first time a woman's preaching by authorizing Sarah Mallet to be a preacher.[16] The authorization of women's preaching by the Methodist Church was the result of Wesley's fundamental principle: "No one, including a woman, ought to be prohibited from doing God's work in obedience to the inner calling of her conscience."[17] In his later years when Wesley was asked why he encouraged women to preach, he replied, "Because God owns them in the conversion of sinners, and who am I that I should withstand God."[18]

After Wesley's death in 1791, however, the egalitarian, democratic spirit of the Methodist movement was not carried by his male successors. In the nineteenth century, the Methodist Church was confronted with the tension between the charismatic and authoritarian views of the church within the Methodist hierarchy and began to search for a coherent doctrine of the church and ministry. At this critical turning point, the question of women's preaching became a crucial issue, and just twelve years after Wesley's death, the majority of conservative male leaders at the Annual Conference resolved to rule women's preaching "unnecessary" because God had currently supplied Methodists with an ample number of male preachers. In 1803, the Manchester Conference, which had already sanctioned women's preaching, limited women's preaching to same-sex groups only and required women preachers to have the official approval of the circuit.[19] The patriarchal male leaders of the Methodist Church officially condemned women preachers by reiterating the literal interpretation of the Pauline passages against women speaking publicly. Consequently, few Methodist women preached from that point in time until the twentieth century, when women's preaching became a live issue again because of the general change in cultural attitudes toward women.[20]

WOMEN AND AMERICAN PREACHING: FROM THE SEVENTEENTH TO THE NINETEENTH CENTURIES

DeWitte T. Holland explains that the American preaching tradition began with the settlement of Plymouth in 1620.[21] The New England colonists, Puritans and nonconformists, came to the new world bringing their entire culture with them from their homelands, including their preachers. The first New England Puritan preachers were orthodox Calvinists in the sense that their sermons were doctrinal lectures, forcefully emphasizing the doctrines of the Word of God as found in the Bible, the sovereignty of God, original sin, predestination, the depravity of human beings, and justification by faith. Every minister in New England in the seventeenth century delivered sermons twice on Sundays, once during the week, and for every significant event in the life of the community. Each sermon lasted between one and three hours and was given in simple and direct language. In worship, sacred images were rejected, and the role of music was restricted. Instead, preaching was the focal point of worship because, among the Puritans, preaching equated to the Word of God. The preacher was supposed to be the best-educated man in town and was regarded as the herald of God or "the man of God appointed by divine decree" to help his people know the will of God for their lives in the new land.[22] Because sermons were expected to be based on *sola scriptura*, the authority of the preacher was gained by his specialized knowledge of the scriptures and his ordination rather than his personal morality or the religious experience of the divine calling. Congregations were responsible not only for obeying the Word of God proclaimed by the preacher but also for reading their Bibles to monitor the preacher to determine whether he held true to biblical doctrines or not. As long as the preacher based his message on biblical truths, the preacher's voice in the pulpit remained sovereign and unchallenged. The congregation assumed that his authority was not human but rather divine.[23]

In addition to having a Calvinist heritage, New England preaching also had the distinctive characteristic of using covenant theology as the unique theological foundation for the colonists' identity. According to the salvation history in the Hebrew Bible, God entered into covenants with the people of Israel and promised that they would be blessed by God's providential might if they would acknowledge no other sovereign and be faithful in keeping God's commandments. The Israelites were the ones chosen to be "God's special instruments entrusted with the task of preparing the way for messianic deliverance." In their sermons, New England preachers identified their congregations as God's "New Israel," the chosen people who were predestined to be "the founders of the American Republic and the custodians of its providential mission." The preachers convinced their listeners that God would stand for them until Christ's return to earth. On the one hand, covenant theology provided spiritual support for the colonists to resist the English and also provided religious justification for the eventual revolution against Great Britain.[24] On the other hand, covenant theology contributed to planting an androcentric imperialistic view in American Christianity, as Eugene E. White critically points out:

> ...the Puritan preaching of the covenants had helped prepare the New England community for the emerging man-dominated world, one in which self-confident humans increasingly rely upon human means in their ongoing struggles to conquer the earth, the universe, matter and energy, the origination of life, and death itself.[25]

Seventeenth-century New England, nurtured by orthodox Calvinism and covenant theology, placed such a high value on patriarchy that it did not grant space for women to participate in the ministry of preaching. Among the early Puritan settlers, two contrasting images of women existed side by side. One image was the traditional misogynist view of women as the "daughters of Eve." As women are wicked sinners and inferior to men, they should subordinate to male authority at home, at church, and in society at large. The other image of women was the religious view of a "good wife." Although Puritan theology mandated social subordination of women, it affirmed the spiritual equality of women and men. In other words, not all women are Eves. Good women, pious and obedient to the norms of social order, are spiritually equal to men. The most significant role for women is within the family as a wife and mother. Good wives have the responsibilities to teach religion to their children and be servants in the home but not to instruct adult males in public. In church, women should be silent except for two cases: when she is to give account of her offense and when she sings forth the praises of the Lord together with the rest of the congregation.[26] Women who preach or question male authority are "stepping out of their place." Women are supposed to be "the Hidden Ones...who make no Noise at all in the World; People hardly Known to be in the World."[27] During the Colonial period, such mainline churches as the Congregationalists in Massachusetts, the Presbyterians in New Jersey and some of the Mid-Atlantic colonies, and the Episcopalians in New York and the southern colonies followed the patriarchal principles that women must silently accept male authority, especially that of the ordained clergy.

However, the patriarchal principles did not keep women silent completely, for some women were convinced that God's calling to preach was more authoritative than the patriarchal norms of social order. In 1634, four years after the Massachusetts Bay colony was founded, Anne Hutchinson (1591–1643), a Puritan who was the wife of a successful merchant as well as a skilled nurse and midwife, arrived in the Colony with her family. She followed her religious mentor, John Cotton, who later became the most influential religious leader of New England, as an immigrant from England. Hutchinson began holding weekly meetings with a small group of women at her home to study the Bible and review Cotton's sermons. Hutchinson criticized clergy who stressed that people could contribute to their own salvation by their works and emphasized that only God's grace could save people from damnation. She also claimed that the religious experience of the Holy Spirit was the primary source of the authority of preaching. Her preaching appealed to the people in the colony. Consequently, her meetings became so popular that up to eighty people began to attend, including men. Threatened by her effective leadership, the Puritan clergy in the Boston area accused Hutchinson of spreading heretical doctrines through public speech. For them, she endangered the traditional authority of the church and state leaders, which were both male monopolies. In spite of her eloquent self-defense for her right to preach and teach religious matters, her opponents in both the civil and ecclesiastical authorities named her the "American Jezebel" and excommunicated her and her supporters.[28] Hugh Peters, one of her opponents, stated in his report at her trial that "You have stept out of your place, you have rather bine a Husband than a Wife and a preacher than a Hearer, and a Magistrate than a Subject."[29]

Under the strict Puritan culture of the early Colonial period of New England, Quakers also fell victim to the patriarchal intolerance. Because Quakers accepted women as preachers and recognized their leadership in the community, the Puritan male leaders regarded Quakers as a troublesome and dangerous sect of heretics and persecuted them. Accordingly, in 1658, Puritan leaders finally banned Quakers from living in Massachusetts by passing a death penalty law for Quakers who would not leave. However, this law did not completely expel Quaker preachers from New England, especially female preachers. Mary Dye, who supported Hutchinson, and other women preached in Boston at the cost of their lives. In Dye's case, after her death sentence in 1659, she wrote a letter to the Geneva Court of Boston in which she insisted that the reason that she preached was a response to God's calling to preach against "the wicked and intolerant law of Massachusetts, which restricted the rights and religious freedom of Quakers."[30]

The seventeenth-century misogynist position of New England and its official persecution of women preachers began to weaken starting in the early part of the eighteenth century because of the impact of some major historical events: the two Great Awakenings in the eighteenth and nineteenth centuries and a women's rights movement in the later half of the nineteenth century. The earliest manifestations of the first Great Awakening occurred in the middle colonies in the 1720s and 1730s under the preaching of a Dutch Reformed pastor, Theodore Frelinghuysen, and a New Jersey Presbyterian family, William Tennent and his sons, Gilbert, John, and William Jr. In its full-fledged, widespread form, the first Great Awakening was triggered in the late 1730s and 1740s by the preaching tours throughout New England of George Whitefield, Gilbert Tennent, James Davenport, and Samuel Davies. They preached extemporaneously and appealed to the "hearts" of the listeners.[31] The Great Awakening was a series of revivals that constituted movements against the formalism and hierarchies of the established churches. The preachers of the Awakening, on the one hand, criticized the inability and laxness of the ministers of the established churches for not helping congregations experience true piety and spiritual regeneration and, on the other hand, encouraged laypeople to take more personal responsibility for their own spiritual lives and assume more power in the churches. The central message of the revivalists was the revitalized religious life and the assurance of eternal salvation that came from conversion. To the revivalists, the authority of preaching was given not by formal theological training or social status but by the preacher's personal experience of conversion and inner regeneration. The Awakening revivals fanned religious passions and enthusiasm and drew many new members into the church by opening a door for them, especially for white women and African American men. Consequently, the Great Awakening contributed to both the undermining of clerical authority and hierarchies based on gender, race, and class and the promotion of a relatively egalitarian environment within the church by increasing the power of laity.

The Great Awakening caused serious theological and homiletical controversy and resulted in the division of the churches in New England. First of all, the revivalists' emphasis on the inward experience of religion was in direct opposition to the intellectual and systematic approach of Calvinist theology. Moreover, the revivalists' preaching, which focused on an emotional appeal, completely disrupted Puritan preaching in its style and content. Whitefield criticized Puritan preaching in which pastors read sermons "in the manner of a prepared essay rather than a living speech" as "a deficiency in faith" because it could not reach popular audiences.[32] Contrarily, Harvard professor Charles Channcy disapproved of revivalists' extemporaneous preaching as "a blind enthusiasm" or "madness." Channcy also blamed the revivalists for encouraging lay exhorters to abandon their proper calling and usurp the role of the minister. Moreover, Channcy contended that women testifying publicly at the revivals violated biblical law.[33]

On the other hand, Jonathan Edwards, who was a Puritan preacher and theologian, tried to synthesize these two opposing positions. He explained that genuine religion begins with the heart and must be experienced. However, any personal experience must be subjected to critical judgments and needs to be tied to understanding because understanding is the integral force between the heart and the will.[34] In addition, Edwards interpreted the supernatural phenomenon of mass conversion held at the revivals and the egalitarian movement of the Great Awakening as the signs of "the Latter-Day Glory"[35] in America as described in Isaiah 2:12–17. Edwards encouraged laypeople to participate in evangelism as divine instruments:

> Let us not refuse to give all that honour which belongs to others as instruments, because they are young, or are upon other accounts much inferior to ourselves and others; and may appear to us very unworthy that God should put so much honour upon them.... God doubtless now expects that all sorts of persons in New England, rulers, ministers and people, high and low, rich and poor, old and young, should take great notice of his hand in this mighty work of his grace, and should appear to acknowledge his glory in it.[36]

Although laywomen were not as fully recognized as laymen and no denominational churches gave women full religious equality as preachers, the Great Awakening did provide further theological justification for women's religious activities through a renewed emphasis on the authority of the individual's conversion experience. Women were encouraged to offer public prayer and testimony and were allowed to organize women's meetings for Bible study and theological discussion. These activities endowed women with greater self-confidence and more spiritual authority. Among the large number of female leaders were Quaker preacher Charity Wright Cook; English evangelical Anne Dutton, who published her religious poems and tracts; Sarah Osborn, who established the Newport society for female Christians and free black people; and Sarah Edwards, the wife of Jonathan Edwards.

Women's participation in evangelism was geared up by the Second Great Awakening. During the first half of the nineteenth century, Lyman Beecher, Charles G. Finney, Asahel Mettleton, and others promoted "the age of revivals"[37] from the established churches in New England to camp meetings on the frontier. The revivals were an ecumenical movement that crossed the denominational lines of the Congregationalists, Presbyterians, Methodists, and Baptists to ensure "America's identity as a Christian nation."[38] The main goal of the revivals was not only to revitalize the spirits of the believers but also to bring nonbelievers to churches by emphasizing the individual experience of "new birth" or conversion as the only means of salvation. Just as in the first Great Awakening, the revivalists — despite denominational differences — had common commitments to emotional, heart-centered preaching, the abandonment of rigid Calvinism, and emphasis on the free will of human beings. The "new birth preaching" of the evangelicals believed that people could be saved only if they went through a dramatic, life-changing experience of spiritual rebirth, by emphasizing Jesus as a personal, individual Savior.[39]

Although Horace Bushnell and other orthodox church leaders vehemently criticized the revivalists' evangelical theology for being so individualistic and emotional that it ignored the significance of the nurturing function of a community of faith, evangelical preaching did contribute to the spreading of Christianity throughout the nation and resulted in women outnumbering men as converts and church members. The representation of women in church membership continued to grow through their active participation in the leadership of the church. Women were encouraged to demonstrate their leadership not only in the private sphere but also in public, by praying, testifying, teaching, exhorting, and even occasionally preaching at revivals and in other public contexts. Finney, the most famous revivalist of the Second Great Awakening, and other male revivalists encouraged women to lead public prayer and speech even in mixed gatherings to promote revivals.[40]

Above all, the holiness doctrine of "spiritual sanctification" supported women's public speech. Sanctification was understood as the result of Christian commitment after conversion. To be sanctified meant to be free from sin. Spiritual sanctification was "a purifying of one's inner disposition to willful sin, a liberation of the soul to follow the indwelling voice of Christ."[41] According to this doctrine, original sin was not the permanent state of humanity. Consequently, the burden of Eve's sin, which had been the theological ground for indoctrinating women's inferiority and sinfulness and injuncting women's preaching, was lessened. Sanctified women and men were spiritually equal to proclaim the grace of God's salvation. Women who were convinced that "salvation made possible the gift of spiritual sanctification" believed that the genuine authority of preaching depended not on the official sanction of the church but on God, who spoke to them through the inspiration of the Holy Spirit.

Both the encouragement from the male leaders of the revivals and the egalitarian doctrine of spiritual sanctification empowered women across races and denominations to stand in the pulpit as preachers. Freewill Baptist Sally Parsons, Holiness Methodist Phoebe Palmer, and African American Methodists Zilpha Elaw and Jarena Lee were among more than a hundred female evangelists who justified their authority as preachers on the grounds of spiritual inspiration rather than educational credentials or ecclesial sanction. According to Catherine A. Brekus, these women invented a new model of female ministry:

> [They] portrayed themselves as *women* who had been called to minister to the family of God as "Sisters in Christ" and "Mothers in Israel." Instead of dressing in "masculine" clothing, advocating celibacy, or denying that they were female, they proudly compared themselves to biblical heroines and prophetesses such as Phebe [sic], Huldah, and Deborah... they explained that they, like Phebe, had been chosen as servants of the church, female laborers in the harvest.[42]

Phoebe Palmer, the wife of a preacher and also a nonordained American Methodist (Holiness) preacher herself, is a good example of the new model of female ministry. She dedicated her life to converting thousands to the church. Although she always spoke of herself as a laywoman, she believed the preaching ministry was open to women as well as men. She defended the right of women to preach and minister not only throughout her own ministry but also in writing. In her book *The Promise of the Father*, she encouraged other women to preach by insisting that Paul's intention in 1 Corinthians 14:34 and 1 Timothy 2:12 was not to exclude women from the pulpit, and that the prohibition of women's preaching was a waste of resources and an offense to Jesus Christ.[43]

Early nineteenth-century women preachers did not push for the ordination of women. Instead, they preached as evangelists, exhorters, and licensed preachers by placing their divine callings and properly translated and interpreted scriptural passages that support women's preaching over ecclesiastical sanctions or institutional authorization. While it may have been too early in the historical context of women's rights to anticipate the struggle women would have faced for institutional procedures to confirm their callings, in the latter half of the nineteenth century, women preachers experienced limitations to their preaching ministry without the authorization granted by ordination. These women were well aware of their privileges as church leaders, yet they could neither greatly influence the mainline Protestant churches in decision-making processes nor provide congregations with sufficient pastoral care nor administer baptism and Eucharist. As a result, women's rights movements that arose from feminism and the development of liberal theology greatly impacted the ability of women to become ordained in the second half of the nineteenth century.

The women's rights movements, initiated by female abolitionists beginning in the 1830s and 1840s, directly raised the issue of the status of all women, which was closely related to the issue of women's ordination. Such female abolitionists as Sarah and Angelina Grimké, Lucretia Mott, and Elizabeth Cady Stanton claimed that women and men not only had an equal role in the antislavery movement but also an equal position in all areas of society. All women must be as free as men to develop their talents and to enjoy useful, respectful, and independent lives.[44]

The first generation of these female reformers challenged younger generations to reexamine their traditional religious beliefs based on patriarchal doctrines of orthodox Calvinism. In fact, these women were proposing an egalitarian theological foundation from a feminist perspective. Some women went so far as publishing books and pamphlets that defended women's right to preach and to be ordained based on a new theological and biblical perspective.[45] Moreover, nineteenth-century liberalism spurred the women's movement and encouraged women preachers to struggle further for their ordination. Liberal theologians claimed not only the possibility but also the necessity of making an egalitarian heaven on earth via social reform. The fastest-growing denominations, the Presbyterians, Methodists, and Baptists, taught the equality of women in the eyes of God. Their "millennial theology," based on Joel 2:28, worked in favor of women preachers and understood women's preaching as heralding the Second Coming of Christ.

Although Lutherans, Presbyterians, Episcopalians, and Methodist Episcopalians did not admit women to the ordained ministry until the twentieth century,[46] some Congregational churches, the Church of Nazarene, the Methodist Protestant Church, Wesleyan Methodists, Free Baptists, Universalists, Unitarians, and the African Methodist Episcopal Zion Church began to ordain women in the late nineteenth century.[47] Antoinette Brown was the first woman to be ordained by a small Congregational church in New York in 1853, following her formal theological education at Oberlin College. Olympia Brown was the first Universalist woman minister ordained in 1863. Anna Shaw was the first Methodist ordained by the Methodist Protestant Church in 1880. Frances Willard reported in her book *Woman in the Pulpit*, published in 1888, that in the United States, 500 women had already entered the pulpit as evangelists, in addition to the 350 Quaker preachers and approximately 20 women serving as pastors, of whom several had already been ordained.[48]

Women's leadership in the Salvation Army is extraordinary. Catherine Mumford Booth, who was greatly influenced by Phoebe Palmer during her preaching tour of England in 1859, later became the cofounder of the Salvation Army with her husband William Booth. She fervently argued for women's right to preach the gospel. At the first annual conference of the Salvation Army held in 1870, she led the organization to grant women the right and authority to preach and hold positions of leadership equal to men.[49] In her defense of women's preaching, she insisted that women's right to preach was based on their natural capacities and qualities, the divine calling, and a "common sense interpretation of the scriptures,"[50] that is, the exegetical method that took into account both the larger context of the biblical passage and its particular historical context. For Booth, the nature of women is different from that of men, and these differences made women especially fit for preaching:

> Making allowance for the novelty of the thing, we cannot discover anything either unnatural or immodest in a Christian

woman, becomingly attired, appearing on a platform or a pulpit. By nature she seems fitted to grace either. God has given to women a graceful form and attitude, winning manners, persuasive speech, and, above all, a finely-tuned emotional nature, all of which appear to us eminent natural qualifications for public speaking.[51]

WOMEN PREACHERS AND AUTHORITY

The biographies of two women preachers — Jarena Lee, the first woman preacher of the African American Episcopal Church as a freed slave during the first half of the nineteenth century, and Anna Howard Shaw, the first ordained Methodist woman preacher during the second half of the nineteenth century — illustrate how women preachers in nineteenth-century America understood their callings to preach and how they gained their authority as preachers. The half-century gap between Lee and Shaw produced different sociocultural and religious contexts for preaching. Moreover, their different racial backgrounds and personal situations led them to understand their roles and authority as preachers differently.

Jarena Lee (1783–?)

Jarena Lee's two autobiographies, *The Life and Religious Experience of Jarena Lee, A Coloured Lady, Giving an Account of Her Call to Preach the Gospel*, published in 1836, and her extended one, *Religious Experience and Journal of Mrs. Jarena Lee, Giving an Account of Her Call to Preach the Gospel*, published in 1849, reveal that Lee was a woman who was a "least of the least": racially discriminated, physically weak, economically poor, and intellectually unlearned. However, she was a woman who lived out God's will as a vessel of God, guided by the irresistible power of the Holy Spirit.

Born into a non-Christian freed slave family in Cape May, New Jersey, in 1783, Lee was sent by her parents at the age of seven to be a servant, sixty miles away from her home. During her deprived childhood and youth, she attempted suicide several times. Her spiritual thirst and feelings of distress drove her to attend revival meetings and search for a spiritual home where she could belong. Lee eventually joined the Bethel Methodist Episcopal Church in Philadelphia, after experiencing an ecstatic moment while listening to the preaching of Rev. Richard Allen, the man who would become the first bishop of the African Methodist Episcopal Church. From that point on, she deepened her understanding of the Christian faith by both experiencing conversion and learning about the doctrine of sanctification.[52]

When Lee first heard the voice of God, telling her to "[g]o preach the Gospel," she was so surprised and fearful that she thought it was a deception of Satan. However, convinced of the consistent calling through visions and dreams, she was encouraged to visit with her pastor Allen and tell him, "the Lord had revealed it to me, that I must preach the gospel." Allen rejected her revelation based on the discipline of the Methodist Church that women should not become preachers. Upon hearing his reply, Lee had mixed feelings: relief from the fear of becoming a preacher but also the extinction of the holy energy for a love of souls burning inside her. She married a pastor and helped his ministry in the town of Snow Hill just outside of Philadelphia. During her marriage, she became terribly ill. Encountering her possible death, she remembered her calling to preach and wished to go throughout the world preaching the gospel before she died. After seeing a vision in a dream of becoming well again, she miraculously recovered from her illness and decided to become a preacher.[53] During her six-year marriage, she lost five members of her family, including her husband. Suddenly a widow, left with two small children, aged two years and six months, Lee returned to Bethel Church.

While attending a service at her church, the Spirit inspired Lee to interrupt the pastor's preaching with her personal testimony in relation to the text used for the pastor's sermon. She confessed in public that like Jonah, who had escaped from God in order not to preach the gospel, she too had resisted God's calling to preach for eight years. After her speech, Lee was afraid of being expelled by Bishop Allen because of her disorderly behavior during the service. Surprisingly, however, Allen stood up in front of the congregation and acknowledged her divine calling to preach. He also gave her credentials to take with her to prove her official authority as a preacher whenever her preaching was questioned because of her gender.[54]

Upon receiving permission from the bishop, Lee began her journey as an itinerant preacher. Her preaching life was a good example of the Methodist circuit riders of her time. No matter what the weather was like, rain or snow, she traveled to wherever she was invited to preach — small and large churches, individual homes, county meeting halls, school classrooms, and camp meetings — from Pennsylvania to Maryland, Ohio, New Jersey, and New York, including slave states. Her listeners were not limited to people of her own race, gender, or denomination. They were often mixed groups of white and African American, male and female, and Methodist and Presbyterian. She was even invited by slaveholders to preach at their homes or churches. On average, she preached seven hundred sermons a year, traveling on foot an average of twenty miles a day from one place to another, mainly accompanied by other women or traveling alone.[55]

Why Lee first resisted the divine call to preach is understandable. For nineteenth-century women, especially African American women, becoming a preacher was one of the most dangerous career choices. As Joycelyn K. Moody explains, no black woman in the nineteenth century was at liberty to leave home without arousing suspicion. "[B]ecause of societal expectations and cultural norms, domesticity bound essentially all women to the hearth."[56] Being an itinerant preacher required Lee to go beyond the restricted "woman's sphere" and break the traditional societal norm of "true womanhood." Furthermore, traveling to unknown places as a freed slave woman, especially at night or daybreak, was literally to risk one's life. In addition, Lee also had to confront sexism by patriarchal male clergy who never thought of the possibility of an egalitarian ministry with an African American woman.

Despite these hindrances, the Spirit of God initiated the course of her life as a preacher. The Spirit continued to be present in her preaching life and became the source of authority for her preaching. To Lee, the inspiration of the Spirit did not mean merely experiencing a temporary ecstatic moment or a supernatural power within herself. She experienced the divine inspiration in various ways throughout her entire life: First of all, even before she was introduced to Christianity, the Spirit of God inspired her to pursue the ultimate destiny of her soul by dwelling in her conscience and giving her a mind that wanted her to know the ways and laws of God.[57] The Spirit helped her to see herself as a "wretched sinner" and led her to faith in Christ Jesus. Next, the Spirit inspired Lee with the conviction that she was called to preach just as Jesus had commanded to his disciples: "Go ye into all the world and preach my gospel to every creature, he that believeth and is baptized shall be saved (Mark 16:15–16)."[58] The same Spirit further prepared the way for Lee to preach by inspiring Allen and other male leaders to recognize the will of God in her.

Most of all, the Spirit inspired in Lee a love for the souls of "the fallen sons and daughters of Adam's race" and the responsibility to proclaim the grace of God to them. She described the feeling she had when Allen prohibited her from preaching as, "I found that a love of souls had in a measure departed from me; that holy energy which burned within me, as a fire, began to be smothered. This I soon perceived."[59] From the time she began her preaching life, her love for others was the major source of power driving her to continue her preaching tour without stopping. Her responsibility to preach was her personal response to God's saving grace for her own soul. She states, "If a man may preach, because the Saviour died for him, why not the woman? [S]eeing he died for her also. Is he not a whole Saviour, instead of a half one?"[60]

Throughout her entire preaching life, Lee experienced the Holy Spirit providing her critical insights and penetrating intuition to interpret the Bible and deepen her theological understanding of the Christian gospel. Although she "never had more than three months schooling,"[61] her understanding of scripture exceeded that of other educated preachers and theologians. Unfortunately, no sermon manuscripts written by her exist today. However, her autobiography provides us with an excellent example of her theological and biblical insights into the issue of women's preaching:

> Did not Mary first preach the risen Saviour, and is not the doctrine of the resurrection the very climax of Christianity—

hangs not all our hope on this, as argued by St. Paul? Then did not Mary, a woman, preach the gospel? [F]or she preached the resurrection of the crucified Son of God. But some will say, that Mary did not expound the Scripture, therefore, she did not preach, in the proper sense of the term. To this I reply, it may be that the term *preach*, in those primitive times, did not mean exactly what it is now *made* to mean; perhaps it was a great deal more simple then, than it is now; — if it were not, the unlearned fishermen could not have preached the gospel at all, as they had no learning. To this it may be replied, by those who are determined not to believe that it is right for a woman to preach, that the disciples, though they were fishermen, and ignorant of letters too, were inspired so to do. To which I would reply, that though they were inspired, yet that inspiration did not save them from showing their ignorance of letters, and of man's wisdom; this the multitude soon found out, by listening to the remarks of the envious Jewish priests. If then, to preach the gospel, by the gift of heaven, comes by inspiration solely, is God straitened; must he take the man exclusively? May he not, did he not, and can he not inspire a female to preach the simple story of the birth, life, death, and resurrection of our Lord, and accompany it too, with power to the sinner's heart? As for me, I am fully persuaded that the Lord called me to labour according to what I have received, in his vineyard. If he has not, how could he consistently bear testimony in favour of my poor labours, in awakening and converting sinners?[62]

For Lee, then, preaching was an address of "a few plain truths."[63] It was a simple announcement about the life, death, and resurrection of Jesus Christ but could have the tremendous power of transforming listeners to a new creation with the intervention of the Holy Spirit. Whenever she stood behind the pulpit, Lee was empowered by the inspiration of the Holy Spirit, and in turn inspired her listeners. Every moment she preached, she felt free; her tongue loosened; her lips touched; and her heart warmed with the love of God and souls. During her preaching, her listeners often wept and mourned for their sins and rejoiced for God's grace of forgiveness. After returning home, Lee often heard that as a result of her preaching, "sinners were converted, backsliders reclaimed, mourners comforted, and believers built up in the most holy faith." For this reason, she was repeatedly invited to preach.[64] These eschatological and spiritual harvests proved that even though Lee was not a licensed preacher, let alone ordained, her preaching had authority as the Word of God. Regardless of her lack of external qualifications based on gender, race, class, and educational background, her audience acknowledged her as a preacher and granted her the authority of a preacher by inviting her to preach for and to them, for they experienced the presence of God during her sermons. Lee compared herself to Paul, Moses, and Isaiah, who were called by God to preach. She understood herself as an instrument or "handmaiden" of God to be used for the will and glory of God:

> By the instrumentality of a poor coloured woman, the Lord poured forth his spirit among the people. Though, as I was told, there were lawyers, doctors, and magistrates present, to hear me speak, yet there was mourning and crying among sinners, for the Lord scattered fire among them of his own kindling. The Lord gave his handmaiden power to speak for his great name, for he arrested the hearts of the people, and caused a shaking amongst the multitude, for God was in the midst.[65]

Lee, as one of the first African American female preachers who lived before the Civil War, was a visionary preacher. She had a special affection for her "own people" and loved to preach to both slaves and freed slaves. By experiencing hospitality offered to her by white Christians, she could imagine a new world where the children of God could live together peacefully without discrimination based on their race, gender, or denomination. Her vision was well-described in her writing: "Oh, I long to see the day when Christians will meet on one common platform — Jesus of Nazareth — and cease their bickerings, and contentions about nonessentials — when 'our Church' shall be less debated, but 'our Jesus' shall be all in all."[66] She continued to preach with this vision until her physical condition no longer allowed her to travel.

Anna H. Shaw (1847–1919)

It is not an overstatement to say that Anna Shaw lived her life by the women, with the women, and for the women. Her life was embroidered with many wonderful women who influenced the directions of her life as a preacher, pastor, medical doctor, lecturer, and prominent leader of the women's suffrage movement.

Shaw was born in England into a Unitarian family. Her maternal grandmother was one of the first Unitarians in England, and she was bold enough to protest against paying tithes to the support of the Church of England. After Shaw's father became bankrupt, her family suffered financial stringency and emigrated to the United States when she was four years old. During the first two years in the United States, Shaw's family lived in New Bedford, Massachusetts, and later moved to Lawrence, Massachusetts, where they lived for seven years until moving to the wilderness of the Michigan frontier. During her childhood in Lawrence, she became friends with the next-door neighbor, a woman of the streets who had been excluded from the community because of her immoral life. Although her friendship with that woman only lasted a short time, her compassion for downtrodden women remained with her for her entire life. She later helped them as both a minister and physician.[67]

Shaw's father, who had "imperishable curiosity" and an adventurous character, built a log house in the wilderness of the Michigan frontier. As much as he was independent, free-thinking, and idealistic, he was equally irresponsible. After moving his family to this wild, new world, he often left his home for months or years at a time without any concern for his eight young children or his wife, who had a nervous disposition. During her youth, Anna Shaw was rebellious toward her father and wanted to preach what she thought was right. She often went to the silent forest and addressed the unresponsive trees, standing up on stumps, feeling within herself an aspiration to preach.[68]

In her early twenties, Shaw left the poverty-stricken wilderness for the big town of Big Rapids, Michigan, where her older sister Mary lived, to learn any kind of a "money-making trade." In Big Rapids, Shaw had the opportunity to hear a sermon from a

Universalist woman minister named Marianna Thompson. During her preaching, Shaw was so thrilled that her previous aspiration to become a preacher rekindled within her. After the service, she introduced herself to Thompson and described her ambition.

Following Thompson's prompt advice to go to school to pursue an education, Shaw gave up her idea of learning a trade and entered Big Rapids High School at the age of twenty-four. There she met another woman who supported her dream to become a preacher. Lucy Foot, the principal of the high school, understood Shaw's dream and enrolled her in speech debate classes. She also introduced Shaw to Dr. Peck, the presiding elder of the Methodist church in Big Rapids. At that time, the Methodist Church in Michigan began to issue licenses to women to preach, and Peck was looking for a woman who was interested in the preaching ministry. When Peck offered Shaw an invitation to preach at a Methodist meeting, her first reaction was, "I've never been converted. How can I preach to any one?"[69] Foot suggested that she would have prayer meetings with Shaw until she experienced the moment of conversion. One night, after several hours of intensive prayer, Shaw felt the conviction that she had been called to preach. From that point onward, she accompanied Peck to preach in his circuit, and she eventually received her license to preach.

Her conversion to Methodism and becoming a Methodist preacher caused a gulf between her and the rest of her family members, who had been pious Unitarians. It took a long time for them to understand Shaw's ministry and reconcile themselves with her. In addition to her family's rejection, Shaw was physically exhausted by completing both her schoolwork and preaching ministry — which was her only source of income — at the same time. She was also severely depressed by her classmates' jeers. At this crisis point in her career, Shaw met Mary A. Livermore, a famous women lecturer, and was encouraged by her words: "My dear, if you want to preach, go on and preach. Don't let anybody stop you. No matter what people say, don't let them stop you."[70] With Livermore's sanction, Shaw pursued her dream of becoming a minister by entering Albion College in Michigan and later the Boston University School of Theology, as the second female student in the school's history.

Shaw spent her student life in Boston in worse conditions than back in Michigan. The sexist policies of the university combined with her being alone in a big, lonely city without her family's financial support caused her to fall into a friendless, penniless, and starving situation. Preaching at revivals and local churches were her major source of income, but that was not even enough to pay for all her meals. When her health began to weaken because of her hectic schedule as a preacher and student and because she had been living on only milk and crackers for several months, Mrs. Barrett, the superintendent of the Woman's Foreign Missionary Society, decided to support her financially, and did so until Shaw graduated. Shaw also had the opportunity to get to know a wealthy widow, Persis Addy, who later became her best friend but died soon afterward, leaving Shaw enough money to visit Europe after her graduation.

Shaw served the East Dennis Church on Cape Cod as her first parish after graduation and, six months later, was asked to take on the temporary charge of the Congregational church at Dennis. She served these two churches as a licensed preacher while at the same time studying at Boston University Medical School until her graduation in 1885. During her parish ministry, Shaw seriously felt the necessity to become ordained, for her ministry was greatly handicapped by the fact that she could preach but not administer baptism or Eucharist. According to her experience as a parish minister, the ministry of preaching was inseparably connected to the ministry of the sacraments. When Shaw applied for her ordination to the Methodist Episcopal Church, her request was rejected. She then did not hesitate to change her church to the Methodist Protestant Church, which allowed ordaining of women. She applied for her ordination to that church with the thought that "I do not intend to fight my Church. But I am called to preach the gospel; and if I cannot preach it in my own Church, I will certainly preach it in some other Church!"[71] Shaw was ordained by the Methodist Protestant Church in 1880 as the first woman minister.

In 1885, at the end of her seventh year on Cape Cod, Shaw resigned from her two churches despite their pleas for her to stay. Her theological and medical education in Boston and frequent invitations by the leading women in society to speak publicly on the topics of temperance, suffrage, and social purity greatly widened her horizons and inspired her to work for the larger world. Shaw lived the rest of her life as a public lecturer, especially as a prominent orator and leader of the women's suffrage movement, in an age filled with other skillful women speakers. She worked collaboratively with such women leaders as Susan B. Anthony, Frances Willard, Lucretia Mott, Olympia Brown, Elizabeth Cady Stanton, and others who were eager to bring a new egalitarian world to American society.

Among her numerous female colleagues in the suffrage movement, Shaw was greatly influenced, for almost twenty years, by the Quaker Susan B. Anthony until Anthony's death in 1906. In her autobiography, Shaw mentions that Anthony was her "unceasing inspiration — the torch" that illumined her life. She admired the "rare beauty of her nature," namely, "her bigness, her many-sidedness, her humor, her courage, her quickness, her sympathy, her understanding, her force, her supreme common-sense, her selflessness."[72] On her deathbed, Anthony encouraged Shaw to continue the women's suffrage movement by giving her the following advice:

> My last word to you is this: No matter what is done or is not done, how you are criticized or misunderstood, or what efforts are made to block your path, remember that the only fear you need [to] have is the fear of not standing by the thing you believe to be right. Take your stand and hold it; then let come what will, and receive blows like a good soldier.... I do not know anything about what comes to us after this life ends, ... But if there is a continuance of life beyond it, and if I have any conscious knowledge of this world and of what you are doing, I shall not be far away from you; and in times of need I will help you all I can.[73]

As a full-time lecturer of the women's suffrage movement, Shaw felt seriously the God-given call to labor for the rights of women. She created sacred space whenever she spoke in the pulpit, on the convention platform, or before legislative bodies. For her, there was no essential difference between her sermons and lectures. Her speeches were replete with scriptural quotations and theological references. In most of her sermons and lectures, she used the Bible as a springboard to present the nature of God and God's creative purposes for women and men alike. Shaw challenged the traditional patriarchal prejudice against women and proclaimed a new concept of womanhood based on her theological conviction that women were human beings who are part of God's plan and purpose, so that men had no right to define the limitations of women. In her lecture, "God's Women," Shaw explained her new image of a woman as follows:

> The highest crown of glory which a woman can wear is not motherhood. It is *womanhood* — true, noble, strong, healthy, spiritual womanhood; the daughter of the King, the child of God, equal with the Bishop or any man in the world. If the woman is first of all a woman, all things shall be to her a crown of glory, whether it be motherhood or spinsterhood ... a woman who, finding any wrong, any weakness, any pain, any sorrow, anywhere in the world, reaches out her hand to right the wrong, to heal the pain, to comfort the suffering — such a woman is God's woman.[74]

God's women, according to Shaw, deserve a place of leadership in the world as well as in the church because they have a vision for the kingdom of God, in which all humanity, both women and men, is lifted out of the subjection into the free and full air of divine liberty, the great principles of universal equality. Shaw believed that this kingdom of Heaven was coming nearer to us because of the loyalty and service of those who believed that God was active in human history, not only on an individual basis but also on the societal level.[75] With this conviction, Shaw motivated American women and men to fight for the equal rights of women not only through her preaching but also through her practicing what she preached. She demonstrated her leadership as the chair of the Woman's Committee of the Council of National Defense as well as the president of the National American Woman Suffrage Association (1904–15). She was instrumental in the passage of the Nineteenth Amendment to the Constitution of the United States — the Women's Rights Amendment — under the presidency of Woodrow Wilson during

World War I. After the war, Shaw went on an exhausting speaking tour in support of the League of Nations until she died in 1919 from a heart attack caused by exhaustion.[76]

Shaw's calling story and her life of ministry are quite different from Lee's. While Lee described hearing the vivid voice of God calling her to preach and that she was convinced of her calling by the physical experience of being miraculously healed, Shaw did not describe in her autobiography such an ecstatic experience of calling. Instead, she was clear that God had given her the aspiration to become a preacher during her childhood and that her dream came true because of God's intervention through women colleagues, ministers, and lecturers. God opened various doors for Shaw to participate in the preaching ministry with authority. Her authority as a preacher came not only from her inner experience of a divine calling but also from external factors such as her theological education, her polished rhetorical skills, her ordination by the church, her medical degree, and her social position as a leader in well-known religious and political associations. Most of all, Shaw's authority as a preacher came from her self-esteem as a woman. During her visit to Europe after graduating from Boston University School of Theology, Shaw had the chance to preach to sailors on the ship. When her preaching was well-received by tough male sailors, the pastor of the ship, who had not previously known that the guest preacher was female, said to her:

"I wouldn't have believed it.... I thought the men would mob you."

"Why should they mob me?..."

"Why," he stammered, "because the thing is so — unnatural."

"Well," I said, "if it is unnatural for women to talk to men, we have been living in an unnatural world for a long time. Moreover, if it is unnatural, why did Jesus send a woman out as the first preacher?"[77]

Another event reveals Shaw's wit and dignified manner in defending herself as a woman. During her ordination interview, Shaw was questioned by a male minister about a Pauline passage:

"Paul said, 'Wives, obey your husbands, ...' Suppose your husband should refuse to allow you to preach? What then?" "In the first place," I answered, "Paul did not say so, according to the Scriptures. But even if he did, it would not concern me, for I am a spinster." ... "You might marry some day," he predicted, cautiously.... "Possibly," I admitted. "Wiser women than I am have married. But it is equally possible that I might marry a man who would command me to preach; and in that case, I want to be all ready to obey him."[78]

Shaw's contemporary audiences and colleagues witnessed that her physical appearance, voice, tone, persona, and delivery style were significant factors for her success in conveying her dignity and authority on a platform. Although she was not physically prepossessing because of her short height, her carriage and demeanor in public were extraordinarily impressive to audiences. They admired her enthusiasm and abundant vitality. She was a person with grit. She was praised as the "golden-voiced orator" who could be easily heard in large halls because of the quality, the clarity, and intelligibility of her voice. Her voice was strong enough to carry a tone of conviction and assertiveness while, at the same time, sounding sweet and musical. In addition to her dignified appearance and voice, her extemporaneous style of delivery had the power to draw listeners into her speech. Her communication style — a combination of rational, emotional, and intuitive approaches — easily led her audiences to engage in her preaching.[79] These rhetorical elements reinforced her dignity and authority as a preacher and contributed to her listeners accepting her sermons and lectures as the Word of God.

AUTHORITY IN PREACHING

The term "authority" is generally defined as a legitimate power or right or ability to exert influence over another. Yet, no explicit definition of authority is evident because it cannot be understood in abstraction apart from a context.[80] When authority relates to preaching, it has traditionally been defined as a special right to preach the gospel or the quality of proclamation that has the power to influence listeners. However, a historical review of preaching from a woman's perspective reveals that various stages in Christian history understood the authority of preaching differently and regarded different elements as major sources of authority in preaching.

The sixteenth-century reformers rejected the authority of the papacy and ecclesiastical hierarchy, which had the supreme power of dominance over the church and society. These reformers declared that the ultimate authority came from God who was the "author," the creator of the world. For the reformers, God was free to call people and to work through all believers. God selected certain people to preach the gospel according to God's free will and endowed them with the rights and privileges to preach on behalf of God. Because the Bible was the key weapon for the reformers to fight against the authority of the pope, they emphasized biblical knowledge as the major source supporting the preacher's authority and identified the preacher as the Bible teacher, whose authority was delegated from God to become God's herald.

Later, the concept of delegated authority from God became the traditional understanding of authority in the Protestant Church. The Orthodox Calvinist churches in Europe and the Puritan churches in the United States in the seventeenth and eighteenth centuries institutionalized themselves according to the traditional patriarchal pattern and understood authority as the power of position and dominance. Only male clergy could have the rights and privileges to preach because masculinity, biblical knowledge from formal theological education, and ordination were considered the major sources behind a preacher's authority.

Although the reformers and their Calvinist posterity could not think about a new reality in which women, traditionally regarded as inferior to men, had special rights to preach and teach the Bible, reformed theology based on the doctrines of *sola scriptura*, the priesthood of all believers, and the activity of the Holy Spirit became a turning point in the history of Christian preaching. The reformed doctrines provided an egalitarian view for understanding the authority of preaching and promised a possibility in the future for the Protestant Church to share the right to preach with women.

The Pietist movement and the two Great Awakenings during the eighteenth and nineteenth centuries challenged the rigid patriarchal clericalism of the established churches by stressing the significance of the individual experience of the Holy Spirit as the most important source of a preacher's authority. For the evangelicals, preaching was not merely intellectual discourse about the Christian faith by educated male clergy but a spiritual event through which listeners experienced sanctification. God called the converted to share their personal experiences of the living God no matter their educational background, race, or gender and empowered them with the transforming power of the Spirit. Therefore, the preacher's conversion experience and divine calling were fundamental to his or her authority in preaching.

The emphasis on the spiritual experience as the major source of authority in preaching loosened the boundaries between clergy and laity and resulted in offering women room to participate in the preaching ministry. During the first half of the nineteenth century, Lee and other evangelical women devoted themselves as itinerant preachers as a means to responding to the divine calling. Without institutional support or official sanction, women preachers did their preaching ministry as the Spirit compelled them. For them, the authority of preaching was not a special right or privilege to speak as traditional male preachers had understood, but a "responsibility" charged by God for saving lost souls. Women preachers identified themselves as God's vessels or instruments, chosen and used by the irresistible power of the Holy Spirit. The Spirit called them to preach, filled their hearts with love for lost souls, gave them intuitive knowledge and wisdom about the Bible, and inspired their listeners to experience the presence of God at the moment of their preaching. Similarly, women's preaching was authoritative not because of such external elements as education, ordination, or gender but because of such spiritual elements as divine calling, compassion for lost souls, and the presence and activity of the Holy Spirit.

On the other hand, churches in the United States, starting in the late nineteenth century, faced a different phase in the history of preaching, for women began to have the opportunity to preach not as itinerant preachers, but as pastors of congregations. Even though the mainline denominations did not ordain women, some women preachers served local churches as licensed preachers. Through their pastoral experiences, women preachers recognized that the ministry of preaching was inextricably bound to pastoral leadership. Authority in preaching was not merely the right to preach as an individual but the ability to guide a congregation on a faith journey. The authority of preaching required pastoral responsibility, inseparable from such pastoral duties as administering Sacraments, guiding a congregation's daily life, and participating in the decision making of a church and denomination. Realizing that such authority came from theological education and ordination, Shaw and other women preachers pursued these goals. Shaw's autobiography illustrates how difficult her struggle was to gain both theological education and ordination.

Luther Lee, who preached the ordination sermon when Antoinette Brown graduated from Oberlin College and was ordained in 1853, emphasized in his sermon that three factors — authorization by the church, qualification by education, and the calling by God — were the sources supporting the authority of a preacher as an ordained minister:

> We are not here to make a minister. It is not to confer on this our sister, a right to preach the gospel. If she has not that right already, we have no power to communicate it to her. Nor have we met to qualify her for the work of ministry. If God and mental and moral culture have not already qualified her, we cannot, by anything we may do by way of ordaining or setting her apart.... All we are here to do... is... to subscribe our testimony to the fact, that in our belief, our sister in Christ, Antoinette L. Brown, is one of the ministers of the New Covenant, *authorized, qualified, and called* by God to preach the gospel of his Son Jesus Christ.[81]

Yet, it is notable that Brown, who was "authorized, qualified, and called by God to preach the gospel," had to resign from her office within a year because of little outside support and the sexist mentality and attitudes of the majority of Christians of her time. Even Shaw had to continually defend her authority as the pastor and preacher against her congregation's sexist mind-set during her seven-year church ministry.

The experiences of these women preachers testify that the so-called legitimate authority of preaching given by institutional authorization, educational qualification, and divine calling was not sufficient for women pastors. Such authority did not automatically guarantee a relationship between the woman preacher and her congregation if the congregation was deeply embedded in the traditional patriarchal culture. Legitimate authority could not provide women pastors with a sense of security, identity, or direction in their ministerial lives. According to their experiences, the authority of preaching also involves a social relation. It was not only a matter between God and the individual preacher or between the preacher and her denomination but also a matter between the preacher and her congregation. Not until her congregants assented to the authority of the preacher could she fully exercise her authority as preacher.

The assent of a congregation has been one of the most crucial issues not only for nineteenth-century women preachers but also for contemporary ordained women preachers. Since the second half of the twentieth century, when some mainline Protestant churches began to open the door to ordain women as ministers of the Word and Sacrament, the number of ordained women preachers has surged in the United States. Before 1965, about one third of the more than two hundred Protestant denominations in the United States had already begun to ordain women. Among these denominations, by 1976, about ten thousand women had been ordained, representing about 5 percent of total clergy numbers.[82] According to research conducted by the Center for Social and Religious Research at Hartford Seminary, mainline Protestant denominations such as UCC, UMC, PCUSA, and RCA had 18 to 30 percent of clergy as women in 1994.[83] Their experiences, however, have been very similar to those of more than a century prior. Despite their legitimate rights to preach, ordained women preachers still experience insecurity and confusion of identity in the sexist environments of their churches and society at large.

The realities of ordained ministry and preaching have challenged women preachers to take seriously the function of the congregation in the ministry of preaching and redefine the authority of preaching. Reflecting on women's particular experience, such feminist theologians as Letty Russell, Catherine Ziel, and Christine Smith give insights into understanding authority from the relational perspective between the preacher and the congregation. Russell states that leadership in the church has "an authority of purpose, as distinguished from authority of position or office." Authority not as a right or privilege but as "the ability to accomplish desired ends" is present in human relationships in the context of particular communities or societies.[84] "Authority in community" is not domination but a "partnership" which "assist[s] members of the congregation in making use of their gifts in the service of Christ's love in the world." It participates in "the common task of creating an interdependent community of humanity and nature."[85]

Like authority in leadership, authority in preaching can be thought of in terms of partnership. According to women preachers' experiences, the authority of preaching initially comes from a divine calling and is finalized by the listeners. It stems from the relationship or "connectedness" between the preacher and the congregation in addition to the sources of ordination, education, and divine calling. As Ziel points out, "office, training, and personal conviction... are not sufficient to evoke the assent of the listeners unless there is also a mutuality which acknowledges that both parties participate in the faith that is being given voice."[86] In other words, the assent of the listeners "is created and experienced in direct relation to the quality of connection and intimacy that humans experience with each other in communication and interaction."[87] Thus, the authority of preaching from a woman's experience is not a possession of the preacher but is in the process through cooperation between the preacher and the listeners. Smith names this sort of authority "integrity and ultimate solidarity."[88] She describes it as follows:

> For feminist women, authority is not something one possesses or the way one dominates a community of people or another

individual; rather it is a quality of humanness that is so persuasive and honest that it calls people into connection and solidarity.[89]

In this sense, authority deals with authenticity. When listeners perceive preaching as authentic, they assent to the authority of the preacher. The authenticity of a message, which "makes the preaching craft and the moment of proclamation credible, honest, and life-transforming for preacher and listener alike," is created only when the preacher weaves together "mutuality, solidarity, and deeper faith sharing" in her sermon.[90]

The concept of authority from the feminist perspective is democratic in the sense that authority is perceived as a social relation among human beings. The formation of the authority of preaching is not a task for the preacher alone but rather a cooperative task for both the preacher and the congregation. This democratic view helps not only women preachers but also men preachers reformulate their authority in our contemporary social context, for the larger context in which American listeners are living is a democratic society. The democratic movement toward recognizing the basic equality of all human beings has challenged the hierarchical view that authority comes only from God, the scriptures, traditions, or institutions. The democratic movement has also led believers to consider the church as a community for all its members and the source behind the authority of preaching as a community of faith.[91]

Based on the experiences of women preachers, the historical review of the authority of preaching reveals that defining the concept of authority and its sources depends on a particular sociocultural fabric and setting. There is no absolute view of the authority of preaching apart from its particular social-cultural context. The definition and sources of authority are contextual, open to the changing situation of the church and larger society and change as needed to better support the proclamation of the gospel.

Chapter Five

PREACHING AND THE POLITICS OF GOD
KOREAN WOMEN PREACHERS DURING THE COLONIAL AND POSTCOLONIAL ERAS

RECENTLY I WAS INVITED by the Iliff Women's Alliance to participate in a panel discussion on the topic, "Women Promoting Peace." This topic immediately reminded me of the Korean women preachers who struggled for peace during the colonial and postcolonial period of Korea. Their preaching lives were great examples of women promoting peace. Peace tends to be understood simply as "a state without war" and is regarded as a political and military issue from which women are traditionally excluded. However, as explored in the first chapter of this book, the concept of peace is more profound and comprehensive than that, because it means the wholeness of God. Women preachers in Korea have considered peace to be the most crucial theological and political issue of all. They have yearned for peace in the form of a vision for a new society, a completely different world from the status quo, in which God's justice, righteousness, and compassion overflow. Women who promote peace through preaching are partners of God, for they directly participate in God's politics. Paul Lehmann defines the politics of God as "humanization" or a "radical social transformation," rooted in the liberating power of God in Jesus Christ. The politics of God generates a revolutionary dynamic and directions "to make and to keep human life human in the world."[1]

The history of Korean preaching includes many women preachers who have participated in the politics of God not only by preaching the gospel of peace, but also by living distinctive lives for peace. This chapter focuses on these women preachers with regard to the following questions: What did preaching mean to them? What did they preach in their particular historical context? How did they live their preaching lives? These theological and homiletical issues are explored in four sections of this chapter.

The first section explores how women became involved in the formation of Korean Christianity during the colonial period. Protestant Christianity, which was introduced by Western missionaries during the late nineteenth century, evolved into a distinctive form of Korean Christianity based on its particular cultural and historical foundation. Christian women played a major role, along with the male leaders of the church, in the formation of Korean Christianity. The second section of this chapter investigates how women preachers in Korea contributed to the development of democracy during the postcolonial period. The third section illustrates the lives of two women preachers; Duk Ji Choi, who preached and suffered during the Japanese occupation of Korea from 1910 to 1945, and Wha Soon Cho, who preached and suffered during Korea's military dictatorship from 1963 to 1992. Their biographies and sermons show how Korean women preachers who lived during the turbulent history of modern Korea participated in the politics of God and how they promoted peace through their preaching. The last section of this chapter develops a theological and homiletical understanding of preaching as an act of the politics of God. This section also extends to the experiences of women preachers in other Asian countries who have promoted peace through their preaching.

THE GOSPEL AND NATIONAL CONSCIOUSNESS

During the late nineteenth century, the Yi dynasty (1391–1910), which was the last Korean dynasty, was on a downward path. National crises caused by governmental corruption, peasant uprisings, natural disasters, plagues, and international hegemony by Japan, China, and Russia over Korea caused political, economic, and social chaos. The political climate was unstable; industries and finances were disorganized; education was neglected; and social morals had degenerated into an increase of bribery, debauchery, gambling, early marriage, slave trade, and concubinage. The Confucian and Buddhist philosophies that had sustained Korean society for over fifteen hundred years became so hardened with formalities and a rigid literati mentality that they failed to provide spiritual leadership during this period. Many Koreans longed for a new leading spirit as an alternative to their traditional religions. At this critical turning point, the Korean government made a Treaty of Amity for the first time with a Western country, the United States, in 1882, and with Great Britain, Germany, and Russia shortly thereafter.[2] The normalization of diplomatic relations between Korea and Western countries made the Korean government officially open a door to Christianity and accept Christian missionaries.

According to historical records, Dr. Horace N. Allen, a Presbyterian medical missionary under the Presbyterian Board, was the first Protestant missionary in Korea. He arrived in Korea via China in 1884. Within three months of his arrival, Prince-General Yong-Ik Min was wounded by the opposite party during a political revolt, and Allen cured him. Because of his successful treatment of Min, Allen gained the respect of the royal family and was officially appointed the court physician. When other missionaries, such as Horace G. Underwood, an ordained Presbyterian minister; Henry G. Appenzeller, an ordained Methodist minister; and Mary F. Scranton, a Methodist woman missionary, arrived in Korea via Japan in 1885, the Korean government was already in favor of Christianity because of Allen's medical practice and, consequently, supported the activities of these missionaries as well.[3]

The U.S. missionaries in Korea, including Allen, Underwood, Appenzeller, and Scranton, were influenced by the nineteenth-century North American evangelical faith. They emphasized personal conversion and piety and viewed a missionary call to preach and teach the gospel to the "heathen" as the highest calling of Christian ministry, based on the doctrine of premillennialism. To them, the world was the scope that the church must conquer with the gospel of Jesus Christ. Missionaries were compared to fighting soldiers (Eph. 6:10–17; 2 Tim. 2:1–7) or competing athletes (Heb. 12:1; 2 Tim. 4:7–8), who should save individual souls from the forces of evil. Missionaries in Korea saw their mission as doing "battle against the 'forces' of evil, darkness, superstition, and the heathen," and their preaching therefore stressed personal salvation through Jesus Christ. Their goal was to "take Korea for Christ."[4] In his writing Appenzeller reveals this theological view as follows:

> The missionary goes to heathen lands for this one purpose. Your schools, your hospitals, your printing offices are all doing much good, ... but let me tell you we go not to heathen lands to do people good in the common acceptance of the word. We go there to deliver our message that in Jesus Christ, by grace, God tasted death for every man. We go there to preach the gospel and we use everything, every agency, to help us in it.[5]

During the early years of Christian missions in Korea, the missionaries did not recognize the internal and external complexities of the country. They simply interpreted idleness as the source behind the poverty and misery in Korea. They regarded Koreans as "poor as church mice, lazy as dogs, dirty as pigs, ravenous as wolves, and proud as hypocrites,"[6] and thought that enhancing individual morality through preaching and teaching the gospel was the key to transforming the situation in Korea. Nevertheless, the missionaries' efforts to reform individual morality and improve social welfare by building hospitals and establishing schools were deeply appreciated by Koreans, who highly respected the missionaries' personal sacrifices in Korea.[7]

Above all, the Christian gospel that the missionaries preached and taught was fantastic news for the Koreans. The gospel's emphasis on equality between men and women, the old and the young, masters and slaves, the literate and the illiterate, and the haves and the have-nots was a completely new message from that of traditional Confucianism, which is based on hierarchism, classism, and sexism and had been the foundation of the personal and social norms of Korean society for centuries. The progressive leaders of the country who were looking for a new leading spirit to reform Korean society, as well as women and the "low class" who were oppressed and marginalized, were attracted to the revolutionary power of the

Christian gospel and accepted the Christian religion as a new leading spirit for their country. They willingly publicized the new truth of the Christian religion and the missionaries' altruistic activities in Korean newspapers and journals.

The Great Revivals (1903–7), which were ignited by a missionaries' prayer meeting held in the town of Wonsan in a northern province of Korea, spread rapidly throughout the country via the Korean church leaders who were active partners with the missionaries. Through their preaching, Bible study sessions, and prayer meetings, Choon Soo Jung, Sun Ju Gil, and other Korean preachers converted to Christianity thousands of people who longed for inner peace in the midst of their chaotic historical situation.[8] The egalitarian view of the Christian gospel especially appealed to Korean women, who had been despised as "no better than a domestic animal" under the traditional sexist culture and social system.[9] Female converts outnumbered men on the membership rosters of the church and shared the leadership with men as evangelists, organizers of revival meetings, and Bible teachers.[10]

The missionaries in Korea also contributed significantly to women's education. The Methodist Church in the United States sent more women missionaries than men to Korea,[11] and these women missionaries devoted themselves to Korean women's education by establishing schools and educational centers for women. After Scranton founded Ewha Hakdang (Ewha School) in 1886 as the first school for women in Korea, the government began to establish schools for girls, and some enlightened Koreans even founded girls' schools with their own money. By 1910, the number of private schools for girls increased to 170. Of these schools, 43 were Christian schools established by missionaries, Korean churches, and/or individual Korean Christians.[12]

During the beginning years of women's education, missionaries had a difficult time recruiting students because of the Confucian regulations and customs that prevented women from public places. Realizing that middle- and upper-middle-class women were more strictly controlled by the Confucian rules, the missionaries instead recruited low-class and marginalized women such as orphans, widows, and concubines. The missionaries educated them to become "useful, practical, Christian women"[13] for the family, church, and society, based on their view of "true womanhood" of nineteenth-century America. Scranton, A. J. Ellers, and other missionary educators limited their curricula to traditional feminine teachings such as sewing, embroidery, music, religion, and the English language with the goal of "making students better Korean women."[14] Realizing the significance of women's leadership for evangelism, the Methodist missionaries established Hyupsung Yeoja Shinhakkyo (The Union Methodist Woman's Bible Training School) in 1920. They trained women seminarians to preach and teach the gospel as evangelists and missionaries in Manchuria as well as within the Korean peninsula.[15] Ten years later, in 1930, the Korean Methodist Church allowed women to be ordained as ministers of the Word and Sacrament.

Korean Christian women who were awakened by the Christian gospel became leaders in society as well as the church. Through their preaching and teaching, they insisted on the importance of educating women; the prohibition of concubinage, early marriage, and slave trade; and the abolition of sexist laws and regulations. In addition, in 1907, Maria Chang, Hester Jung, and other Christian women leaders organized a nationwide movement for reducing the national debt. In 1924, the first temperance organization, Chosen Yeoja Kydokkyo Juljaehoe Yonhabhoe (Korean Women Christian Temperance Unified Society), was founded by Christian women in response to an increase in alcoholism, smoking, opium usage, and prostitution. In April 1938, Gunwoohoe, a Korean women's national organization for social and moral reform, persuaded the government to enact a law protecting youth from drinking and smoking.[16]

Although the Western missionaries and Korean Christians worked together on social and moral reform, the missionaries' policies toward political issues conflicted with Korean Christians. From the beginning of their mission in Korea, missionary organizations kept church and state separate and ordered their missionaries not to get involved in Korea's political situation. Korea was at that time in the process of being colonized by Japan. From the early Meiji era (1860–94), Japan was preoccupied with the illusion of establishing a

Pan-Asian Japanese empire. Japan's victories from the Sino-Japanese War (1894–5) and the Russo-Japanese War (1904), both of which were fought on Korean soil, accelerated the colonization of Korea. The United States and the United Kingdom provided Japan with financial support during the Russo-Japanese War, and the United States supported Japan in its efforts to colonize Korea based on Japan's willingness to remain indifferent to U.S. colonialism in the Philippines.[17] The end of the Russo-Japanese War brought a Japanese protectorate over Korea in 1905 and full annexation by Japan in 1910. The organizations that had sent missionaries to Korea welcomed Japanese rule over Korea because the main missionary organizations in Korea were also strongly represented in Japan. They did not want to offend Japan nor "damage" the existence of Christianity there. As journalist F. A. McKenzie indicates, "there was a feeling — a quite honest feeling — that they might accomplish more by appealing to the better side of Japan than by frankly proclaiming the truth."[18] In 1912, Arthur Brown, the secretary of the Presbyterian Board of Foreign Mission, wrote the following as a guideline for the mission in Korea:

> What is the attitude of the missionaries toward the Japanese? There are four possible attitudes: First, opposition; second, aloofness; third, cooperation; fourth, loyal recognition... the fourth, loyal recognition, is I believe, the sound position. It is in accord with the example of Christ, who loyally submitted himself and advised his apostles to submit themselves to a far worse government than the Japanese and it is in line with the teaching of Paul in Romans xiii.[19]

Following this guideline, missionary-governed Korean churches officially adopted the position of "loyal recognition."[20] The missionaries tried to avoid conflict between the Japanese government and their churches by advising Korean Christians not to get involved in any political activities that opposed Japan.

However, Korean Christians who were conscious of the national crisis caused by Japanese imperialism understood that there would be no true freedom in Christ if they lost their nation. They identified their political struggle for national independence with Jesus's movement against the unjust forces that suppressed the freedom and liberty of the innocent and weak. Many Korean Christians viewed their movement for national independence as the movement for the reign of God, who is the source of justice and freedom. They believed that their mission as Korean Christians was to participate in God's politics against Japanese imperialism through both prayer and action in the independence movement. This belief justified the political involvement of Korean Christians.

Christian women played a major role in the nationalist movement. Along with male leaders, they organized political clubs and meetings to inspire a national consciousness and identity. Women preachers interpreted the biblical stories about political liberation in the Hebrew Bible in relation to their particular historical situation and understood the independence movement to be the will of God. By preaching and teaching, they encouraged their listeners to support the national independence movement. As the Korean church became a well-organized social group, the Japanese government in Korea perceived it as a potential threat to Japan's occupation of Korea.

During the Japanese annexation of Korea, Korean Christians assassinated two key politicians: the U.S. diplomat Durham White Stevens and Marquis Ito Hirobumi, the resident general in Korea. Myung Woon Chun and In Hwan Chang, two members of the Korean Methodist Church in San Francisco, assassinated Stevens in San Francisco in 1908. Stevens was the chief advisor to Marquis Ito Hirobumi, who was responsible for the Japanese colonization of Korea. Hirobumi was the resident general in Korea since 1905 and supported the Japanese polices in Korea, stating that all Koreans wanted to be ruled by Japan. Stevens forced the Korean emperor to sign a treaty giving away the independence of Korea to Japan. Chun gave a written statement explaining why he assassinated Stevens:

> Stevens is an enemy of the world and a disturber of its peace. ...If I kill him and I die, it will be a warning to others who take his place to rule justly and to deal with [the] people in his care with kindness and humanity. I will make no complaint to the punishment that will be meted out to me and, should my

act aid my country in struggles for freedom, I will die nobly and well.[21]

The second assassination occurred one year later in 1909, in Harbin, Japan, when Choong Gon Ahn, a Roman Catholic, killed Hirobumi at the Harbin train station, injuring three other Japanese officials as well. Ahn believed that the Japanese forces, which were waging an unjust war in Korea and East Asia, were committing the greatest sin before God.[22] In his interrogation, he responded to the question of why he committed murder, which was against the Christian faith, as follows:

> I know that the Bible says that killing a person is a sin. However, wresting the nation from the innocent people by force and taking their lives are worse sins. I simply eliminated these vicious sins because the ignorance of these sins is a bigger sin than killing a person.... I thank God for the death of Ito.[23]

These two assassinations resulted in the severe persecution of the Korean church by the Japanese government. According to McKenzie, in the town of Sunchon, located in a northern province of Korea, a Korean pastor who preached about "the Kingdom of Heaven" was arrested and warned by the Japanese police that "there is only one kingdom out here, and that is the kingdom of Japan." Missionary G. S. McCune and other Christian educators were also arrested because they preached the story of David and Goliath, pointing out that a weak man armed with righteousness was more powerful than a mighty enemy. The Japanese police understood this message as a direct incitement to the weak Koreans to fight strong Japan. Christian hymns such as "Onward, Christian Soldiers" and "Soldiers of Christ Arise" were also regarded as rebellious against Japan.[24] Furthermore, in 1911, the Japanese police manipulated a conspiracy case to oppress Korean Christians. The police arrested 149 Christian leaders, including preachers, teachers, students, and elders, in the city of Pyungyang and Sunchon on a charge of conspiracy to assassinate Count Terauchi, the governor-general of Korea. Because of brutal torture by the Japanese gendarmes, 3 people were killed, and 23 people were exiled without a trial. Eventually, 123 innocent prisoners were arraigned at the local court in Seoul, and 105, including prominent church leaders such as Chi Ho Yun and Ki Tak Yang, were found guilty.[25]

Despite these persecutions, Korean Christians continued to fight for independence. Maria Kim, a Korean student studying in Japan, raised funds for the independence movement and delivered the funds to the movement's leadership in Shanghai. Along with a number of other Korean students, she also led the February Eighth Independence Movement in Tokyo in 1919 and issued the historic "February Eighth Declaration of Independence."[26] The continued underground activities of Korean Christians for national independence enabled Korean Christians to greatly contribute to the emergence of the March First Independence Movement of 1919. The March First Independence Movement was a series of mass movements, initiated by religious leaders of Chundokyo (the indigenous Korean religion), Confucianism, Buddhism, and Christianity. Out of the 33 leaders who signed the Declaration of Independence in 1919, 16 were Christians. The movement began in Seoul and continued for two months, quickly spreading throughout the entire nation. Soon Ai Kim, Esther Whang, Kwan Soon Yoo, Young Shin Rim, and other Christian women led the movement along with male leaders. The March First Independence Movement Collective consisted of nonviolent actions, including a total of 1,214 demonstrations at 311 different locations in Korea. Christians led 25 percent of the demonstrations, and 66 percent of the females arrested were Christians. The participation of Christians in the March First Independence Movement was amazing, considering the fact that, at that time, only 1.3 percent of the total population of Korea was Christian.[27]

The Japanese government accused Korean Christians of being the primary instigators of the March First Independence Movement and arrested nearly every Korean Christian pastor in Seoul. Churches were burned, leading Christians were jailed, and their congregations were flogged.[28] Many of them were severely tortured by the Japanese gendarmeries and even martyred.[29] One of the most brutal, tragic attacks made by the Japanese police was the massacre of the Cheamni Church in the province of Kyunggi. In April

1919, the police called thirty members of the congregation into the church, locked them in, and killed them by setting the church on fire as revenge for the independence movement.[30] An American who witnessed the persecution of Koreans stated that

> The Belgian Government has recently announced that during the more than four years that the Germans held the country, six thousand civilians were put to death by the Germans. Here in this land it is probably safe to say that two thousand men, women and children, empty handed and helpless, have been put to death in seven weeks.[31]

Persecution was extended to the missionaries as well. Many of them were searched, attacked, and severely beaten by the Japanese gendarmerie. However, missionary organizations in the United States and other Western countries were indifferent to the suffering of Korean Christians and slow to respond to the missionaries' reports on the persecution of Christians in Korea. McKenzie criticized the missionary organizations for their indifference:

> You, the Christians of the United States and of Canada, are largely responsible for these people. The teachers you sent and supported taught them the faith that led them to hunger for freedom. They taught them the dignity of their bodies and awakened their minds.... Your teaching has brought them floggings, tortures unspeakable, death.... I would mourn for you if you were willing to leave them unhelped, to shut your ears to their calls, to deny your practical sympathy.... What can we do? you ask. You can exercise the powers that democratic government has given you to translate your indignation into action.... "The Koreans are a degenerate people, not fit for self-government," says the man whose mind has been poisoned by subtle Japanese propaganda... but it has already indicated that this charge is a lie.... When you ask me if I would risk a war over Korea, I answer this: Firm action to-day might provoke conflict, but the risk is very small. Act weakly now, however, and you make a great war in the Far East almost

certain within a generation. The main burden of the Western nations in such a war will be borne by America.[32]

As McKenzie prophesied above, the political climate changed in the 1930s. In Tokyo, the military party was expanding its political influence and engaging in terrorist activities to suppress the liberal democratic elements emerging in Japanese politics. In 1932, Japan used force to occupy Manchuria and officially recognized it as one of its states. When the League of Nations criticized Japan for its invasion, Japan withdrew from the League. The military government of Japan abandoned the ideas of democracy and deified the Japanese emperor by reinforcing Shinto ceremonies as religious expression for paying homage to the emperor. Koreans were forced to attend Shinto ceremonies and bow down in Shinto shrines established in every village in Korea.[33] As an assimilation policy, the Japanese government did not allow Koreans to use the Korean language or even their Korean names. Instead, Koreans were forced to adopt the Japanese language and use Japanese names. When the Sino-Japanese War began in 1937, Japan drafted approximately 160,000 young Korean women into systemized sexual slavery as Jungshindae (military comfort women)." These women were forced to provide sexual services to the Japanese soldiers fighting in Teinchin, Manchuria, Peking, Shanghai, and Singapore and on La Paul Island, Saipan Island, and the South Pacific Islands. According to some of the survivors, the comfort women were confined to small rooms about the size of a double bed and were not allowed to leave except for time for their basic needs. They were raped by dozens of soldiers every day of their confinement. If a woman escaped but was later captured, she was brutally tortured.[34]

Korean Christians strongly resisted worshiping the emperor. To them, worshiping the emperor was a violation of their Christian faith based on the monotheistic belief that there is only one God who liberated the oppressed Israelites from the oppressor, the Egyptian Pharaoh, and the same God revealed the truth through the life and ministry of Jesus Christ. The Japanese government persecuted Korean Christians who resisted worshiping the emperor: two hundred churches were closed; two thousand Christians were jailed; seventy ministers and church leaders, including women preachers such as Duk Ji Choi and Ai Na Yeom, were tortured; and fifty ministers were martyred in jail.[35] The Japanese government also prohibited the Korean church from preaching from the Hebrew Bible because of its liberating power from oppression. The subsequent persecution succeeded in that the Methodist and Presbyterian churches, the two major Protestant denominations in Korea at that time, officially assented to worshiping the emperor. Christian activists could no longer remain in the Korean church; they were either jailed, martyred, or exiled to foreign countries. Only those who were quiet about the national crises and obedient to the Japanese political and religious polices could survive. The remaining Christian leaders led the Korean church to the evangelical-conservative faith based on the principle of separation between church and state. They preached the salvation of individual souls after death as the essence of the Christian gospel. Their sermons were full of escapism and pessimism, avoiding responsibility for this world to which they belonged.[36]

In 1940, the Japanese government ordered all Americans, including missionaries, to leave Korea. In 1941, Japan attacked Pearl Harbor. In July 1945, all Protestant churches in Korea were forced to abolish their denominational distinctions and combine into the Nihon Kirishto-Kyo Chosen Kyodan (the Korean division of the Japanese Christian Church).[37] All the way up until Japan was defeated in World War II on August 15, 1945, Japan ruined Korea's natural and human resources by using Korea as the springboard for Japanese invasions of other Asian countries. Until the day of national emancipation in Korea, many Korean Christian women and men continued their struggle against Japanese imperialism either in jail or in foreign countries, sometimes at the cost of their lives.

PREACHING AND THE STRUGGLE FOR DEMOCRACY

Korea was emancipated from Japan on August 15, 1945, the same day Japan surrendered to the United States. Emancipation brought another tragedy to the history of Korea. Despite the desire of Koreans to create a united, democratic, and independent country, two superpowers — the Soviet Union and the United States — divided Korea into North and South with the assumption that such a division would "provide a convenient allocation of responsibility for the acceptance of the Japanese surrender."[38] North Korea was occupied by communists supported by the Soviet Union, and South Korea by the Liberal Party supported by the United States.

To this day, the division of the country has been the major cause of conflict and difficulty for establishing a democratic society in Korea. The Korean War (1950–53) devastated both halves of the country and resulted in more than six million casualties and the destruction of approximately 80 percent of Korea's industry, public utilities, residential dwellings, and transportation.[39] Technically, the Korean War never ended because Korea remains a divided country.

After the emancipation, the Korean church suffered divisions, too. The schisms of the church were caused by the conflicts between the Christian nationalists who came back from prison and exile and the pro-Japanese church leaders who appeased imperialist Japan with the evangelical-conservative faith; hegemony between the conservative-orthodox Christians who wanted to preserve the legacy of the nineteenth-century Western missionaries and the liberals who were exposed to the early twentieth-century American liberal theology; and an influx of diverse denominations from North America and Europe after the emancipation.[40]

During the political and religious chaos that ensued after the emancipation, Christian women made a strong effort to unite the church. Sung Mu Kim, Young Sook Lee, and Pil Rye Kim organized the National Presbyterian Women's Missionary Society and sought solidarity among Christians by preaching nationally and internationally.[41] Furthermore, Christian women leaders actively participated in establishing a new democratic government by demonstrating their leadership in the fields of politics, legislation, and economics. For example, Young Shin Rim and other Christian women organized Taehan Yeoja Kukmindang (The People's Party of Korean Women) with the following three claims:

1. We, Korean women, participate in establishing a democratic society because the democratic society cannot be established

by men only. 2. We, Korean women, participate in establishing a healthy economic system that can protect women and laborers from the pitfalls of capitalism. 3. We, Korean women, as the people of an independent nation, participate in promoting world peace and the prosperity of humanity by improving our national culture.[42]

Because of the national campaign of the women leaders, the People's Party gained over three hundred thousand members. Young Shin Rim, the party leader, attended the Second General Assembly of the United Nations as the Korean ambassador in 1946 and later served as both a congresswoman and as the secretary of trade and industry.[43] Moreover, Eu Kyung Shin and nine other female Christian legislators helped create the Constitution and other laws, making sure that women's rights were properly included in them.[44]

From 1945 until today, the United States has used South Korea as a military base for the defense of Northeast Asia against North Korea, Russia, China, as well as for the general protection of Japan.[45] This political and military situation has maintained the division of Korea and fostered long-term military dictatorships in both North and South Korea. The military dictatorship in South Korea began with the regime of Chung Hee Park (1963–79) and was followed by the regimes of Doo Whan Chun (1980–87) and Tae Woo Rho (1987–92). The dictatorial governments rigidly exercised anticommunist and anti–North Korean policies and imposed martial law to restrict freedom of speech and the freedom to criticize the government in the name of so-called national security. The Park regime, in particular, envisioned a nation that was an economically established utopia and accelerated rapid industrialization by exploiting poor workers and abandoning human rights.

The majority of the Korean church, which was conservative-fundamentalist, supported the dictatorships by stressing national security and survival as the most crucial issues. Messages from the pulpits of the Korean church were aligned with the governmental propaganda. Their sermons emphasized the Christian faith as a key to the individual's worldly success, ignoring the Christian responsibility for the greater society and the world.[46] However, some liberal

Christian leaders, such as Chai Choon Kim, Hyung Kyu Park, and Ik Hwan Moon, were conscious of the lack of democracy in Korea and resisted the dictatorships by indicting the usurpation of political and military power as intolerable and detrimental to the development of democracy in Korea. These Christian dissidents opposed the anticommunist policies of the military government as a means of unjust political repression and a strong obstacle against the reunification of the nation. The prophetic role that these Christian leaders envisioned for democracy in Korea was the revival of national consciousness among Korean Christians during the Japanese occupation. By preaching and engaging in political activities, Christian dissidents defended the human rights of poor laborers, abandoned urban squatters, and impoverished farmers.

The liberating message of Christian dissidents developed into Korean liberation theology — "minjung theology"[47] — which became the theological foundation for the sociopolitical struggles for democracy in Korea during the 1970s and the 1980s. Minjung preachers, along with like-minded university students and professors, laborers, farmers, journalists, intellectuals, and writers, criticized the dictatorial government as evil, a government that hindered peace in Korea. The minjung preachers preached an alternate vision for a new democratic society.[48] To them, preaching democracy was the same as preaching the dominion of God, for establishing a democratic society meant actualizing ultimate peace on earth.

The dictatorial government of South Korea severely oppressed minjung preachers by accusing them of being procommunists controlled by North Korea. The Korean Central Intelligence Agency (KCIA) examined their sermons and put their churches under surveillance. Female minister Wha Soon Cho and other Christian leaders who belonged to the Urban Industrial Mission were held under particularly close guard by the KCIA, for their preaching and teaching the liberating power of the Christian gospel generated subversive power among the industrial laborers, who were deprived of their human rights and dignity under the dictatorial government. The government considered such democratic activity dangerous to both national security and economic growth and accused the Christian leaders of being agents of North Korea.

When many prominent leaders of the democracy movement were arrested and tortured under the Park and Chun regimes, Kyohoe Yeosung Yeonhaphoe (The United Association of Church Women) and other groups of women Christians organized nationwide meetings for prayer services both within and across their denominations. They also raised funds to support the families of arrested church leaders and to pay for their legal fees. For example, one female Christian leader, Ah Ra Cho, organized a council for the release of those who were jailed under the Park regime and led prayer meetings for them. During the Chun regime, she was arrested and convicted of conspiracy to incite rebellion and sentenced to three years in prison, with a probation of six years.[49]

Through their suffering and pain under the various dictatorships, many South Korean Christians realized that the subsequent national tragedies were rooted in the national division of their country and felt a serious sense of urgency for national reconciliation and reunification. Although the dictatorial military government prevented civilians from discussing national reunification, female theologian and professor Soon Kyung Park and other Christian leaders exerted themselves to propose new ideas and strategies to make national reconciliation and reunification possible. Park was invited to give a lecture on peaceful reunification and Christian mission at the conference held by the Korean Japanese University Church in Tokyo, Japan, in July 1991. In her lecture, Park indicted the superpowers of Japan and the United States for monopolizing the world market and dominating the political and military arenas of the world. She also reminded the audience that North Korea was not the only country ruled by a dictatorial government. Because of this lecture, Park was arrested by the KCIA as soon as she came back to Korea and sentenced to one year and six months in prison with a probation of two years. She was also disqualified from teaching for one and a half years.[50]

Since the 1980s, a feminist movement has emerged among Korean women preachers. Women Christian leaders, who realized that women were the primary victims under dictatorial governments, became conscious of women's issues and have subsequently struggled to gain equal rights in both society at large as well as in the church. One of the results of their struggles was the ordination of women. Today, the major denominations of the Korean church officially ordain women to be ministers of the Word and Sacrament and encourage them to participate in the ministry of the gospel equal to male clergy.[51] Women ministers have greatly contributed to the development of an egalitarian structure of the Korean church. For example, Young Kim and Sook Ja Chung developed a "Women-Church" modeled after feminist theology. Sung Ja Park and other women ministers established minjung churches for the poor and marginalized and have proclaimed the gospel from the perspective of liberation theology. These women preachers have promoted peace in Korea by preaching human rights, democracy, and national reunification as well as gender issues.

The struggle for democracy in South Korea was not in vain. South Koreans finally succeeded in establishing a democratic government through a democratic presidential election in December 1992. Since then, the democratic government has campaigned to restore justice and peace, and the public has regained the freedoms of speech and press. However, contemporary Korea still has the formidable tasks of national reunification, equitable distribution of wealth, and equal rights ahead of them. Many South Korean Christian leaders, especially women preachers, are conscious of the national crises. They are facing ecological crisis, economic instability, the absence of moral and spiritual guidance, and the loss of identity under the neocolonialism of Western cultures, to name a few. The struggle to promote peace also engages contemporary women preachers in South Korea.

WOMEN PREACHERS AS PEACEMAKERS

During the turbulent history of modern Korea, women preachers have continually fought for promoting peace. The lives of two women preachers — Duk Ji Choi and Wha Soon Cho — are concrete examples of how Korean women preachers have struggled for justice and peace on earth in their particular historical contexts. Choi proclaimed the liberating gospel against Japanese imperialism and Cho against the subsequent military dictatorships. Both Choi and Cho participated in the politics of God at the cost of their lives. They both believed that God was present and working in human history by breaking the oppressive authorities and powers of the status quo and that the work of God would ultimately overcome evil in this world, bringing peace to the children of God.

Duk Ji Choi (1901–56)

Duk Ji Choi was born into a Christian family in the town of Tongyoung,[52] located in a southern province of Korea, four years before the protectorate of Japan over Korea began. Her fraternal grandmother was the first Christian in her family, and her parents later joined the church. Choi received a Christian education from private elementary and high schools established by missionaries. Her Christian schoolteachers awakened a national consciousness in her and inspired her to fight for national independence. Her parents raised her with their full attention and affection. However, their love and care did not last long, as they both died at a young age. Choi's mother died of an illness when Choi was fifteen years old, and her father died four years later.[53]

After graduating from Eushin Girls' High School, Choi became a kindergarten teacher in her hometown. She taught her children the story of Esther, who saved her people from the imperial kingdom of Persia with the resolution that "If I perish, I perish" (Esther 4:16). Choi also ran a night school to teach illiterate adults the Korean alphabets, math, history, and music and inculcated in them the urgency for national independence. Choi was active in leading the March First Independence Movement in 1919. In June of that same year, she organized Tongyoung Aikook Booinhoe (the Association of Women Patriots in Tongyoung) and went from house to house to raise funds to support the provisional government of Korea in Shanghai.[54] At the age of twenty, Choi married a man from the next village. As he was studying in Japan, they actually only saw each other during his vacations. During the fourth year of their marriage, they had a daughter. Choi's husband visited her and their daughter shortly after the baby was born. However, he became infected with typhoid fever and died two months later. In the midst of her despair over losing her husband as well as her parents at such a young age, she made the decision to live the rest of her life only for Christ.

From that point forward, Choi put her hopes not on earthly aspirations but on heavenly ones. She moved to the city of Pyungyang with her young daughter to enter the Pyungyang Women's Seminary. During her seminary studies, for which she received a full scholarship, Choi demonstrated her leadership as the president of the student association. In 1935 when she graduated from the seminary, she became a circuit evangelist, covering the area of Masan City located in the southeast of Korea. Her responsibility was to tour and supervise eighty-three small churches with other evangelists and Western missionaries by providing pastoral care through teaching, preaching, and leading worship.[55]

When Choi began her ministry, the Japanese government compelled Christian schools and churches to worship the emperor at Shinto shrines established in every village as a duty of the people to the Japanese empire. The leaders of the church resisted worshiping the emperor for political and religious reasons. First, they understood that the Japanese imperialists were demanding that Koreans worship Japanese gods and the emperor in order to exterminate the national spirit of Koreans and assimilate them into the Japanese culture. Second, worshiping the emperor was a violation of the first two of the Ten Commandments: "You shall not make for yourself an idol," and "You shall not bow down to them or worship them." Last, the forcible demand of worshiping the emperor violated the freedom of religion, which was guaranteed to the Koreans even under the Japanese Constitution.[56]

Christian schools that disobeyed worshiping the emperor were forcefully closed by the Japanese government. This repression extended to the churches as well. This state of oppression made almost impossible a unified resistance of the Korean church against worshiping the emperor. Most denominations and churches officially submitted to worshiping the emperor by reinterpreting it not as a religious ceremony but as an expression of honoring the Japanese king. However, Ki Chul Joo, Sang Dong Han, other pastors, evangelists, and laity of the church did not accept their denominations' surrender and protested against worshiping the emperor by organizing a national network of antiemperor worship. Through their sermons, they tried to persuade other Christians that imperial Japan was committing the greatest sin before God by forcing Christians to worship idols and that Korean Christians must fight against the evil power of Japan by witnessing the living God over the false gods of Japan.[57]

In 1936, Choi was appointed to be a teacher at the Kyungnam Women's Bible School, where she participated in the antiemperor worship movement. She and other schoolteachers were arrested by Japanese police in 1940 and were horribly tortured. During the seventeen days in jail, said Choi, "I experienced hell."[58] Jong Kyu Choi mentions in his biography of Choi that the methods the police employed were so horrifically cruel that he cannot describe them in writing. According to McKenzie's report on the forms of torture the Japanese used on Korean Christian and nationalist prisoners, these prisoners suffered stripping, beating, kicking, and flogging. The police burned women by pressing lit cigarettes against their tender areas and/or used hot irons to sear the bodies of women, men, and children. The police also strung up prisoners by their thumbs, beating them with bamboo and iron rods until they became unconscious. The police would then restore them and repeat the process, sometimes until death. The prisoners were also confined for long periods of time under torturous conditions, such as being so tightly packed into a room that one could not lie or sit down for days at a time.[59]

Although many Christian prisoners gave up on their Christian faith and human dignity because of the persecution they suffered, such violence and torture had no effect on Choi. After being released, she organized a house church in her hometown and held regular prayer meetings with a dozen other Christians. She also toured some churches, where she preached to others to love God and fight against false gods, by telling the story of Elijah who fought against the Baal worshipers (1 Kings 18:20–40).[60]

In 1941, the Japanese police arrested Choi again along with her church members. This time, she was tortured more severely than before. As a way of overcoming the unbearable torture, Choi decided to fast for twenty-one days even without drinking water, remembering Daniel who fasted during his captive life in Babylon (Dan. 10:2). While fasting, she prayed to God that the Japanese emperor and imperialists should repent and give Christians the freedom to worship God. Because the police were afraid of her possibly dying from fasting, Choi was released.[61]

In 1942, Choi was arrested a third time when she was leading a prayer meeting. She was charged with forming a secret association against the Japanese government. This time, she was moved to the state prison. Her interrogators offered her release under the condition that she would no longer preach the Christian gospel. She refused their offer, however, claiming that she could not help proclaiming the truth of Christ against Japanese idols.[62]

The following year, Choi was moved to the Pyungyang Prison, which was notorious for its terrible treatment of political and religious prisoners. Until her release two days after the national emancipation, she fought Japanese imperialism by means of worshiping four times a day in her cell. Her service began with singing a hymn, followed by confessing her faith by reciting the Apostles' Creed, memorizing biblical verses, praying, and closing with the Lord's Prayer. Choi recited the entire order of service in a loud voice so that the other prisoners and the prison guards could hear. Through her worship in prison, she prophesied that Japan would perish because God was living and working to destroy evil in this world.

Choi suffered severe forms of torture because of her worship sessions in prison — not only beating and kicking but also having her hands handcuffed behind her back, having a stick or dust cloths stuffed in her mouth, and having her mouth covered with a rubber mask. Nevertheless, Choi fearlessly continued her daily schedule of worship. She sang hymns prohibited by the Japanese government, such as "All Hail the Power of Jesus's Name," "A Mighty Fortress Is Our God," and "God Is Our Refuge."[63] She also prayed loudly to God to empower Korean Christians to endure the oppression until God's reign was restored over Korea. Choi based her faith on Matthew 10:28: "Do not fear those who kill the body but cannot kill the soul; rather fear him who can destroy both soul and body in hell." She believed that "what we must fear is only God." Eventually, the prison guards gave up on trying to stop her worshiping in jail.[64]

While Choi was struggling in the Pyungyang Prison, Yi Sook Ahn was also imprisoned there because she distributed fliers in the Japanese Congress with the message that Japan must repent its imperial sin before God. Ahn was inspired by Choi's invincible spirit and gave witness to it in her autobiography as follows:

> One day, late afternoon, a woman who seemed to be pretty aged was placed in Ward five. She was pale and weakened because of torture by the police and malnutritious food in jail. Her height loomed large because of her skinny body so much that she looked like a tall giant.... At supper time, I and other prisoners heard her singing a hymn, loudly echoed from her ward. A prison guard ran to her and beat her, yelling at her to stop singing. But her voice was getting stronger and stronger. After singing all three verses, the woman recited a biblical passage and began to pray as loud as all the prisoners could hear. My heart was beating from shock and fear.... In the early morning, we heard her singing again... and the prison guard beating and yelling.... Around three o'clock in the afternoon, we heard it again.... I assumed that this woman began her afternoon service as Daniel did in the Bible. This time, the chief guard handcuffed her two hands behind her back and put a damp duster in her mouth, treating her like a lunatic.... She continued her worship four times a day despite the frantic punishments of the prison guards.... My heart was broken not by my sympathy for her but by my weak faith. I was not as bold as she was. Even though I wanted to cry for her suffering and pain, I couldn't because of shock and fear. Her courageous effort to witness to the living God drew me to hold on to God desperately.... I asked a prison guard who was kind to me to allow me a moment to look at her face.... When I saw her, I could not help being amazed; although I anticipated a miserably dying old lady, her face was shining with joy and happiness; I saw a strong light in her eyes; I saw something

miraculous in her face. Her determined attitude raised infinite respect and awe for her inside of me.... Mrs. Choi would fight against evil until she died of beating. But she is not alone. Almighty God is standing by her side.... Choi is a magnificent woman. How can she be so ardent without agitation in her mind and so resolute in her attitude as a woman? She is the miracle of the miracles. She is the soldier of the soldiers. Her faith is like that of Moses. Her fighting is the war with flesh, blood, and bones against cannons. However, her fists and flesh of faith melts the violent weapons.... Oh, Soldier of faith, how splendid and honorable![65]

The Japanese police scheduled the execution of Choi and other Korean Christian prisoners on August 18, 1945. However, they were miraculously set free on August 17, one day before their execution, immediately following Japan's surrender to the United States. Choi and other released Christian leaders made an effort to reconstruct the Korean church by stressing ecclesiastical repentance for the churches and Christian leaders who worshiped the emperor. Choi held revival meetings nationwide and preached about the presence of God based on her experience in jail. Her powerful message inspired listeners to renew their faith through the purifying Spirit of God.

In 1948, Choi and her colleagues organized a new denomination, the Yaesukyo Jaekun Kyohoe (the Reconstruction Church of Jesus), separate from the mainline Korean Presbyterian Church. This new church grew to include over fifty member churches in just three years. When her ordination was proposed to the General Assembly in 1951, it became a controversial issue because mainline Presbyterian churches did not ordain women at that time because of the influence of American Presbyterian missionaries who believed in patriarchal gender ideology. In order to support her ordination, the moderator of the General Assembly of the Korean Reconstruction Church stated, "We do not ordain a woman but ordain Duk Ji Choi, who is the true servant of victory. I doubt if our church can have such a wonderful woman again within fifty or one hundred years."[66] Then Choi stood up and said, "If you ordain me as a special case,

I will not receive ordination. If the church agrees to ordain women officially from the biblical perspective, I will be ordained."[67] The ministers who attended the General Assembly discussed the issue of women's ordination further, and the majority voted positively. In her sermon, "Imitate Their Faith," Choi states her understanding of women's rights as follows:

> The issue of women's rights is contentious within the Korean church. Some say that women cannot be ordained to be ministers or elders. Some women say that they regret being born as female. However, I never regretted my gender.... The role of women is as great as men's, for they are equally created in the image of God (Gen. 1:27). If I have regret, it is not for my gender but that I am not a great person who can fulfill God's will on earth.... Is the ordination of women illegal? Not at all! The Christian Church was created by the work of the Holy Spirit on Pentecost. Did only men receive the Holy Spirit? Not at all! Everyone — women and men, old and young, slaves and masters — that gathered in the room experienced the presence and work of the Holy Spirit. The Holy Spirit did not discriminate between women and men.... Therefore, women are able to stand in the same ecclesial rank as men.[68]

Until her death in 1956 from the aftereffects of torture, Choi put all her time and energy into preaching the Christian faith. Isaiah 42 was the foundation of her theology:[69]

> Here is my servant, whom I uphold, ... he will faithfully bring forth justice.... I am the LORD, that is my name; my glory I give to no other, nor my praise to idols. See, the former things have come to pass, and new things I now declare; before they spring forth, I tell you of them.

Wha Soon Cho (1934–present)

Wha Soon Cho was born in 1934, when Japan was escalating its political and military power over China by exploiting colonized Korea for its imperialistic ambitions. Cho's father, who attended the March First Independence Movement in 1919, had to leave his hometown to escape from the Japanese police and finally settled with his family in Inchon, a harbor city on the west coast of Korea. He was successful enough in his transportation business to provide economic stability for his family until he became bankrupt during the Korean War. Cho had an older sister, whose parents quickly arranged for her to be married to save her from being one of the military comfort women. However, her husband was a debauchee and ruined the rest of her life. Cho felt terrible pity for her sister and made the decision to live out her life as a single woman because of her negative impression of marriage.[70]

Cho's parents were devout Christians and raised their children in a relatively free and democratic environment, compared to more traditional Korean families. Cho was a delightful, spirited child who loved music and dance. She dreamed of becoming a musician, actress, or dancer when she grew up. From her middle school years onward, however, she became awakened to a national consciousness through the teaching and preaching of her Sunday school teacher, who later became a minister. He often told his youth group about the colonized situation of their country and reminded them of their national identity and responsibility as Korean people. Cho took the situation of her country seriously. She often wept, looking at the miserable and hopeless realities of the Korean people; She wanted to live her life serving those in need, especially poor farmers.[71]

The Korean War began when Cho was sixteen years old. She joined her church choir, which was organized to sing for soldiers and refugees. When the group arrived in Pusan, the southernmost city of Korea, the war had become so fierce and bitter that she and other members could not return home. They had to remain in Pusan for four months, waiting for the situation to improve. During that time, Cho was hired as a nurse assistant in an army hospital. Although she had no medical training, she was dispatched to an intensive care unit because of the shortage of working hands. She overcame the hardships of hospital work by realizing that her job caring for dying soldiers was "given by God's grace and love." To Cho, the intensive care unit was the field of her peacemaking ministry:

For the bored patients, I sang songs, and for those with worries I listened to all their stories.... I encouraged them to have hope in the future by reminding them of their memories of [their] hometown, family, and beautiful things that had happened in the past.⁷²

One cold winter day, Cho's love and sympathy for her patients led her to make socks for them because they were lying barefoot and cold in the hospital unit. She retrieved some old blood-stained blankets from the storage room, went to the frozen creek, broke the ice, and scrubbed the blankets. During the night, she sewed ten pairs of socks and put them on her patients' feet the next day. Her joy was beyond expression as she watched the happy faces of her patients.⁷³

After the Korean War, Cho made her teenage dream come true. She became an elementary school teacher in a remote rural area in Kyonggi Province, with the vision of uplifting poor farmers' lives. In addition to teaching children by day, she also taught illiterate adults by night how to read. She also taught courses such as health, cooking, and everyday knowledge necessary for healthy living. What she learned from this experience was that this type of social work is not enough to improve the lives of farmers unless their spiritual and moral lives are also transformed.⁷⁴

While Cho was reflecting on religious education for the farmers and praying for God's guidance, a friend of hers encouraged her to study at the Methodist seminary in Seoul and become a pastor. During her seminary studies, her classmates often praised her when she spoke from a platform. They admired her voice, as beautiful as the sound of "a rolling gem bead," and clear and loud enough to be heard even in the back.⁷⁵

After graduating from the seminary in 1961, Cho's first appointment was to the Neungdong Church, located in a small village of twenty-seven families in Dokjokdo, an abandoned island, seven hours away by boat from the mainland city of Inchon. Most of the residents on the island were poor war refugees who made their living fishing, and they lived in small shacks along the shore. Without toilets or a sewer system in the village, the roads stank and were full of excrement and trash.

When Cho arrived at her church, which had been built by the General Conference a few years prior, she discovered that the villagers had been using the church as a public toilet since the former pastor had left three months prior. The building had no electricity or heating. She also learned that the villagers had a superstitious belief that if they were converted to Christianity, the village would perish, and that if they came close to a Christian, they would have bad luck.

Cho spent several days cleaning the church building, and then eagerly prepared her sermon for her first Sunday worship. On that Sunday, only one person appeared, a mentally deranged man from a neighboring village:

> He sat with a dull expression, often laughing to himself. I hesitated to preach in front of just this one person who was not even normal. I sat down facing him as I pondered what to do, then suddenly I thought, "Did not Jesus suffer on the cross for this very person? Jesus said he would leave ninety-nine sheep to go and find the one that was lost. This disturbed man is that very one to whom I must preach God's word."[76]

Cho began her preaching life in this manner. The deranged man was her only listener for an entire month. However, she was clear about the role of her church: The church must exist for the community. She visited the villagers at their homes and even at their workplaces. She introduced herself to them and soon became their friend. In addition to opening a Sunday school for children and a night school for adults, she developed many programs to help the villagers reduce poverty. The chief official of the town asked Cho to give some public lectures and sermons when he organized township meetings for the villagers. Whenever she preached, Cho challenged the villagers to think about how to make their island a better place to live, rather than evangelizing by claiming "Believe in Jesus and go to heaven."[77]

After three years in Dokjokdo, Cho was appointed to Dalwol Church, located in a rural area in Kyonggi Province. Dalwol Church was considered a headache to the General Conference because the existing pastor had had constant conflicts with the congregation because of his lack of leadership. The General Conference intentionally sent Cho to this church with the thought that a woman pastor might better solve the problems caused by an authoritarian male and heal the wounds of the congregation. Although Cho was under enormous stress during the beginning of her ministry at Dalwol, she was successful in handling all the problems within the church. In three years, the membership increased from 20 to 150.[78]

In 1966, while she was enjoying her ministry at Dalwol, the Urban Industrial Mission (UIM) contacted Cho and asked her to work for a group of female factory workers. Cho realized that urban ministry was just as urgent as rural ministry because of the exploitative economic policy of the Park regime. She also concluded that the need for a woman minister was essential for female factory workers, who were treated worse than male workers by the company owners. Although she was sad to leave her church, Cho decided to accept the assignment with the UIM.

The UIM required Cho to work six months at a factory where the majority of employees were women. Cho disguised herself as a real factory worker to learn about the true situation of the employees. She was hired by the Dong-il Textile Company, a government-supporting enterprise. The factory had over one thousand female laborers out of thirteen hundred employees. Everyone lived in extreme poverty. The company paid the women much lower wages than the men. Although the women had to work overtime almost every day to complete their allotted work, they were not compensated for their overtime. From their small income, far below their living expenses, most of the women sent a portion of their earnings to their parents, who were poor farmers in rural areas. Some of the workers saved their earnings to pay for the school tuition of their brother(s).[79]

Through her experience as a worker, Cho learned how company owners and the government had been victimizing female workers. In fact, the major leading factor for the economic growth of Korea during the 1970s was female workers who worked for low wages in the textile, electronics, sewing, and wig-making industries, producers of the main export products. The government and businesses were able to exploit their labor force because of women's unequal status in society. Most of the women laborers were uneducated and had been raised in poor rural families. They were being victimized by the factory owners because they did not know how to claim their human rights.

After her six months of intensive training, Cho began to work for the Dong-il women workers. She invited them to Sunday worship held at the UIM center and gave them lectures on the history, laws, and socioeconomic functions of the labor union. She also led small-group discussions on topics that the workers were interested in. During group discussions, the workers shared their work experiences and were gradually "conscientized" to the idea that they must elect women leaders who could defend their rights and welfare. In the labor union election of 1972, female workers supported in solidarity a woman candidate, Kil Ja Chu, and elected the first chairwoman in the history of Korean labor unions. The executive committee was also composed entirely of women.[80]

When women became leaders of the union at Dong-il and began to demand their rights from the factory owner, both the company and the government became nervous about union activities and worked together to attempt to manipulate and dissolve the union. However, women workers occupied the leadership positions in the union even in the following elections (1975 and 1978). The union fought for fair treatment of the laborers regarding not only their wages and working environment but also their freedom and right to elect their leaders and organize democratic activities. Whenever the union went on strike by holding sit-ins and/or fasting after negotiations with the company failed, the leaders of the union were arrested and violently tortured, and in some cases even sexually molested by the police.[81]

Despite such hardships, the labor movement spread quickly to other companies. Cho organized a group of twenty-four women laborers who were working at different factories and provided them with training to lead the labor movement at their companies. In addition, Cho traveled all around the country, preaching and leading prayer meetings. She stunned the public by addressing the oppressive situation of women laborers caused by selfish company owners and the inhumane economic policy of the government. Through her preaching, Cho accused the Park regime and the Korean Federation of Trade Unions of vicious political oppression. Cho succeeded in raising solidarity among conscientious listeners to support the labor movement.[82]

The KCIA condemned the UIM of being a communist organization and watched Cho closely, accusing her of being the controller behind the laborer revolts. On April 28, 1974, Cho gave the sermon "Search for the Kingdom and for Righteousness" to UIM members. The following month, she was imprisoned for this sermon because it was deemed "impure." In her sermon, Cho said,

> Our reality is completely the opposite of the justice of God. In our society, if we say "white" when we see white or "black" when we see black, we will be arrested. Now many students and ministers are suffering for this reason. We as workers should not be afraid of arrest, but must fight against the injustices in our working places.[83]

When Cho was interrogated in the basement of the KCIA headquarters, she was afraid. However, she overcame her fear because of her faith in Christ Jesus:

> I was told to sit in a chair, whereupon three interrogators came and began abusing me with terrible, ugly language, mostly connected with sex.... I felt unbearably ashamed and scared. My body trembled with fear and my mind couldn't focus. I closed my eyes. This time they cursed at me and demanded that I open my eyes. I felt my body shrinking from the fear.... Then, suddenly two things vividly came to my fear-filled mind. One was "When they bring you to be tied..., do not be worried about how you will defend yourself, or what you will say. For the Holy Spirit will teach you at that time what you should say" (Luke 12:11–12). I seemed to hear Jesus' voice clearly. The other was a joke I used to use when I talked to the

> workers about all humans being equal. "You go to the toilet, right? Don't all human beings go to the toilet just the same? Who is the most scary person to you? The company president? He goes to the toilet.... You should not be afraid of anyone, because everybody is the same human being who eats rice and goes to the toilet...." I found self-confidence and composure.... My attitude toward the interrogators had turned 180 degrees. I even felt the calling to use that moment to let them know the will and life of the Lord.[84]

Cho was expecting to be sentenced to a minimum of fifteen years and a maximum of the death penalty. However, she was released after only three months as the result of a flood of petitions that were sent to the government by many national and international women's organizations.[85]

Cho's lecture at the YMCA in Pusan in November 1978 caused her second imprisonment. In her speech, she indicted the government's injustice and brutality against the movement of the Dong-Il laborers, stating that "our country is world-famous for two things: one is dictatorship, and the other is torture."[86] Cho was charged with violating Presidential Emergency Decree No. 9 and the Law on Meetings and Demonstrations. Her defense statement at her trial was an inspiring sermon, which moved the audience to tears. They stood up and clapped warmly when she finished her speech as follows:

> When I was a child my home was the richest one in the village; I did not know the suffering of the poor.... When I went to the factory to work and live with the laborers, I could not help weeping in repentance. At first I met them simply to evangelize and teach the gospel, but it was no use.... I realized that there is a systematic evil, and that to solve this problem it is necessary not only to worship but also to demolish that systematic evil.... In Luke's gospel, some people came to Jesus and warned, "Herod is trying to kill you! Please hurry and escape!" But instead of escaping Jesus told them, "Go and tell the fox that today and tomorrow, I will chase Satan away and heal the sick, then the third day I will finish my work...."

> As a disciple of Jesus, I am doing this work with the same mind as Jesus.... Even though a crowd of devils like Herod tries to kill me, I will fight against them without fear of death. My friends the workers are the same. We will fight the devil of this land, not fearing death. The *han* [righteous anger] of all the oppressed, poor, and marginalized will turn into the sword — the dagger — of God's judgment and stab deep into the hearts of the devils. Our chief, Jesus, is leading us. We will surely have victory. Hurrah for the workers of this land! Hurrah for God![87]

Cho was sentenced to three years in prison. While she was serving her sentence, President Park was assassinated on October 26, 1979. A few months later, she was released.[88]

When Chun took power via a military coup d'état on May 18, 1980, he promulgated emergency martial law and arrested Kim Dae Jung, the democratic symbol of Korea, and other democratic leaders. Cho was arrested again by the KCIA and forced to give a false confession that Kim had financially supported her labor movement. After suffering seventy days of interrogation, she was finally released.[89]

In 1984, Cho retired from the UIM and resumed her rural ministry as a local pastor at Dalwol Church, which she had left in 1966 to work for the UIM. This time, however, the goal of her ministry was women's liberation. Throughout her work with women laborers over eighteen years, she recognized how sexism was deeply embedded in Korean society and how women — particularly women of the "have-not" class — were oppressed and victimized by sexist social and economic systems as well as by a sexist culture and public mentality. She believed that true human liberation could be accomplished only when women were fully liberated. Through preaching, prayer, home visitation, and church administration, she imbued the spirit of equality between women and men within her congregation. In selecting her sermonic texts, Cho intentionally chose biblical texts related to women's issues or biblical stories in which women were the main characters. Through her preaching, she instilled self-esteem into women listeners and enlightened male listeners to envision a new world where women and men were equal partners.⁹⁰

In her sermons, "Women Who Are Making Peace" (Eph. 2:14–16) and "Let My Sisters and Brothers Go to Galilee" (Matt. 4:12–17), Cho states that peace does not mean a state of no accidents or disputes. Rather, real peace is based on justice and love and is a process including many conflicts, hardships, sacrifices, courage, and decision making. Cho says that the powerful do not talk about justice but security, and they justify their violence in the name of security based on their belief that peace comes from guns. In contrast, however, real peace originates from the power of love, that of the weak, just as Jesus showed his power through his suffering and pain.⁹¹

To Cho, peace is God's commandment to all human beings but especially to women. Cho offers at least two reasons that women are the subjects tasked by God to make a new history of peace in the world. First, God fulfills peace on earth by giving power to the weak, who cry out for justice under oppression. Korean women have been victimized throughout Korean history—politically, economically, socially, and culturally. However, Korean women have demonstrated their power by resisting injustice and violence at the cost of their lives to bring forth a new world. Second, women themselves are the "symbol of peace" because of their inherent potential for motherhood. Cho says that just as most women are naturally pleased to sacrifice themselves for children and others, so they have sympathy and love for the oppressed and the marginalized in society. Therefore, women are more qualified than men to become preachers and pastors who promote peace.⁹²

When I visited Cho in the summer of 2001 to personally interview her, she had already retired from her ministry and was living in the mountains in Kangwon Province. Reflecting both on her rural and urban ministries spanning forty years, Cho said that preaching should be based on the "theology of feet,"⁹³ because the ground on which the preacher's feet are standing is the real locus of preaching. In other words, preaching must stem from the real situation that the preacher encounters socially, politically, historically, and culturally. Cho continued to state that the preacher's role is not to negotiate with the status quo but to proclaim the peace of God against the false peace of the world and to proclaim the reign of God that is fundamentally different from the present world. Cho's involvement in the farming community, the labor movement, and the women's rights movement illustrates that preaching is not simply speaking but acting. After all, preaching is a political event, in which the preacher participates in God's politics.[94]

ASIAN WOMEN'S PREACHING AND THE POLITICS OF GOD

The history of women's preaching in Korea reveals that preaching is a political event, responsive not only in words but also through the actions of the preacher toward the problems raised from the particular sociopolitical and cultural context in which the preacher lives. The compelling issue in Korean women's preaching during the colonial and postcolonial period was "To whom does the sovereignty of the world belong?" This is closely related to the questions of authority and power and their exercise in the world: "What is power, and by whose authority is power considered power?"

Duk Ji Choi, Wha Soon Cho, and other women preachers have witnessed to the sovereign power of God against an oppressive world power. They convinced their listeners that suffering was temporary and that God would end the oppressors' evil power by using God's sovereign power, which is the source of creating a new world, to intervene in their history by breaking through the old way of life. Women preachers were the symbols of God's humanizing politics rather than victims of an oppressive ruling power. The suffering and pain of Korean women preachers are testimony to the sins of the imperialism, colonialism, and militarism of human politics. Their resistance and struggle against evil presented God's involvement in the liberating power and activity of a human situation.

Soon Kyung Park provides a theological interpretation for the political aspect of Korean women's preaching, by claiming that "the pure gospel" does not ignore the political power of oppression but "transcends it by penetrating the evil power of the oppressors through the eyes of God's justice."[95] She further explains that

The transcendence and purity of the gospel do not mean irresponsibility for the injustice of society, as evangelical, pietist Western missionaries stressed to Koreans during the colonial period, but the transcendence of God's righteousness.... The transcendental righteousness of God means God's judgment and power that leads the world to the recognition of the dominion of God, which does not point to the other world after death but to the future of salvation that was already revealed in the proclamation, life, and death of Jesus Christ.... Repentance does not mean a level of individual morality but decision making and obedience, corresponding to the dominion of God that is coming near us.... Christians in the world must bring the power structure of the world to stand behind the bar of God's judgment so that the world may have the spiritual opportunity to overcome evil structures.[96]

Women's preaching in Korea demonstrates this political aspect of the Christian faith. Korean women preachers proclaimed the dominion of God that is coming toward us with revolutionary power. According to the experiences of Korean women preachers, preaching brings oppressive human politics before the judgment of God and grants freedom to the oppressed. In this sense, preaching is an act of God's politics. Preaching as the politics of God concerns itself with what God is doing in the world to make and keep human life human, because its primary goal is to invite listeners to participate in the politics of God by providing concrete guidelines and directions toward humanization in a particular context.

The women preachers in Korea described in this chapter were the Spirit-led politicians who participated in the politics of God as God's co-workers. Their important task was to discern the paradigmatic acts of God in a particular historical context. They had the eyes to see and the ears to hear a fragmented dominion of God, even in the midst of their despairing reality. These women were able to discover God's humanizing activity in their particular contexts. They not only spoke about what God had done and was doing in their particular historical situations to make and keep human life human but also lived their lives for God's humanizing politics.

The legacy of Korean women preachers is a theological and ministerial model for women preachers in other Asian countries. All the Asian countries, except Thailand and hinterland China, have been under colonial rule by either Western countries or Japan. Although the extent and length of their colonial experiences vary from country to country, Asian women have a common experience of suffering and pain because of military imperialism.[97] In addition, even though political colonialism was dismantled in 1945, countries within Asia are still suffering under economic colonialism by the political and economic consolidations of their former colonizers. The economy of Asia is still being run by foreign capital, especially that of the former colonial countries. Furthermore, international militarism is also a threat to Asian countries. Under the ideology of national security and integration, repressive regimes have mushroomed all over Asia, where fundamental human freedom and rights are being suppressed in various forms. As a result, the oppression and exploitation of the powerless by the powerful continues in Asia.[98]

During this postcolonial period, Asian women have been more and more oppressed not only sociopolitically but also economically and physically. Women have been the victims of capitalism and militarism as well as feudalism and patriarchal culture. They are paid lower wages to boost their nations' economies while working under inhuman working conditions. Moreover, the governments in Asia sexually exploit women by promoting sex tourism as a source of earning foreign currency.[99]

In Asia, Christians are a minority. Although Korea is unique in that 25 percent of its population is Christian, in Asia as a whole, only about 2 percent of the population is Christian.[100] Because of this reality, women preachers are rare, yet they still play a tremendously significant role in transforming their respective societies. Asian Christian women preach against the oppressive power of violence and injustice. Their concerns are related to promoting peace and living a full life, one in which human beings reconcile with God, other people, and nature. On the one hand, Asian women preachers articulate in their sermons their anger, pain, frustrations, tears, and anguish over oppressed Asian women. On the other hand, they describe their joy, hope, aspirations of the future in the power of Christ Jesus, and their commitment to promoting peace.

Asian women preachers understand that women's rights and freedoms cannot be separated from their national independence and democratic social structures. Women's liberation is not simply concerned with gender issues but is tightly related to the ultimate freedom and equality of all humanity. Thus, Asian women preachers' calling to preach the gospel is God's invitation to join the politics of God, in which all those without status and power in the world are called to be the children of God. Asian women preachers continue their political struggle by proclaiming the dominion of God, even at the cost of their lives, until oppressed women, who are the oppressed of the oppressed, are fully humanized. Until this happens, the liberation of all humanity will not be complete on earth.

It is worth noting the activities of Japanese women preachers. Yoshiko Isshiki, Hisako Kinukawa, and other Japanese women preachers take their responsibility seriously to reconcile their country with other Asian countries that were colonized and oppressed by Japan. To this day, Japan has still refused to apologize for its imperialist invasion and oppression of other Asian countries. Japanese women preachers consider their role to be peacemakers in search of solidarity, hope, and true reconciliation. They preach that the Japanese should repent to God and other Asians their national sins based on ethnic superiority: discrimination against other ethnic groups in Japanese society, legitimized subjugation and colonization of other Asian countries, and the ideological vestiges of the emperor system.[101]

When I visited Japan in August 2001, the Japanese government was coming under close scrutiny by other Asian countries because of two events. First, the Japanese government had just erased the Japanese expansionism of the early twentieth century from the revised Japanese high school history textbooks. Second, the Japanese prime minister had recently revived emperor worship as a symbol of nationalism. Japanese Christian leaders demonstrated against the government's poor decision making on these two political issues.

The Japanese women preachers whom I met in Japan were especially critical of their government's inappropriate actions. In the Sunday worship service I attended in Reverend Sunohara Suzuko's church, she preached about how to live as followers of Christ Jesus in an unjust society, and she led the congregation to pray for the correction of the government's false policies. When I interviewed two women pastors, Suzuko and Isshiki, they both said that although Japanese Christians were a minority group and had been persecuted by the military and imperialist government, they felt, in particular, that women Christians did not fear standing on the side of truth.

Asian women preachers believe that God is present and acting to make and keep human life human in the world and that the oppressive power of evil will soon be judged by the power of Almighty God, to whom all worldly authority and power should eventually submit. With this conviction, women preachers proclaim true peace against the false peace propagandized by the oppressors, without losing hope for a new world even in the midst of their severe persecution. Asian women preachers are true partners of God, fulfilling the politics of God on earth.

Conclusion

PARTNERSHIP IN PREACHING

THE HISTORY OF PREACHING FROM A WOMAN'S PERSPECTIVE, explored in the previous four chapters, reveals that Christian preaching has been in partnership with God. God has always initiated partnership with women preachers by calling them to become God's partners and working together to actualize peace in the world. The Spirit of God has constantly invited women preachers in many different ways across time and space to work as agents of reconciliation and transformation. Women preachers, who live in the margins of society, are Spirit-led people. They have responded to the initiating grace of the Spirit with amazement and commitment, and the Spirit has liberated them from the bondage of misogynist traditions and cultures and empowered them to become new marginal people. The margins of women preachers have been changed into a new creative core where the Spirit of God is present and at work, transforming the old order of the world into a new creation. From these new margins, the women preachers described in the previous chapters proclaimed peace, the gift of the wholeness of God, with courage.

The first women preachers in the Bible and in the early church were called into the ministry of preaching by witnessing the transforming power of the risen Christ. Their preaching was based on the conviction that God would overcome evil in the world and restore sovereignty in Jesus Christ. The women preachers were missionaries who invited their listeners into a new creation in Jesus Christ.

Despite the sexist oppression of the institutionalized, patriarchal church, some medieval women partnered with God through preaching. The irresistible power of the Spirit led them to preach a new vision for the world, one in which the wholeness of God is fully revealed. Through subversive rhetoric, the women preachers publicly disclosed the falsity of gender ideology and revealed the holistic nature of God, even in the midst of the misogynist oppression by the church.

In the Protestant Church, women have continued for centuries to partner with God through preaching. During the early period of the Protestant Church, women's responses to God's initiating grace to partnership were not tolerated by patriarchal churches and often put the lives of women preachers at risk. Despite persecution both inside and outside the church, however, women preachers continued to struggle for their right to preach, and eventually transformed many Protestant pulpits to be gender-inclusive. Nowadays, many Protestant churches officially sanction the ordination of women to become ministers of the Word and Sacrament.

Women in Korea and other previously colonized countries have been victims of racism, classism, capitalism, and militarism, as well as sexism. In this predicament, Asian women preachers understood their calling to preach as God's invitation to become God's partners for the politics of God. They have been the active agents of God's politics by participating in the transformation of the old order of human politics into a new order of God's new creation, by proclaiming ultimate freedom and equality for all humanity.

Contemporary women's experiences as pastors and ministers of local churches challenge us to reconsider the significance of the concept of partnership in preaching. Partnership in preaching is not limited to the relationship the preacher has with God but includes relationships with the congregation, the larger church, the world, and particularly those living in the margins of society. Letty Russell helps explain the multilateral relations of partnership:

> Partnership [is] a new focus of relationship in which there is continuing commitment and common struggle in interaction with a wider community context.... By definition, partnership

involves growing interdependence in relation to God, persons, and creation so they are constantly in interaction with a wider community of persons, social structures, values, and beliefs that may provide support, correctives, and negative feedback.[1]

Partnership as interaction with a wider community context leads us to remember that preachers need their partners who can work with them on the vision of a new creation. Just as the preacher-as-pastor becomes the partner of God, so the members of the congregation and particularly the marginalized in society need to become partners of the preacher. The preacher can represent their voices by collecting their diverse experiences of God through theological reflection. However, partnership with the congregation demands a more active role from the congregants. In other words, preaching is no longer a clergy-only ministry; the pulpit is no longer exclusively the place for professionally trained preachers. Instead, partnership with the congregation suggests inviting laity to the ministry of preaching. They share their own experiences in the pulpit, partial and fragmentary, as a way to participate in revealing the wholeness of God.

The notion of sharing the pulpit with the congregation reminds us of Lucy Rose's egalitarian view on preaching. She states in her book *Sharing the Word: Preaching in the Roundtable Church* that the goal of preaching is "to gather the community of faith around the Word.... The preacher and the congregation are colleagues, exploring together the mystery of the Word for their own lives, as well as the life of the congregation, the larger church, and the world."[2] Partnership as colleagueship between the preacher and the congregation proposes that "the clergy should relinquish their monopoly of the pulpit, since the right to preach derives from baptism and from each believer's experiences of God."[3] Therefore, partnership in preaching breaks down the wall between clergy and laity and understands preaching as teamwork or a shared ministry with the congregation.

Members of a congregation who participate in the act of preaching are so-called "amateur theologians" or "worldly theologians," who do theology for the "love of it."[4] One of the preacher-as-pastor's roles is to teach them how to interpret biblical and church traditions in relation to their experiences in a variety of worldly contexts. Trained congregants are able to represent voices from the margins, which the pastor may have ignored in her preaching. The term "preacher," then, is not "a synonym for one who is ordained or for the minister who controls access to the pulpit" but the one whose responsibility is to "encourage and equip the laity to preach"[5] and provide them with space and time to share their personal and communal experiences of the risen Christ with other members of the congregation.

One pastor I know is especially effective at getting others to partnership in preaching. In the Sunday worship at his church, children's sermons are always preached by parents and Sunday school teachers. While they preach to the children, sharing their personal and communal experiences of the Christian faith, the adult congregation overhears their messages. On one Mother's Day Sunday, the sermon was given as a team project between the pastor and three congregants. A teenager, a young adult, and a middle-aged member of the church shared their experiences of God as mother, and afterward the pastor concluded the sermon by reminding the congregation of the biblical women who became the spiritual mothers of the Christian Church.

Preachers who practice partnership with their congregants have no need to fear a loss of leadership in the church because the key to good leadership is participating in God's partnership by inviting the congregation to become active partners of God. Partnership with the congregation makes it possible for preaching to become a cross-cultural conversation, a beautiful kaleidoscope, revealing the wholeness of God in harmonious ways. Our partnership together in God's liberating actions brings us closer to the day when the wholeness of God is fully revealed and actualized on earth. At this point, preaching from a woman's perspective is a communal journey, i.e., a partnership in God's liberating actions with the anticipation of actualizing the wholeness of God on earth.

Sermon 1

STORIES AFTER SILENCE

TEXT: MARK 16:1-8

*Preached at the Albuquerque
Worship and Music Conference 2002*

"They said nothing to anyone, for they were afraid." (vv. 8)
As most of you know,
earlier and important manuscripts of the Gospel of Mark end here.
"They said nothing to anyone, for they were afraid."
Hmmm...
What an odd ending!
If you had a chance to read the entire book of Mark,
you would probably agree with me that
the ending is strange.

Mark recounts the life story of Jesus of Nazareth
with a lively and direct style.
The plot develops dynamically:
A young Jewish man, Jesus, is baptized in the Jordan River,
calls disciples,
announces the kingdom of God,
and performs mighty works as the signs of the coming kingdom.
Crowds of marginalized people follow him
with a hopeful anticipation that
"He may be the Messiah
who will set us free from oppression."

However,
the dominant group of society cannot tolerate his ministry
and finally sentences him to death.
In the horrified scene of his crucifixion,
the crowds disappear,
his twelve disciples disappear,
and even the sun disappears.
The dead body of Jesus is laid in the tomb
and a big stone covers its entrance.
Now, the stage fades away.
But, wait!
This is not the end of the story.
There is one more scene, which is our text today.
In the final chapter of the book,
the flow of the story toward tragedy reverses itself
180 degrees.
Peter, James, John, and other male characters,
who were present throughout most of the story,
no longer appear,
but new characters arrive on the stage.
They are three women—
Mary Magdalene,
Mary the mother of James,
and Salome.
They visit Jesus's tomb early in the morning
to anoint his body with spices.
On arriving,
they hear for the first time the news
that the crucified Jesus has now been raised from the dead.
They are commissioned to tell the good news to his disciples.
However,
these three women are so shocked and amazed by the news
that they flee from the tomb in fear
and say absolutely nothing to anyone,
for they are afraid.
Mark puts down his pen here.

Well, we readers would like to shout,
"Mark, wait!
You didn't tell us the whole story, yet.
Give us all the facts:
Who are these three women?
You simply mentioned in the previous chapter that
these women were the ones
who followed Jesus from Galilee
and witnessed his death from a distance.
But,
we want to know more about these three women.
Were they really scaredy-cats,
so terrified that they couldn't say anything to anyone?
Did they lose their voices forever?
If not,
what would they say after their silence?
How would they live the rest of their lives after such a shock?"
Mark doesn't answer these important questions.
Instead, he closes his story by leaving these three women in veil.
Hmmm...
What an odd ending!

My dear friends,
Have you ever met these three women in your lives?
Have you ever heard their stories about the risen Christ?

Well, I think I have.
In my life,
I have three Korean women
who have broken the silence
and witnessed the risen Christ
with joy and amazement.
They were first my mother,
who planted a seed of the Christian faith in me;
second, a Korean Methodist woman preacher,
who watered my faith with her preaching;
and last, a Korean woman professor,

who helped me bear the fruits of my faith.
These three women have taught me
to become who I am today
by telling their stories to me.
Let me tell you a little bit more about these three women.
First, my mother.
My grandmother often told me a funny story
about my mother's birth.
My mother was born the third child after two brothers.
Since my grandfather was a medical doctor,
he helped his wife deliver all their children.
When my mother was born,
my grandfather was very upset
because the newborn baby was a girl.
So, he wept,
completely forgetting to cut the umbilical cord.
The woman who was born in her father's tears
grew up to be a Christian.
When she graduated from an all-girls' high school,
she wasn't given the chance to go to college
because of her parents' sexist mind-set.
Although her two older brothers were busy attending college,
she had to learn all the domestic things around the home,
under her mother's guidance—
how to make kimchi,
how to clean the house,
how to wash blankets,
and how to serve her future husband and in-laws—
so that she would one day become a "good wife."
She married the man
whom her parents had arranged for her.
As my father was an only son,
his parents expected a grandson
in order to continue the family line.
However,
my mother didn't bear a son
until after she had first had five daughters.

During that long wait,
she had to live as a "sinner,"
which her traditional patriarchal society determined her to be.
In spite of her husband's faithfulness and love,
my mother often cried to God with bitterness and tears
to help her become free
from the psychological oppression and guilty consciousness
that were imposed by her society's sexist culture.
When she finally had a son, her sixth child,
the entire family expected that
her son would become her idol.
But, this was not to be.
As soon as my brother was weaned,
my mother announced to the family that
she was going to college to become a pastor.
This was a real shock for me and the entire family.
At the age of thirty-eight,
my mother finally began
what she had always wanted to do.

When raising her children,
my mother treated her five daughters and only son equally.
She never forced her daughters to behave
like subordinate women in a male-centered society,
nor did she discourage their ambitions
because of their gender.
Rather, she always told us
to live as God's children
and reminded us of the freedom
to live for the glory of God.
As her oldest child,
I grew up hearing my mother's liberating message,
and this message became a seed of my faith in God.

The second woman who taught me about the risen Christ was
a Methodist woman preacher.
When I was twelve years old,

I once went to a revival meeting with my parents.
The preacher was a woman.
About thirty years ago,
it was very rare
to see women preachers in Korea.
I still remember vividly
her beautiful white Korean traditional dress
in the high pulpit.
She preached about how she met Christ
in the midst of her suffering
and how she had now become a witness to the risen Christ.
The message she preached was so powerful
that those who packed the sanctuary were moved by her sermon.
Many of them experienced the presence of God
through the irresistible power of the Spirit
during her preaching
and decided to live new lives.
On the way home that night,
I told myself,
"I want to be just like her.
I want to be a preacher
who proclaims the risen Christ."

The third woman was a professor
in Seoul, Korea.
My intellectual curiosity about Christianity and the Bible
led me to study biblical theology
at the Graduate School of Ewha Women's University.
My advisor was the first Korean female biblical theologian.
She had received her M.Div. degree from Yale
and her Ph.D. from Princeton Theological Seminary.
Today she is the president of Ewha Women's University.
She taught me how to study the Bible
with the gift of human rationality given to us by God,
and she helped me broaden and deepen my theological perspective.
When I was finishing my master's degree,
she encouraged me to continue my studies at Princeton, saying,

"The Christian Church must continue to reform
and contribute to the renewal of the world.
For this goal, sooner or later,
churches will need more women leaders
who are well-trained theologically and spiritually."
Ecclesia reformata reformanda!
This is the message that I learned from her about the risen Christ.

Although the dominant group of society tried
to suppress Jesus's liberating messages
by crucifying and burying him,
no one could lock up his messages in the tomb.
The three women
who first heard the amazing news of the risen Christ
were shocked into silence.
However,
I have heard their stories after their initial silence
through my mother,
the woman preacher,
and my professor.
I have also heard their voices, asking,
"What is *your* story about the risen Christ?
What is *your* life in him?"

Oh, now, I understand why Mark's gospel ends so strangely.
Today's text is *not* the end of the story.
Mark doesn't mean to close his Gospel here
but wants us the readers to write the ending.
He tells us,
"You are the ones who are going to break the silence
and conclude the Gospel
with your *own* stories."
Friends,
what story of *yours* will end the Gospel?

Sermon 2

COULD WE SING THE LORD'S SONG?

TEXTS: PSALM 137; REVELATION 21:1-4

*Preached at the Anna H. Shaw Center,
Boston University, 2002*

Rivers...
Wherever we are from,
our cities and towns are located along the waters of rivers.
The thick and thin threads of streams and creeks,
meandering shadowed valleys,
steep and tall mountains,
flat prairies and wilderness
meet one another
and change into swift and deep currents of the rivers.
Over thousands of years,
rivers have attracted people to dwell along the water.

Most of us have probably never been to Mesopotamia,
the relics of ancient Babylon,
where the Psalmist lived long ago.
However,
we can imagine its vast array of beauty
along the waters,
snaking through the dense waterway bushes and undergrowth
until the waters finally meet the major river Euphrates.
Along the waters,
luxuriant foliage of willow trees and leafy branches of poplars

mesmerize people to come and take rest
under their shade.
The Psalmist and his people are sitting on this riverbank.
They are not tourists who visit that site
to admire the novelty
or wonder at the natural scenery of the rivers,
but they are Jewish exiles,
deported to Babylon and forced to live for the rest of their lives
on the margins of the imperial kingdom of Babylon.
Shhhhh... Listen!
Do you hear a sound,
a sound of mourning among the exiles,
floating on the silent surface of the water?
During their long, exhausting journey into exile
and their oppressed lives as captives in a captor's land,
they may not have had time to lament
until they reached the waters of Babylon.
They once sang songs of joy,
to the melody of harps,
in the promise of God for the City of Zion,
where the Lord will reign forever
with righteousness and justice.
But, now, being captive,
their spirits are down.
They hang their harps on the willow,
and lament by saying,
"How could we sing the Lord's song in a foreign land?"

"How could we sing the Lord's song in a foreign land?"
Perhaps, many of us want to join their lamentations,
because of our similar experiences with captives.
Along the rivers of North America,
many of us feel that
we are not quite at home in our homeland.
We live in one of the so-called
most advanced and egalitarian countries of the world.
Women are now participating in many areas of society

as politicians, lawyers, entrepreneurs, teachers, medical doctors,
and senior administrators.
Even in the church,
some mainline denominations ordain women
as ministers of the Word and Sacrament
and allow them to demonstrate their leadership
in local churches and institutions.
But, we still hear weeping of victims
of family violence,
sexual harassment and rape,
racial prejudice and gender discrimination.
In addition,
I hear from my students that many experience
rejection, abandonment, and condemnation
from their families and churches and at work
because of their sexual orientation.
Many of my female colleagues deplore
the prevailing sexist mentality of the congregations
that crave a "white male" as their pastor.
Many churches and clergy still repeat
the literal sense of the biblical text that
"Women shall not preach."
Our nation is at war against terror.
Under the name of justice and peace,
The vicious circle of warfare continues
Victimizing thousands of innocent people,
particularly women and children.
Our modern technology is helpless
to fix our prejudiced mind-sets,
to heal our broken relationships and the scars
engraved deeply inside us
by our family members, neighbors, colleagues, and friends.
Living in this world,
who can sing the Lord's song among us?
How can we sing the joyful songs of Zion?
We who gather together by the Charles River
mourn in despair and hopelessness

like the Psalmist and his people
who wept by the rivers of Babylon.

The riverbank of Babylon, however,
was not only a place for weeping and lamenting.
It was also a place for hearing the voice of God.
When the captives are weeping
by the rivers of Babylon,
the Psalmist reminds them that
they are not alone even in the captor's land.
Whenever Israel is exiled,
the Lord is exiled with them:
when they were oppressed in Egypt,
the Lord was with them.
When they are now exiled to Babylon,
the Spirit of the Lord is exiled with them, even there.
God listens to their lament and says,
"Even if Israel forgets me
and refuses to sing the joyful songs of Zion
in a foreign land,
I do not forget my divine promise with Israel."
So, in the poem,
God renews the promise by singing,
"If I forget you, O Jerusalem,
Let my right hand wither!
Let my tongue cling to the roof of my mouth,
if I do not remember you,
if I do not set Jerusalem above my highest joy!" (vv. 5–6)
On the riverbanks of Babylon,
God was weeping with those
who were on the margin of the kingdom
and sang to them a song of promise.

Remember,
The exiles were not the only people
who heard the promise of God.
John the Prophet also heard the promise

on the island of Patmos.
He heard the voice of God,
singing the vision for a new Jerusalem.
The voice says:
"See, the home of God is among mortals.
God will dwell with them as their Lord.
They will be the peoples,
and God will be with them;
the Lord will wipe every tear from their eyes.
Death will be no more;
mourning and crying and pain will be no more,
for the first things have passed away." (Rev. 21:4)
Can you hear it?
Can you see
the City of God, the New Jerusalem,
which is coming down out of heaven?
Only those who hear the promise of God,
Only those who see the vision for a new world
can sing again the Lord's song,
even in a foreign land,
even on the margins of society.
Thus, the Psalmist invites those
who hear God's promise
to sing together the last stanza of the poem:
"Remember, O Lord, against the Edomites...
O daughter Babylon, you devastator!...
Happy shall they be who take your little ones
and dash them against the rock!" (vv. 7-9)
When God is with us,
and when we listen to God's promise for the future,
we can dare to join the chorus on the day
when God finally overcomes the oppressive powers of this world
by dashing them against the rock.
When God is with us,
we can dare to anticipate the day
when a new heaven and a new earth come down to us
where there is no more mourning, crying, or pain.

Our foresisters —
Mary Magdalene, Lydia, St. Nina,
Hildegard of Bingen, Julian of Norwich, Sor Juana Inés de la Cruz,
Ann Hutchinson, Phoebe Palmer, Sojourner Truth,
Jarena Lee, Susan Anthony, Anna Howard Shaw,
Duk Ji Choi, Wha Soon Cho, Isshiki Yoshiko....
These women preachers sang the Lord's song
because they saw the vision of the New Jerusalem
and held on to the promise of God.
Even in their severe suffering
from the cruel patriarchal structure and sexist cultures
of their societies and churches,
they had faith that
God was with them and at work in their margins
to transform the old world into a new one.
The riverbanks,
where they lamented the famine of
justice and righteousness,
love and mercy,
were also the celebrating places
with the joyful song of Zion
because the Spirit of God was there,
suffering and weeping with them,
and responding to them with the power of life.

My dear friends,
are you still weeping,
hanging up your harp on a tree?
Please wipe your tears and take down your harp.
And let's play and sing the Lord's song together,
as our foresisters did,
louder and louder,
until our singing echoes
wherever the waters of our world reach.
Amen!

Sermon 3

HAVE YOU EVER IMAGINED...?

TEXTS: MATTHEW 22:23-33; EPHESIANS 4:1-6
*Preached at the Albuquerque Worship
and Music Conference 2002*

Good morning!
It is my great pleasure to share the Word of God with you
throughout this entire week.
I would especially like to thank
Reverends Fane Dawn, Marney Wesserman,
and Michael Waschevski
for working together in organizing all services
with genuineness and creativity.

I believe there is diversity in this sanctuary.
Among us there are age and gender differences.
Most of us are from different states,
different churches, and different ethnic backgrounds.
In spite of our differences,
I think we have at least one common experience.
It may be, and I hope you agree with me,
that all of us are allergic to exams.
If you are a student right now, you know what I mean.
If you graduated long ago,
remember how you were stressed out by midterms and final exams
while you were in college.
Even for me, remembering my student years,

Have You Ever Imagined...? 175

taking exams was never fun.
One of the best things that
I now enjoy about my life as a teacher is that
I don't have to take exams anymore
but instead give exams to students.
As you and I have experienced, exams are like growing pains.

In today's Gospel lesson,
Jesus seems to take an exam too.
If his three temptations in the wilderness
in Matthew chapter 4
represent the entrance exam
for his three-year messianic ministry,
it seems to me then that
chapter 22 tells us about his final oral defense
for completing his ministry on earth.
In chapter 22, from verses 15 on,
Jesus is tested by three questions.
The examiners are from two different theological schools,
the Pharisees and the Sadducees.
Both are well-known theological parties
with their intellectual and scholarly qualities.
First, the Pharisees ask a question related to Christian ethics,
"Is it lawful to pay taxes to the emperor, or not?"
Their next question is pretty much like a Bible content exam,
"What is the greatest commandment in the Pentateuch?"
Between these two questions,
the Sadducees ask a profoundly theological
but extremely complex and tricky question
with a hypothetical case.
The question goes like this:
"There is a woman who has been married seven times.
Her first husband had six brothers,
but he died childless.
So, in order to give birth to keep her husband's family line,
the woman married her husband's first brother
according to Moses' law.

However, her second husband also died childless.
And the third, fourth, fifth, and six...
all the brothers died without leaving any children.
Finally the woman also died.
Then, the question is,
'Of these seven brothers,
which one is going to take this woman
as his wife in the resurrection?'"
Well, at a glance,
this question seems to expect a simple answer.
Seven husbands and one wife but no children!
Who is going to be her husband in the resurrection?
Number one? Number two? Number three?
Four? Five? Six? Seven?

We know, however, that
the school of Sadducees didn't believe in resurrection.
Why, then, are they questioning life in the resurrection?
What is their real intention
behind asking Jesus this question?
Jesus seems to penetrate this trickiness.
Rather than being trapped by the examiners' mocking question,
he grasps the real query inside this twisted puzzle
and cross-questions them,
"Oh, you think that if this woman is resurrected,
she will marry again, don't you?
But, that's not true!
In the life of the resurrection,
the people neither marry nor are given in marriage.
In the resurrection,
this woman will no longer be shared among the brothers
as property to preserve the family line,
for people in the resurrection are not interested
in repeating the life of this world
but live like angels in heaven."
"No more marriage? Live like angels in heaven?
How can this be?"

I guess Jesus's answer must be a shock,
not only to the examiners
but also the crowds who were observing Jesus's oral exam.
Even if they believe in the resurrection,
it is hard for them,
who have become used to this worldly life,
to imagine such an absolutely different life in the resurrection.
It was impossible for the first-century Jews
to imagine a new world
where women and men are equally free
to glorify God's name like angels,
because in their patriarchal society,
women were not regarded as humans but rather as property.
According to some historical researches
of first-century Jewish communities,
when a Jewish girl is born,
she becomes the possession of her father.
When she becomes twelve years old,
her father yields his right to possession
to a man who brings money to marry her.
From that point forward,
the woman becomes the property of her husband.
Her duty as a married woman is like that of a slave's:
She must call her husband "master,"
serve her husband's daily meals,
and wash his hands and feet every day.
Furthermore,
the most important responsibility for a married woman
is to continue the family line by bearing a son.
If she fails to do this with her husband,
she must continue to try again and again
with her husband's brothers until she bears a son.
How, then, can women, who are treated as property,
become angels in the resurrection?
How can slaves be equal to their masters?
Oh, no!
Jesus's audience couldn't imagine

such a new world in the resurrection.
Particularly, the Sadducees,
who were the descendants of the privileged class,
were not able to,
or refused to imagine any other world
where they would have to give up their vested interests.
For them,
even if there is life in the resurrection,
It must be a continuation of this world:
Men must still be masters,
women must still be slaves,
the rich must still be rich,
the poor must still be poor,
the Sadducees must still be in authority,
and peasants must still remain in the margins.

Well, even for us,
it is difficult to imagine something totally new,
because our imagination is biased toward our present experiences —
what we see, what we hear,
what we taste, and what we touch.
Just as the Sadducees imagined life in the resurrection
as a continuation of this world,
so may we believe consciously or unconsciously that
the privileges we enjoy in this world,
resulting from our nationality, class, gender, religion, and race,
will continue even in the life of the resurrection.

Well, it seems that
Jesus grasped our suspicion of his answer.
So, he reminds us of a passage from scripture:
"Have you not read what was said to you by God,
'I am the God of Abraham, the God of Isaac, and the God of Jacob'?
He is God not of the dead, but of the living."
The God who is living
in the promise of Abraham, Isaac, and Jacob
is the one who fulfills the promise for the New World.

The life-giving Spirit of God is already working on
breaking human history and restoring everything
to bring us new life in the resurrection.
Thus, life in the resurrection is not for the dead
but for the living.
It can be tasted in advance even in this world
by those who live and believe in the promise of God.

Matthew reports that
the crowds who had been observing Jesus's oral exam
were astounded at his teaching.
I can imagine them shouting to one another such things as,
"Wow, what an amazing answer!
I've never thought that
life in the resurrection is for the living!
I've never been able to imagine such a wonderful world
where women and men and haves and have-nots
live equally like angels,
free to glorify God's name!"

In fact, Jesus's answer was the core
of his teaching and preaching
throughout his three years of messianic ministry.
He not only taught and preached
the good news of the dominion of God
but also had the people taste this New World in advance
by showing them signs, expelling demonic powers,
and healing every disease and sickness.
The New World, Jesus proclaimed, is
neither a revival nor a continuation of this world.
Rather, it is a totally new creation
in which all of God's creatures
restore their dignity in the image of God
and live as sisters and brothers in God's presence.
As a result, God is so pleased to exclaim,
"It is good to see! It is good to see!"

Jesus of Nazareth saw this New World coming near us
with the transforming power of the Spirit.
Those who followed Jesus were amazed to experience
this strange new life in the resurrection
in their present lives.
Yet,
Jesus's answer to the question about life in the resurrection
was not good news for everyone,
but a serious threat
to those who were taking advantage of the status quo.
They wanted to keep
their sociopolitical, economic, religious, and cultural systems
because they wanted to enjoy
their vested interests and privileges forever.
Consequently,
Jesus's name was placed on the top of their blacklist.
Although Jesus is now taking his oral exam
in the center city, Jerusalem,
the next destination on his messianic journey is Golgotha.
Because of his vision for the New World,
he is going to be judged and crucified.
But...
We know that no one could keep Jesus dead in the tomb;
no one could keep in the darkness
his vision for a new heaven and a new earth.
Instead,
this vision has spread with the risen Christ,
like water, gushing from a dammed pool,
breaking the boundaries between men and women,
masters and slaves, Jews and Gentiles,
the rich and the poor, and the literate and the illiterate.
Through Jesus's followers,
who had witnessed the risen Christ,
God created a new community, the church,
the community of the resurrected.
Baptized with the irresistible power of the Holy Spirit,
the early Christian Church began to practice

a strange new life in the resurrection:
"They devoted themselves
to the apostles' teaching and fellowship,
to the breaking of bread and the prayers." (Acts 2:42)
They were called to live a new life
"with all humility and gentleness, with patience,
bearing with one another in love,
making every effort to maintain the unity of the Spirit
in the bond of peace." (Eph. 4:2–3)
Through this practice, the members of the church
felt as one in the faith of the risen Christ.
Among them, "there [was] one body and one Spirit,
one Lord, one faith." (Eph. 4:5)
By experiencing this new life in the church,
they could now finally understand
what Jesus had taught them about life in the resurrection.

Have you ever tasted life in the resurrection —
a strange new world
where there is no more male dominance over females,
no more rich over poor,
no more majority over minority,
no more first world over third world,
but a world where only the children of God live together
as sisters and brothers,
like angels living in God's presence?
Have you, have you ever been able to imagine this? ...

I believe that you and I are called to this vision
and invited to live the life worthy of the calling
to which we have been called.

May the blessings of the risen Christ
be with you and your churches forever,
so that we may continue to live life in the resurrection
even in this world!
Amen.

NOTES

Chapter 1: A Theological Reflection

1. Carl J. Schneider and Dorothy Schneider, *In Their Own Right: The History of American Clergywomen* (New York: Crossroad, 1997), 1.
2. Louis Charles Willard, ed., *Fact Book on Theological Education 1999–2000* (Pittsburgh: Association of Theological Schools in the United States and Canada, 2000), 46–47.
3. Barbara Brown Zikmund, Adair T. Lummis, and Patricia M. Y. Chang, *Clergy Women: An Uphill Calling* (Louisville, Ky.: Westminster John Knox Press, 1998), 5.
4. Christian M. Smith, *Weaving the Sermon: Preaching in a Feminist Perspective* (Louisville, Ky.: Westminster/John Knox Press, 1989); Carol M. Norén, *Woman in the Pulpit* (Nashville: Abingdon Press, 1992); Lee McGee, *Wrestling with the Patriarchs: Retrieving Women's Voices in Preaching* (Nashville: Abingdon Press, 1996); Lucy A. Rose, *Sharing the Word: Preaching in the Roundtable Church* (Louisville, Ky.: Westminster John Knox Press, 1997); Mary D. Turner and Mary L. Hudson, *Saved from Silence: Finding Women's Voice in Preaching* (St. Louis: Chalice, 1999).
5. Sheila Ruth, *Issues in Feminism: A First Course in Women's Studies* (Boston: Houghton Mifflin Company, 1980), 84.
6. Quoted in Vern L. and Bonnie Bullough, *The Subordinate Sex* (Baltimore: Penguin, 1974), 114.
7. Ruth, *Issues in Feminism*, 151.
8. Margaret R. Miles, "Violence against Women in the Historical Christian West and in North American Secular Culture: The Visual and Textual Evidence," in *Shaping New Vision: Gender and Values in American Culture*, ed. Clarissa W. Atkinson, Constance H. Buchanan, and Margaret R. Miles (Ann Arbor: University of Michigan Research Press, 1987), 12.
9. Turner and Hudson, *Saved from Silence*, 93.

10. Ibid., 55.

11. bell hooks, *Feminist Theory: From Margin to Center* (Boston: South End Press, 1984), 15.

12. Ibid., 37–38.

13. Jung Young Lee, *Marginality: The Key to Multicultural Theology* (Minneapolis: Fortress Press, 1995), 60.

14. Daniel L. Migliore, *Faith Seeking Understanding: An Introduction to Christian Theology* (Grand Rapids, Mich.: Wm. B. Eerdmans, 1991), 24.

15. Rebecca S. Chopp, "Feminist Theology as Political Theology: Visions on the Margins," in *Theology, Politics, and Peace*, ed. Theodore Runyon (Maryknoll, N.Y.: Orbis Books, 1989), 150.

16. Sheila Davaney, "The Limits of the Appeal to Women's Experience," in *Shaping New Vision: Gender and Values in American Culture*, 46.

17. Rebecca S. Chopp, *The Power to Speak: Feminism, Language, God* (New York: Crossroad, 1991), 100.

18. Robert Schreiter, *The New Catholicity: Theology between the Global and the Local* (Maryknoll, N.Y.: Orbis Books, 1997), 49.

19. Ibid.

20. Leonora T. Tisdale, *Preaching as Local Theology and Folk Art* (Minneapolis: Fortress Press, 1997), 15–16.

21. Ibid., 38.

22. Ibid., 32–33.

23. Schreiter, *The New Catholicity*, 51.

24. Ibid.

25. Ibid., 54.

26. Ibid.

27. Ibid.

28. Schreiter, *The New Catholicity*, 4.

29. Ibid.

30. Fred Craddock, *Overhearing the Gospel* (Nashville: Abingdon Press, 1978).

31. Mary M. Fulkerson, *Changing the Subject: Women's Discourses and Feminist Theology* (Minneapolis: Fortress Press, 1994), 391.

32. Sharon D. Welch, *A Feminist Ethic of Risk* (Minneapolis: Fortress Press, 1990), 133.

33. M. Shawn Copeland, "Toward a Critical Christian Feminist Theology of Solidarity," in *Women and Theology*, ed. Mary Ann Hinsdale and Phyllis H. Kaminski (Maryknoll, N.Y.: Orbis Books, 1994), 14.

34. Ibid., 32, 29–30.

35. Fulkerson, *Changing the Subject*, 375.

36. Rebecca S. Chopp and Mark Lewis Taylor, eds., *Reconstructing Christian Theology* (Minneapolis: Fortress Press, 1994), 7.

37. Marjorie Hewitt Suchocki, *God, Christ, Church: A Practical Guide to Process Theology* (New York: Crossroad, 1989), 70.

38. Marjorie Hewitt Suchocki, "Spirit in and through the World," in *Trinity in Process: A Relational Theology of God*, ed. Joseph A. Bracken, S.J., and Marjorie Hewitt Suchocki (New York: Continuum, 1997), 176.

39. Claus Westermann, "Peace (*Shalom*) in the Old Testament," in *The Meaning of Peace: Biblical Studies*, ed. Perry B. Yoder and Willard M. Swartley (Louisville, Ky.: Westminster/John Knox Press, 1992), 19.

40. Walter Brueggemann, *Living toward a Vision: Biblical Reflections on Shalom* (New York: United Church Press, 1982), 15–16.

41. Ibid, 16–17.

42. Paul Hanson, "War and Peace in the Hebrew Bible," *Interpretation* 38 (1984): 356.

43. Ibid., 360–61.

44. Fulkerson, *Changing the Subject*, 4.

45. Paul Lehmann, *Ethics in a Christian Context* (New York: Harper & Row, 1963), 112.

46. Suchocki, *God, Christ, Church*, 61.

47. Gloria L. Schaab, S.S.J., "Feminist Theological Methodology: Toward a Kaleidoscopic Model," *Theological Studies* 62 (2001): 342.

48. Ibid.

49. Suchocki, *God, Christ, Church*, 3–4.

50. Schaab, "Feminist Theological Methodology," 343.

51. Ibid.

Chapter 2: Preaching the Risen Christ

1. Ronald E. Osborn, *Folly of God: The Rise of Christian Preaching* (St. Louis: Chalice, 1999), 110.

2. James J. Murphy, *Rhetoric in the Middle Ages: A History of Rhetorical Theory from St. Augustine to the Renaissance* (Berkeley: University of California Press, 1974), 272.

3. Yngve Brilioth, *A Brief History of Preaching* (Philadelphia: Fortress Press, 1965), 5–6.

4. Bonnie Thurston, *Women in the New Testament* (New York: Crossroad, 1998), 17–18.

5. Ibid. See also Joachim Jeremias, *Jerusalem in the Time of Jesus: An Investigation into Economic and Social Conditions during the New Testament Period* (Philadelphia: Fortress Press, 1969), 359–76.

6. Quoted in Thurston, *Women in the New Testament*, 18.

7. Osborn, *Folly of God*, 80–100.

8. Ibid., 73.

9. The first three books of *De doctrina Christiana* (*The Christian Doctrine*) were written in 396 CE and the fourth in 426 CE.

10. C. H. Dodd, *The Apostolic Preaching and Its Developments* (Chicago: Willett, Clark & Company, 1937), 1.

11. Ibid., 1–2.

12. Rudolf Bultmann, *Theology of the New Testament*, vol. 1, trans. Kendrick Grobel (London: SCM Press, 1952), 3.

13. Brilioth, *A Brief History of Preaching*, 7.

14. David Buttrick, *Preaching Jesus Christ* (Philadelphia: Fortress Press, 1988), 23, 25.

15. Robert H. Smith, *Easter Gospels: The Resurrection of Jesus According to the Four Gospel Evangelists* (Minneapolis: Augsburg Publishing House, 1983), 27.

16. Ibid., 29.

17. Ibid., 71.

18. Osborn, *Folly of God*, 256.

19. Esther De Boer, *Mary Magdalene: Beyond the Myth*, trans. John Bowden (Harrisburg, Pa.: Trinity Press International, 1997), 116.

20. St. Augustine, *Sermon*, 232.2, quoted in ibid., 64.

21. Jeremias, *Jerusalem in the Time of Jesus*, 359–76.

22. Cf. John 19:25–27.

23. Carla Ricci, *Mary Magdalene and Many Others: Women Who Followed Jesus* (Minneapolis: Fortress Press, 1994), 26–27.

24. In these passages, the women persecuted are in silence. However, such names of the martyrs of the second century as Blandina, Biblis, Perpetua, Felicitas, and Agatha are known to us. The martyrdom story of Perpetua and Felicitas, which is assumed as one of the earliest pieces of Christian literature written by a woman in the second or early third century, includes vivid descriptions of women's experiences as martyrs. See Elizabeth A. Clark, *Women in the Early Church* (Wilmington, Del.: Michael Glazier, 1983), 97–106.

25. Valerie Karras, "Women in the Eastern Church: Past, Present and Future," *Sourozh: A Journal of Orthodox Life and Thought* (February 1998): 34.

26. It is noteworthy that there was a group of female prophets at the end of the second century called the "New Prophecy" or "Montanists." Their preaching activities as prophets initiated a resurgence of prophecy based on the experience of the Spirit by ecstatic visions. See Karen Jo

Torjesen, "Reconstruction of Women's Early Christian History," in Elisabeth Schüssler Fiorenza, *Searching the Scriptures* (New York: Crossroad, 1993), 298.

27. Paul J. Achtemeier, ed., *Harper's Bible Dictionary* (San Francisco: Harper & Row Publishers, 1985), 40; there are more names of women leaders in Acts and the Epistles who are called disciples or fellow workers, such as Tabitha (Acts 9:36–43), Chloe (1 Cor. 1:11), Apphia (Phil. 2), Nympha (Col. 4:15), and Lois and Eunice (2 Tim. 1:5).

28. Quoted in Osborn, *Folly of God*, 369.

29. Karen Jo Torjesen, "The Early Christian *Orans:* An Artistic Representation of Women's Liturgical Prayer and Prophecy," in Beverly Mayne Kienzle and Pamela J. Walker, eds., *Women Preachers and Prophets through Two Millennia of Christianity* (Berkeley: University of California Press, 1998), 42–56.

30. Thurston, *Women in the New Testament*, 50.

31. Karen Jo Torjesen, *When Women Were Priests: Women's Leadership in the Early Church and the Scandal of Their Subordination in the Rise of Christianity* (San Francisco: HarperCollins, 1993), 10.

32. Susan Haskins, *Mary Magdalen: Myth and Metaphor* (London: HarperCollins, 1993), 88–89.

33. Ibid., 16; the early church fathers combined the four different women in the Bible and re-created a new character of Mary Magdalene as a symbol of seductiveness and penitence in their commentaries and sermons in order to serve the purpose of the patriarchal ecclesial hierarchy in the late sixth century. See Ricci, *Mary Magdalene and Many Others*, 33–39.

34. Ricci, *Mary Magdalene and Many Others*, 130.

35. Haskins, *Mary Magdalen*, 65.

36. Katherine L. Jansen, "Maria Magdalena: *Apostolorum Apostola*," in Beverly Mayne Kienzle and Pamela J. Walker, eds., *Women Preachers and Prophets through Two Millennia of Christianity* (Berkeley: University of California Press, 1998), 260.

37. De Boer, *Mary Magdalene*, 64–65.

38. For example, in the *Gospel of Peter*, Mary Magdalene is called "a disciple of the Lord"; Peter in the *Gospel of Thomas* requests Jesus to exclude Mary Magdalene from the circle of the disciples. However, Jesus says, "I myself shall lead her in order to make her male, so that she too may become a living spirit resembling you males" (Logion 114). In the *Gospel of Mary*, Peter is portrayed as a jealous opponent to Mary and challenges her authority because of her gender but was defeated by her.

39. De Boer, *Mary Magdalene*, 74–76.

40. Haskins, *Mary Magdalen*, 107.

41. Jacobus de Voragine, *The Golden Legend: Readings on the Saints*, vol. 1, trans. William G. Ryan (Princeton, N.J.: Princeton University Press, 1993), 374–82.

42. E.g., *Apostolorum Apostola. Psalter of St. Albans*, Hildesheim: Dombibliothek, MS St. God. I (Property of St. Godehard, Hildesheim). See Jansen, ""Maria Magdalena," 64.

43. A. I. Natroshvili, Mtskheta and Sveli Tskhoveli, *Cathedral: An Historical-Archeological Description* (Tiflis, 1901), 158–62, quoted in V. Nikitin, "St. Nina, Equal to the Apostles, and the Baptism of Georgia," *Journal of the Moscow Patriarchate* no. 3 (1986): 52.

44. Cf. Eva M. Synek, "The Life of St. Nino of Georgia: A Country's Conversion to Its Female Apostle," *Ostkirchliche Studien* 47, nos. 2–3 (1998): 140.

45. Ibid., 144.

46. "The Life of St. Nina, Equal of the Apostles and Enlightener of Georgia with the Service" (Jordanville: Holy Trinity Monastery, Printshop of St. Job of Pochaev, 1988), 8.

47. According to Rufinus, Nina came to Georgia as a "slave woman." See Rufinus, *Historia ecclesiastica*, I, 10–11. The excerpt of Rufinus's book is included in David Braund, *Georgia in Antiquity: A History of Colchis and Transcaucasian Iberia 550 BC–AD 562* (Oxford: Clarendon Press, 1994), 248–50.

48. "The Life of St. Nina, Equal of the Apostles and Enlightener of Georgia with the Service," 5–20.

49. Ibid., 23–31; "*Akathist* to the Holy Equal-to-the-Apostles, Nina, Enlightener of Georgia," *Orthodox Word* 36, nos. 3–4 (May–August 2000): 123–37.

50. Riassaphore-monk Adrian, "Following the Cross of St. Nina," *Orthodox Word* 36, nos. 3–4 (May–August 2000): 113–15.

51. Ibid., 121.

52. The early fathers' Christology based on the doctrine of atonement is criticized in Susan Bond, *Trouble with Jesus: Women, Christology, and Preaching* (St. Louis: Chalice, 1999).

53. Jürgen Moltmann, *The Spirit of Life* (Minneapolis: Fortress Press, 1992), 63–66.

54. Eunjoo M. Kim, *Preaching the Presence of God: A Homiletic from an Asian American Perspective* (Valley Forge, Pa.: Judson Press, 1999), 61–62.

55. Jürgen Moltmann, *God for Secular Society* (Minneapolis: Fortress Press, 1999), 240.

56. Kim, *Preaching the Presence of God*, 63–65.

Chapter 3: Preaching as Subversive Rhetoric

1. Ronald E. Osborn, *Folly of God: The Rise of Christian Preaching* (St. Louis: Chalice, 1999), 371.

2. *Fragments on 1 Corinthians 74*, quoted in Karen Jo Torjesen, "Reconstruction of Women's Early Christian History," in Elisabeth Schüssler Fiorenza, *Searching the Scriptures* (New York: Crossroad, 1993), 306.

3. *Constitutions of the Holy Apostle*, Book III, IX in *Ante-Nicene Fathers*, vol. 7, ed. Alexander Roberts, D.D., and James Donaldson, LL.D. (Grand Rapids, Mich.: Wm. B. Eerdmans, 1985), 429.

4. Susan Haskins, *Mary Magdalen: Myth and Metaphor* (London: HarperCollins, 1993), 87–89.

5. Larissa Taylor, *Soldiers of Christ: Preaching in Late Medieval and Reformation France* (New York: Oxford University Press, 1992), 176.

6. IX, 5, quoted in Elizabeth A. Clark, *Women in the Early Church* (Wilmington, Del.: Michael Glazier, 1983), 28–29.

7. Gary Macy, "The Ordination of Women in the Early Middle Ages," *Theological Studies* 61, no. 3 (September 2000): 483–84.

8. E.g., 1 Tim. 2:12–14: "I permit no woman to teach or to have authority over a man; she is to keep silent. For Adam was formed first, then Eve; and Adam was not deceived, but the woman was deceived and became a transgressor."

9. *Corpus Iuris Canonici*, ed. Aemilius Friedberg, vol. 1, col. 1367, quoted in Ida Raming, *The Exclusion of Women from the Priesthood: Divine Law or Sex Discrimination?* (Metuchen, N.J.: Scarecrow Press, 1976), 13.

10. Malcolm Lambert, *Medieval Heresy: Popular Movements from the Gregorian Reform to the Reformation* (Cambridge: Blackwell, 1992), 44–87.

11. Bernardi Abbatis Fontis Calidi, "Adversus Waldensium sectam liber VIII," in *Patrologiae: Cursus Completus*, accurante J.-P. Migne, 16, 520 (Brepols, 1882), 826–87: "But the enemies of truth say women may teach; and so this is what the Apostle says to Titus: 'The old women,' he naturally exhorts, 'should be saintly in their bearing... so that they teach the young women to be prudent... (Titus II).... These enemies are to be repelled lest intellectual women teach heresies; secondly, lest they preach any words, unless they are old women, near the end of life, and even then they may not teach except young women.'" I am indebted in this translation to Merle Marie Troeger.

12. Nicole Bérlou, "The Right of Women to Give Religious Instruction in the Thirteenth Century," in Beverly Mayne Kienzle and Pamela J. Walker, eds., *Women Preachers and Prophets through Two Millennia of*

Christianity (Berkeley: University of California Press, 1998), 137. *Decretals* are papal letters, strictly those in response to a question. They have the force of law within the pope's jurisdiction.

13. Ibid., 138.

14. Humbert of Romans, *De eruditione praedicatorum* [Sebastian a Cormelias, 1607], 31, quoted in Taylor, *Soldiers of Christ*, 176; Katherine L. Jansen, "Maria Magdalena: *Apostolorum Apostola*," in Kienzle and Walker, *Women Preachers and Prophets*, 68.

15. Raming, *The Exclusion of Women from the Priesthood*, 23.

16. Talyor, *Soldiers of Christ*, 20; James Murphy, *Rhetoric in the Middle Ages: A History of Rhetorical Theory from St. Augustine to the Renaissance* (Berkeley: University of California Press, 1974), 269–355.

17. Quoted in Richard Lischer, *Theories of Preaching: Selected Readings in the Homiletical Tradition* (Durham, N.C.: Labyrinth Press, 1987), 10.

18. Alan of Lille, *The Art of Preaching*, Cistercian Fathers Series, No. 23, trans. Gilian R. Evans (Kalamazoo, Mich.: Cistercian Publications, 1981), 15–22, quoted in Lischer, *Theories of Preaching*, 9–13. The seven steps to Christian moral perfection are confession, prayer, the act of grace, the study of scripture, the more serious study of scripture, the exposition of scripture, and preaching.

19. Alan of Lille, *The Art of Preaching*, 311–15; Taylor, *Theories of Preaching*, 60–69.

20. Beverly M. Kienzle, "The Typology of the Medieval Sermon and Its Development in the Middle Ages: Report on Work in Progress," in *De L'Homélie Au Sermon: Histoire De La Prédication Médiévale, Actes du Colloque international de Louvain-la-Neuve*, ed. Jacqueline Hamesse and Zavier Hermand (Louvain-la-Neuve: Publications de l'Institut d'Etudes Médiévales, 1993), 84.

21. Quoted in Murphy, *Rhetoric in the Middle Ages*, 345.

22. Roberto Rusconi, "Women's Sermons at the End of the Middle Ages," in Kienzle and Walker, *Women Preachers and Prophets*, 173–74.

23. Bernard McGinn, "The Changing Shape of Late Medieval Mysticism," *Church History* 65 (January 1996): 209.

24. Bérlou, "The Right of Women to Give Religious Instruction in the Thirteenth Century," 139.

25. Rose of Viterbo received an ecclesiastical permission to preach in the church pulpit. Darleen Pryds, "Proclaiming Sanctity through Proscribed Acts: The Case of Rose of Viterbo," in Kinzle and Walker, *Women Preachers and Prophets*, 159–73.

26. Claire L. Sahlin, "Preaching and Prophesying: The Public Proclamation of Birgitta of Sweden's Revelations," in *Performance and Transformation: New Approaches to Late Medieval Spirituality*, ed. Mary A. Suydam and Joanna E. Ziegler (New York: St. Martin's Press, 1999), 69–96.

27. Cf. ibid., 71; Paul Scott Wilson, *A Concise History of Preaching* (Nashville: Abingdon Press, 1992), 77.

28. Kienzle, "The Typology of the Medieval Sermon and Its Development in the Middle Ages," 86.

29. Murphy, *Rhetoric in the Middle Ages*, 303.

30. Kienzle, "The Typology of the Medieval Sermon and Its Development in the Middle Ages," 86; Peter Dronke, *Women Writers of the Middle Ages: A Critical Study of Texts from Perpetua (203) to Marguerite Porete (1310)* (Cambridge: Cambridge University Press, 1984), 183.

31. Julia Dietrich, "The Visionary Rhetoric of Hildegard of Bingen," in *Listening to Their Voices: The Rhetorical Activities of Historical Women*, ed. Molly Meijer Wertheimer (Columbia: University of South Carolina Press, 1997), 200.

32. Ibid., 202.

33. *Epistola 49*, quoted in Barbara Newman, *Sister of Wisdom* (Berkeley: University of California Press, 1987), 27.

34. Hildegard of Bingen, *Scivias*, trans. Mother Columba Hart and Jane Bishop (New York: Paulist Press, 1990), 59.

35. Dietrich, "The Visionary Rhetoric of Hildegard of Bingen," 212.

36. Hildegard of Bingen, *Scivias*, 162.

37. Ibid., 169–71.

38. Julian of Norwich, *Showings*, trans. Edmund Colledge, O.S.A., and James Walsh, S.J. (New York: Paulist Press, 1978), 19.

39. Ibid., 18–21.

40. Brad Peters, "A Genre Approach to Julian of Norwich's Epistemology," in *Julian of Norwich: A Book of Essays*, ed. Sandra J. McEntire (New York: Garland, 1998), 133.

41. Julian of Norwich, *Showings*, Long Text, chap. 42, 252.

42. Elizabeth Alvilda Petroff, *Medieval Women's Visionary Literature* (New York: Oxford University Press, 1986), 300.

43. Elisabeth K. J. Koenig, "Julian of Norwich, Mary Magdalene, and the Drama of Prayer," *Horizons* (Spring 1993): 26.

44. Julian of Norwich, *Showings*, Long Text, chaps. 58–59, 293–97.

45. Ibid., chaps. 60–62, 299–303.

46. Cf. Hos. 11:3–4; 13:13–14; Ps. 36:8; 84:4; 123:2; Isa. 42:14; 49:15; 66:13; Jer. 30:7; Ezek. 34:16; Matt. 23:37; Luke 13:34; Col. 2:7; 1 Pet. 1:3; James 1:18; Rev. 2:17; 21:6; etc.

47. Caroline Walker Bynum, *Jesus as Mother: Studies in the Spirituality of the High Middle Ages* (Berkeley: University of California Press, 1982), 129–30.
48. Ibid., 143.
49. Julian of Norwich, *Showings*, Short Text, chap. 6, 135.
50. Julian of Norwich, *Showings*, Long Text, chap. 57, 292.
51. Jennifer P. Heimmel, *"God Is Our Mother": Julian of Norwich and the Medieval Image of Christian Feminine Divinity* (Salzburg: Universität Salzburg, 1982), 72.
52. Ibid., 71.
53. Some resources mention 1648 as her birth year.
54. Sor Juana Inés de la Cruz, "The Reply to Sor Philothea," in Alan S. Trueblood, trans., *A Sor Juana Anthology* (Cambridge: Harvard University Press, 1988), 211.
55. Heimmel, *"God Is Our Mother,"* 46.
56. George H. Tavard, "The Pilgrimage in the Works of Juana Inés de la Cruz," *Dialogue and Alliance* 6, no. 4 (1993): 51.
57. Stephanie Merrim, "Mores Geometricae: The "Woman Script" in the Theater of Sor Juana Inés de la Cruz," in *Feminist Perspectives on Sor Juana Inés de la Cruz*, ed. Stephanie Merrim (Detroit: Wayne State University Press, 1991), 96.
58. Octavio Paz, *Sor Juana, or, the Traps of Faith*, trans. Margaret Sayers Peden (Cambridge, Mass.: Belknap Press of Harvard University Press, 1988), 19–23, 57. *La Respuesta* reveals that Sor Juana wrote the criticism of a prominent Jesuit Antonio Vieira's sermon at the behest of Manuel Fernández de Santa Cruz, the bishop of Puebla. He published Juana's written copy without her permission, appending his letter as a preface disguising him as Sor Filotea. In the letter, he threatened her to be silent.
59. Alfonso Méndez Plancarte and Alberto Salceda, eds., *Obras Completas de Sor Juana Inés de la Cruz*, vol. 1–4 (México–Buenos Aires: Fondo de Cultura Económica, 1951–57), 202–3. Quoted in Pamela Kirk, "Sor Juana Inés de la Cruz — Precursor of Latin American Feminism," *Journal of Hispanic/Latino Theology* 5, no. 3 (February 1998): 16.
60. Josefina Ludmer, "Tricks of the Weak," in Merrim, *Feminist Perspectives on Sor Juana Inés de la Cruz*, 91.
61. Trueblood, *A Sor Juana Anthology*, 213–14, 225–26.
62. Ibid., 111, 113.
63. Paz, *Sor Juana*, 303.
64. Pamela Kirk, "Christ as Divine Narcissus: A Theological Analysis of 'El Divino Narciso' by Sor Juana Ines de la Cruz," *Word and World* 12, no. 2 (Spring 1992): 146–53.

65. Stephanie Merrim, "Toward a Feminist Reading of Sor Juana Inés de la Cruz: Past, Present, and Future Directions in Sor Juana Criticism," in Merrim, *Feminist Perspectives on Sor Juana Inés de la Cruz*, 28.

66. Electa Arenal and Amanda Powell, trans., *The Answer/La Respuesta: Including a Selection of Poems, Sor Juana Inés de la Cruz* (New York: Feminist Press, 1994), 21.

67. Trueblood, *A Sor Juana Anthology*, 233, 235.

68. Arenal and Powell, *The Answer/La Respuesta*, ix.

69. Brian Wren, *What Language Shall I Borrow? God-Talk in Worship: A Male Response to Feminist Theology* (New York: Crossroad, 1990), 64.

70. Elizabeth A. Johnson, "Naming God She: The Theological Implications," *The Princeton Seminary Bulletin* 22, no. 2 (2001): 135.

71. Wren, *What Language Shall I Borrow?* 82.

72. Sallie McFague, *Models of God: Theology for an Ecological, Nuclear Age* (Philadelphia: Fortress Press, 1987), 33.

73. Wren, *What Language Shall I Borrow?* 158.

Chapter 4: The Authority of Preaching

1. Martin Luther, "The Misuse of the Mass," in *Luther's Works*, vol. 36, ed. Abdel Ross Wentz (Philadelphia: Fortress Press, 1959), 149.

2. Ibid., 152.

3. John Calvin, *Institutes of the Christian Religion*, vol. 2, ed. John McNeill, trans. Ford Lewis Battles (Philadelphia: Westminster Press, 1960), 1206–8.

4. John Calvin, *Sermons on the Epistles to Timothy and Titus* (1579; reprinted, Carlisle: Banner of Truth Trust, 1983), 212–13.

5. Jane D. Douglass, *Women, Freedom, and Calvin* (Philadelphia: Westminster Press, 1985), 54–59.

6. Martin Luther, "The Estate of Marriage," trans. Walter I. Brandt, in *Luther's Works*, vol. 45, ed. Walter I. Brandt (Philadelphia: Fortress Press, 1962), 38–46.

7. Martin Luther, *Sämmtliche Werke* (Erlangen and Frankfurt, 1826–57), 61, 212, quoted in Merry Wiesner, "Luther and Women: The Death of Two Marys," in *Feminist Theology: A Reader*, ed. Ann Loades (London: SPCK, 1990), 123.

8. *Sämmtliche Werke*, 61, 125, 20, 84, 33, 112, quoted in Wiesner, "Luther and Women," 123, 126.

9. Luther, "The Misuse of the Mass," 151–52.

10. Douglass, *Women, Freedom, and Calvin*, 63.

11. Barbara J. MacHaffie, *Her Story: Women in Christian Tradition* (Philadelphia: Fortress Press, 1986), 70.

12. Paul W. Chilcote, *John Wesley and the Women Preachers of Early Methodism* (Metuchen, N.J.: American Theological Library Association and Scarecrow Press, 1991), 10.

13. Document R2a.43b, II (26) at Unity archives, Herrnhut, quoted in Peter Vogt, "A Voice for Themselves: Women as Participants in Congregational Discourse in the Eighteenth-Century Moravian Movement," in Beverly Mayne Kienzle and Pamela J. Walker, eds., *Women Preachers and Prophets through Two Millennia of Christianity* (Berkeley: University of California Press, 1998), 238–39.

14. Paul W. Chilcote, *Her Own Story: Autobiographical Portraits of Early Methodist Women* (Nashville: Abingdon Press, 2001), 19.

15. Vicki Tolar Collins, "Women's Voices and Women's Silence in the Tradition of Early Methodism," in *Listening to Their Voices: The Rhetorical Activities of Historical Women*, ed. Molly Meijer Wertheimer (Columbia: University of South Carolina Press, 1997), 236–37.

16. Ibid., 238.

17. Chilcote, *Her Own Story*, 18.

18. Quoted in Chilcote, *John Wesley and the Women Preachers of Early Methodism*, 182.

19. Collins, "Women's Voices and Women's Silence," 245.

20. Chilcote, *John Wesley and the Women Preachers of Early Methodism*, 237.

21. DeWitte T. Holland, *The Preaching Tradition: A Brief History* (Nashville: Abingdon Press, 1980), 51.

22. Ibid., 51–52; Harold Bosley, "The Role of Preaching in American History," in *Preaching in American History: Selected Issues in the American Pulpit, 1630–1967*, ed. DeWitte Holland (Nashville: Abingdon Press, 1969), 27; Eugene E. White, "Puritan Preaching and the Authority of God," in Holland, *Preaching in American History*, 36.

23. Harry Stout, *The New England Soul: Preaching and Religious Culture in Colonial New England* (New York: Oxford University Press, 1986), 19.

24. Ibid., 7–9.

25. White, "Puritan Preaching," 73.

26. John Cotton, "Singing of Psalms a Gospel-Ordinance, 1650," quoted in Sussan Hill Lindley, *"You Have Stept Out of Your Place": A History of Women and Religion in America* (Louisville, Ky.: Westminster John Knox Press, 1996), 19.

27. Cotton Mather, *El-Shaddi. A Brief Essay . . . Produced by the Death of . . . Mrs. Katharin Willard* (Boston, 1725), 21, quoted in Gerald Moran, "'The Hidden Ones': Women and Religion in Puritan New England,"

in *Triumph over Silence: Women in Protestant History*, ed. Richard L. Greaves (Westport, Conn.: Greenwood Press, 1985), 127.

28. Lindley, *"You Have Stept Out of Your Place,"* 5-6.

29. "A Report of the Trial of Mrs. Ann Hutchinson before the Church in Boston," in *The Antinomian Controversy 1636-1638: A Documentary History*, ed. David Hall (Middletown, Conn.: Wesleyan University Press, 1968), 203, quoted in Lindley, *"You Have Stept Out of Your Place,"* 5.

30. Lindley, *"You Have Stept Out of Your Place,"* 8.

31. Ibid., 40; Williston Walker, et al., *A History of the Christian Church*, 4th ed. (New York: Charles Scribner's Sons, 1985), 607-8.

32. Stout, *The New England Soul*, 192.

33. Ibid., 201.

34. Jonathan Edwards, "A Treatise Concerning Religious Affections," in *Puritan Sage: Collected Writings of Jonathan Edwards*, ed. Vergilius Ferm (New York: Library Publishers, 1953), 447-50; cf. Edward Collins Jr., "The Rhetoric of Sensation Challenges the Rhetoric of the Intellect: An Eighteenth-Century Controversy," in Holland, *Preaching in American History*, 116-17.

35. Jonathan Edwards, "Some Thoughts Concerning the Present Revival of Religion in New England," in Ferm, *Puritan Sage*, 392.

36. Ibid., 395.

37. D. Ray Heisey, "On Entering the Kingdom: New Birth or Nurture?" in Holland, *Preaching in American History*, 153.

38. Catherine A. Brekus, *Strangers and Pilgrims: Female Preaching in America, 1740-1845* (Chapel Hill: University of North Carolina Press, 1998), 126.

39. Ibid., 123; Heisey, "On Entering the Kingdom," 155-61.

40. Lindley, *"You Have Stept Out of Your Place,"* 62.

41. William L. Andrews, ed., *Sisters of the Spirit: Three Black Women's Autobiographies of the Nineteenth Century* (Bloomington: Indiana University Press, 1986), 4; Betty Collier-Thomas, *Daughters of Thunder: Black Women Preachers and Their Sermons, 1850-1979* (San Francisco: Jossey-Bass Publishers, 1998), 12.

42. Brekus, *Strangers and Pilgrims*, 119-20.

43. Phoebe Palmer, *The Promise of the Father*, reprinted (New York: Garland, 1985), 20-33.

44. Blanche Glassman Hersh, "To Make the World Better: Protestant Women in the Abolitionist Movement," in Greaves, *Triumph over Silence*, 173-84.

45. E.g., Sarah Grimké, *Letters on the Equality of the Sexes, and the Condition of Women* (Boston: Isaac Knapp, 1838; reprinted, New

York: Source Book Press, 1970); Frances E. Willard, *Woman in the Pulpit* (Boston: D. Lothrop Company, 1888); Louisa M. Woosley, *Shall Woman Preach? Or the Question Answered* (Caneyville, 1891; reprinted, Memphis: Frontier Press, 1989).

46. With the exception of the Cumberland Presbyterian Church, which ordained Louisa M. Woosley in 1889.

47. MacHaffie, *Her Story*, 112.

48. Willard, *Woman in the Pulpit*, 94.

49. Pamela J. Walker, "A Chaste and Fervid Eloquence: Catherine Booth and the Ministry of Women in the Salvation Army," in Kienzle and Walker, *Women Preachers and Prophets*, 288–95.

50. Ibid., 292.

51. Catherine Booth, *Female Teaching: Or, the Rev. A. A. Rees versus Mrs. Palmer, Being a Reply to a Pamphlet by the Above Named Gentleman on the Sunderland Revival* (London: G. J. Stevenson, 1861), reprinted in Victorian Women Writers Project (Bloomington: Library Electronic Text Resource Service, Indiana University, 1996), 3.

52. Jarena Lee, *The Life and Religious Experience of Jarena Lee, A Coloured Lady, Giving an Account of Her Call to Preach the Gospel* (Philadelphia: Printed and Published for the Author, 1836), in *Sisters of the Spirit: Three Black Women's Autobiographies of the Nineteenth Century*, ed. William L. Andrews (Bloomington: Indiana University Press, 1986), 27–34.

53. Ibid., 40–41.

54. Jarena Lee, *Religious Experience and Journal of Mrs. Jarena Lee, Giving an Account of Her Call to Preach the Gospel* (Philadelphia: Printed and Published for the Author, 1849), at http://digilib.nypl.org/dynaweb/digs/wwm9716/@Generic_BookView.

55. E.g., ibid.

56. Joycelyn K. Moody, "On the Road with God: Travel and Quest in Early Nineteenth-Century African American Holy Women's Narratives," *Religion and Literature* 27, no. 1 (Spring 1995): 37.

57. Lee, *The Life and Religious Experience of Jarena Lee*, 27.

58. Ibid., 32.

59. Ibid., 36.

60. Ibid.

61. Ibid., 48.

62. Ibid., 36–37.

63. Lee, *Religious Experience and Journal of Mrs. Jarena Lee*.

64. Ibid.

65. Lee, *The Life and Religious Experience of Jarena Lee*, 45–46.

66. Lee, *Religious Experience and Journal of Mrs. Jarena Lee*.
67. Anna Howard Shaw, D.D., M.D., *The Story of a Pioneer* (New York and London: Harper & Brother Publishers, 1915; reprinted, New York: Kraus Reprint Co., 1970), 18.
68. Ibid., 45.
69. Ibid., 60.
70. Ibid., 65.
71. Ibid., 124.
72. Ibid., 191.
73. Ibid., 232.
74. Anna Howard Shaw, "God's Woman," lecture at a meeting of the National Council of Women of the United States in 1891, quoted in Wil A. Linkugel and Martha Solomon, *Anna Howard Shaw: Suffrage Orator and Social Reformer* (New York: Greenwood Press, 1991), 137–38.
75. Shaw, "The Heavenly Vision," a sermon, in Linkugel and Solomon, *Anna Howard Shaw*, 118–19.
76. Ralph W. Spencer, "Anna Howard Shaw," *Methodist History* 13, no. 2 (January 1975): 33.
77. Shaw, *The Story of a Pioneer*, 102.
78. Ibid., 126–27.
79. Linkugel and Solomon, *Anna Howard Shaw*, 12–18.
80. Richard T. De George, *The Nature and Limits of Authority* (Lawrence: University of Kansas Press, 1985), 67–68.
81. Luther Lee, "Woman's Right to Preach the Gospel," in *Five Sermons and a Tract*, ed. Donald W. Dayton (Chicago: Holrad House, 1975), 99, quoted in Lindley, "You Have Stept Out of Your Place," 123. Emphasis is mine.
82. Carl J. Schneider and Dorothy Schneider, *In Their Own Right: The History of American Clergywomen* (New York: Crossroad, 1997,) 185.
83. See Appendix 1.3, "Change in Number of Clergy Women as Percent of Total Clergy," in *Clergy Women: An Uphill Calling*, ed. Barbara Brown Zikmund, Adair T. Lummis, and Patricia Mei Yin Chang (Louisville, Ky.: Westminster John Knox Press, 1998), 139.
84. Letty M. Russell, *Church in the Round: Feminist Interpretation of the Church* (Louisville, Ky.: Westminster/John Knox Press, 1993), 67.
85. Letty M. Russell and J. Shannon Clarkson, eds., *Dictionary of Feminist Theologies* (Louisville, Ky.: Westminster John Knox Press, 1996), 19.

86. Catherine A. Ziel, "Mother Tongue/Father Tongue: Gender-Linked Differences in Language Use and Their Influence on the Perceived Authority of the Preacher" (Ph.D. dissertation, Princeton Theological Seminary, 1991), 21.
87. Christine Smith, *Weaving the Sermon: Preaching in a Feminist Perspective* (Louisville, Ky.: Westminster/John Knox Press, 1989), 50.
88. Ibid.
89. Ibid., 48.
90. Ibid., 47.
91. De George, *The Nature and Limits of Authority*, 94.

Chapter 5: Preaching and the Politics of God

1. Paul Lehmann, *The Transfiguration of Politics* (New York: Harper & Row, 1975), 7, 10, 293.
2. Wi Jo Kang, *Christ and Caesar in Modern Korea: A History of Christianity and Politics* (Albany: State University of New York, 1997), 7.
3. Allen D. Clark, *A History of the Church in Korea* (Seoul: Christian Literature Society of Korea, 1971), 88-90.
4. Everett N. Hunt Jr., *Protestant Pioneers in Korea* (Maryknoll, N.Y.: Orbis Books, 1980), 91.
5. Henry G. Appenzeller, *The Henry G. Appenzeller Papers* (New York: The Missionary Research Library, Union Theological Seminary, 1910), quoted in Hunt, *Protestant Pioneers in Korea*, 89-90.
6. Henry G. Appenzeller, *The Henry G. Appenzeller Correspondence* (New York: The United Mission Library, 1886), quoted in Hunter, *Protestant Pioneers in Korea*, 59.
7. "Editorial," in *Dokrip Shinmoon (Independence Newspaper)*, August 20, 1896, quoted in Yong Ok Park, "Kidokkyowa Yeosungeu Kaewha (Christianity and the Enlightenment of Women)," in *Yeosung! Ggaelggiada, Ilanalggiada, Noraehalggiada: Hankuk Kydokkyo Yeosung Paikyeonsa (Women! Awake, Rise, and Sing: The History of Korean Christian Women Over One Hundred Years)*, ed. Committee on the Centennial Celebration of Korean Christianity (Seoul: Korean Christian Press, 1985), 93-94.
8. Hankuk Kydokkyo Yoksa Yonkuso (The Institute of Korean Church History Studies), *Hankuk Kydokkyoeu Yoksa (A History of the Korean Church)*, vol. 1 (Seoul: Christian Literature Press, 1989), 268-75. The Great Revivals brought a 268 percent increase in the number of Korean churches from 1905 to 1907. In 1907, there were 642 churches, 1,045 mission centers, and approximately 120,000 Christians.

9. Kwang Su Yi, "What Christianity Has Done for Korea," *Chung Choon (Youth): A Korean Monthly* (August 1918), trans. T. H. Yun, quoted in *Kidokkyosa Jaryogip (Resources for the History of Korean Christianity)*, vol. 3, ed. Ok Soong Cha (Seoul: Korean Research Institute for Religion and Society, 1988), 629.

10. Min Ji Choi, "Minjokeu Konankwa Kidokkyo Yeosung Woondong (National Suffering and Christian Women's Movement)," in *Women! Awake, Rise, and Sing*, 166.

11. Hae Won Yoon, "Kidokkyo Hakkyowa Yeosung Kyoyook (Christian Schools and Women's Education)," in *Women! Awake, Rise, and Sing*, 116.

12. Park, "Kidokkyowa Yeosungeu Kaewha (Christianity and the Enlightenment of Women)," 97.

13. Ibid., 82.

14. Ibid.; translation mine.

15. Choi, "Minjokeu Konankwa Kidokkyo Yeosung Woondong (National Suffering and Christian Women's Movement)," 167.

16. Ki-Young Shin, "Christianity and Nation-Building in Korea, 1885–1945" (Ph.D. dissertation, Arizona State University, 1993), 51; The Institute of Korean Church History Studies, vol. 2, 60.

17. Donald S. Macdonald, *The Koreans: Contemporary Politics and Society* (Boulder, Colo.: Westview Press, 1988), 237.

18. F. A. McKenzie, *Korea's Fight for Freedom* (New York: Fleming H. Revell Company, 1920), 308.

19. "Letter from Arthur J. Brown to Masanao Hanihara," February 16, 1912, in the Presbyterian Library, New York, quoted in Kang, *Christ and Caesar in Modern Korea*, 44.

20. Ibid.

21. *San Francisco Call*, March 24, 1908, 1, quoted in Kang, *Christ and Caesar in Modern Korea*, 41.

22. Kang, *Christ and Caesar in Modern Korea*, 42.

23. "An Interrogation" in *The History of Korean Independence Movements*, 284, quoted in the Institute of Korean Church History Studies, vol. 1, 337–38; translation mine.

24. McKenzie, *Korea's Fight for Freedom*, 219–20.

25. The Institute of Korean Church History Studies, vol. 1, 308–23.

26. Peggy Billings, *Fire Beneath the Frost: The Struggles of the Korean People and Church* (New York: Friendship Press, 1984), 28.

27. Shin, "Christianity and Nation-Building in Korea," 51; The Institute of Korean Church History Studies, vol. 2, 38.

28. By the end of the year 1919, 3,426 Christians were arrested because of their participation in the March First Independence Movement. The number of the arrested Christians was 17.6 percent of the total of 19,525 prisoners. Presbyterian and Methodist churches lost 88 churches and 22,409 members by the persecution of the Japanese government. See the Institute of Korean Church History Studies, vol. 2, 38.

29. Choi, "National Suffering and Christian Women's Movement," 162.

30. Ibid., 36.

31. McKenzie, *Korea's Fight for Freedom*, 267–68.

32. Ibid., 316–19.

33. Kang, *Christ and Caesar in Modern Korea*, 61–62, 67.

34. Yani Yoo, "Han-Laden Women: Korean "Comfort Women" and Women in Judges 19–21," *Semeia* 78 (1997): 37–39.

35. Shin, "Christianity and Nation-Building in Korea," 63.

36. The Institute of Korean Church History Studies, vol. 2, 302–23.

37. Kang, *Christ and Caesar in Modern Korea*, 69.

38. Ibid., 71.

39. David I. Steinberg, *The Republic of Korea: Economic Transformation and Social Change* (Boulder, Colo., and London: Westview Press, 1989), 52.

40. Eunjoo M. Kim, "The Preaching of Transfiguration: Theology and Method of Eschatological Preaching from Paul Lehmann's Theological Perspective as an Alternative to Contemporary Korean Preaching" (Ph.D. dissertation, Princeton Theological Seminary, 1996), 94.

41. Sun Ai Ju, "Kwangbok Yhooeu Kidokkyo Yeosung Eundong (The Movement of Christian Women After the Emancipation)," in *Women! Awake, Rise, and Sing*, 187.

42. Ibid., 185; translation mine.

43. Ibid., 186.

44. Ibid., 187–89.

45. Kang, *Christ and Caesar in Modern Korea*, 72.

46. Kim, "The Preaching of Transfiguration," 62.

47. *Minjung* is a Korean word which means the people who are poor and weak politically and economically. However, minjung has the power to sustain the history of the nation. Minjung theology is a theological reflection of the sociopolitical struggles of the Korean people throughout the Japanese occupation, the division of the nation, and the dictatorship in North and South Korea. See ibid., 78.

48. Ibid., 71–72.

49. Sang Bin Rim, "Kidokkyo Yeosungeu Heonjaejuk Zeungun (Current Witnesses of Christian Women)" in *Women! Awake, Rise, and Sing*, 347.

50. Soon Kyung Park, *Tongil Shinhakeu Kotongkwa Seungri (The Suffering and Victory of the Theology of Reunification)*, (Seoul: Hanwool, 1992), 67, 116.

51. Two major Presbyterian denominations now ordain women as ministers of the Word and Sacrament. The liberal denomination, Kichang (Christian Presbyterian), began the ordination in 1976, and the moderate, Yeachang Tonghap (Unified Presbyterian of Jesus), in 1996.

52. Tongyoung is now called Choongmoo City.

53. Jong Kyu Choi, *Y Han Moksum Jureul Wihae: Choi Duk Ji Moksa Jungi (My Life for the Sake of Christ: A Biography of Rev. Duk Ji Choi)* (Seoul: Dosuh Chulpan Jinsuhchun, 1981), 18–24.

54. Ibid., 28–30.

55. Ibid., 31–55.

56. Ibid., 63.

57. Ibid., 73–78.

58. Ibid., 81.

59. McKenzie, *Korea's Fight for Freedom*, 8–9.

60. Choi, *My Life for the Sake of Christ*, 82.

61. Ibid., 83.

62. Ibid., 83–89.

63. Eun Soon Koo, ed., *Modeunkut Da Burigo: Yeo Moksa's Okjoong Kanzeung Sulkyojip, Duk Ji Choi Moksa Sulkyo (Discarding Everything: A Collection of a Woman Pastor's Sermons As the Witness of Life in Prison, Sermons of Rev. Duk Ji Choi)* (Seoul: Somangsa, 1981), 259.

64. Ibid., 201.

65. Yi Sook Ahn, *Chookeumeun Chookeurira (If I Perish, I Perish)* (Seoul: Kidokkyomoonsa, 1976), 278–86; translation mine.

66. Choi, *My Life for the Sake of Christ*, 122; translation mine.

67. Ibid., 123; translation mine.

68. Koo, *Discarding Everything*, 130–32; translation mine.

69. Choi, *My Life for the Sake of Christ*, 142–43.

70. Wha Soon Cho, *Let the Weak Be Strong: A Woman's Struggle for Justice*, dictated and trans. Lee Sun Ai and Ahn Sang Nim (Bloomington, Ind.: Meyer-Stone Books, 1988), 12, 131; translation mine.

71. Ibid., 13–14.

72. Ibid., 18.

73. Ibid., 18–19.

74. Ibid., 20–22.

75. Ibid., 30.

76. Ibid., 32.
77. Ibid., 35.
78. Ibid., 44–46.
79. Ibid., 47–54.
80. Ibid., 55–61.
81. Ibid., 62–73.
82. Ibid., 74–83.
83. Ibid., 89.
84. Ibid., 90–91
85. Ibid., 94.
86. Ibid., 96.
87. Ibid., 100.
88. Ibid., 101.
89. Ibid., 120.
90. Eunjoo M. Kim, "Interview with Rev. Wha Soon Cho" (Summer 2001), unpublished.
91. Wha Soon Cho, "Women Who Are Making Peace," in *From the Place of Suffering to a Flame of Love*, ed. Association of Korean Women Theologians (Seoul: The Christian Literature Society of Korea, 1992), 299–308.
92. Wha Soon Cho, "Tell My Sisters and Brothers to Go to Galilee," in *From the Place of Suffering to a Flame of Love*, 321–25.
93. Kim, "Interview."
94. Ibid.
95. Soon Kyung Park, "Hankook Minjokkwa Kidokkyo Sunkyoeu Moonjae: Sunkyoeu Miraewa Yeosung (Koreans and the Problems of Christian Mission: The Future of Mission and Women)," in *Women! Awake, Rise, and Sing*, 415; translation mine.
96. Ibid., 445–46, 449; translation mine.
97. The draft into the military comfort women was one of the common experiences of Asian women under military imperialism. From 1932 to the end of World War II, the Japanese government recruited girls from its colonies in Asia into sexual slavery for the Japanese military by force, coercion, or deception. Of two hundred thousand comfort women, 80 percent came from Korea, and another large percentage came from Japanese-occupied China. Others were taken from the Philippines, Burma, and Indonesia. In addition, some women who were Netherlands subjects were included in the immense roundup (www.comht.com/casewatch/cases/cwcomfort2.htm, "Japan's Mass Rape and Sexual Enslavement of Women and Girls from 1932–1945: The 'Comfort Women System'").

98. Franklyn J. Balasundaram, *Contemporary Asian Christian Theology* (Delhi: Indian Society for Promoting Christian Knowledge [ISPCK], 1995), 173–203.

99. Oo Chung Lee, *In Search for Our Foremothers' Spirituality* (Seoul: Asian Women's Resource Center for Culture and Theology, 1994), 36–37; Yayori Matsui, "Violence against Women in Development, Militarism, and Culture," in *Feminist Theology from the Third World*, ed. Ursula King (Maryknoll, N.Y.: Orbis Books, 1994), 126–29.

100. Balasundaram, *Contemporary Asian Christian Theology*, 176.

101. See Yoshiko Isshiki et al., *Women Moving Mountains: Feminist Theology in Japan* (Kuala Lumpur: Asian Women's Resource Center for Culture and Theology, 2000).

Conclusion: Partnership in Preaching

1. Letty M. Russell, *Growth in Partnership* (Philadelphia: Westminster Press, 1981), 29.

2. Lucy A. Rose, *Sharing the Word: Preaching in the Roundtable Church* (Louisville, Ky.: Westminster John Knox Press, 1997), 4.

3. Elisabeth Schüssler Fiorenza, "Response," in *A New Look at Preaching*, ed. John Burke (Wilmington, Del.: Michael Glazier, 1983), 48–55, quoted in Rose, *Sharing the Word*, 97.

4. Russell, *Growth in Partnership*, 105–6.

5. Ibid., 97, 123.

INDEX

Addy, Persis, 107
African Methodist Episcopal Church, 100
African Methodist Episcopal Zion Church, 98
Ahn, Choong Gon, 126
Alan of Lille, 54
Albion College, 106
Allen, Dr. Horace N., 120
Allen, Rev. Richard, 100
Anthony, Susan B., 108
Appenzeller, Henry G., 120
Ars Praedicandi, 54
asceticism, 56
Asian women preachers, 154
Association of Theological Schools, 2
Atto, Bishop of Vercelli, 52
authority
  in evangelicalism, 113
  feminist perspectives on, 117
  papal, 112
  in preaching, 79, 111, 113–17
  reformist views of, 112
  relational perspective, 116

Beecher, Lyman, 94
Bernard of Clairvaux, St., 57
Birgitta (Bridget) of Sweden, St., 57
Book of Decretals, 53
Booth, William, 98
Bosanquet, 87
Brekus, Catherine A., 96
Brilioth, Yngve, 24, 27
Brown, Antoinette, 98
Brown, Arthur, 124
Brown, Olympia, 98, 108
Brueggemann, Walter, 16
Buddhism, 127
Bushnell, Horace, 95
Buttrick, David, 27
Bynum, Caroline W., 66

Calvin, John
  Institutes of Christian Religion, 81
  theology of, 82
  on women in the church, 82, 84
Celsus, 34
Center for Social and Religious Research, 115
Chang, Maria, 123
Channcy, Charles, 93
Cho, Ah Ra, 134
Cho, Wha Soon, 119, 135–36, 142–52
  speech of, 149–50
Choi, Duk Ji, 119, 130, 136–42
  theology of, 142
Chosen Yeoja Kydokkyo Juljaehoe Yonhabhoe (Korean Women Christian Temperance Unified Society), 123
Christ. *See* Jesus
Christian church
  masculine imagery of, 48
  medieval, 52
  mission of, 45

Christian doctrine
  Kingdom of God, 109
  premillennialism, 120
  sanctification, 95, 96, 100
Christian theology, righteousness of God, 153
Chu, Kil Ja, 147
Chun, Doo Whan, 132
Chundokyo, 127
Church of Nazarene, 98
clericalism, 55
colonialism, 154
Confucianism, 121, 127
contextual theology, 11–12
Copeland, M. Shawn, 14
Cotton, John, 91
Council of National Defense Woman's Committee, 109
covenant theology, 89
Crosby, Sarah, 87
culture, 12

Davaney, Sheila, 10
Davenport, James, 92
Davies, Samuel, 92
deacons, women, 35
dialogue, crosscultural, 21
disciples of Christ, female, 31
diversity, 20
divinity schools. *See* seminaries
Dodd, C. H., 26
Douglass, Jane, 84
Dutton, Anne, 94
Dye, Mary, 92

early Christianity, women in, 35
East Dennis Church, 107
ecclesiastical regulations, medieval, 53
Edwards, Jonathan, 93
Elaw, Zilpha, 96
Elijah, 138
Ellers, A. J., 123
Eustache of Arras, 56

evangelists, female, 96, 98
Ewha Hakdang (Ewha School), 122

feminism, 6
  in Korea, 134
  of Sor Juana Inés de la Cruz, 73
feminist theory, 5, 8
Finney, Charles G., 94
Ford, Ann, 87
Forma Praedicandi (The Form of Preaching), 55
Fox, George, 85
Free Baptist Church, 98
Frelinghuysen, Theodore, 92

Gauthier of Château-Thierry, 53
gender ideology, 49–50
General Assembly of the Korean Reconstruction, 141
Georgian Orthodox Church, 40
Gil, Sun Ju, 122
Gnostic writings
  Gospel of Mary, 36
  Gospel of Philip, 36
  Gospel of Thomas, 36
  Pistis Sophia, 36
God
  concept of, 15
  masculine imagery of, 49
  as mother, 75–76
  nature of, 15–16, 49, 75, 77
  revelation of, 21
  wholeness of, 17–21
Golden Legend, The 37
Gratian, 52
Great Awakening, 92–94
  women's role in, 94
Gregory IX, Pope, 53
Grimké, Angelina, 97
Grimké, Sarah, 97
Guibert of Nogent, 57
Gunwoohoe, 123

Index

Hall, Cross, 87
Henry of Ghent, 56
Hildegard of Bingen, 58–61
  rhetorical strategies of, 59
  sermons of, 60
  theology of, 59
  visions of, 60–61
Hirobumi, Marquis Ito, 125
holiness doctrine. See Christian doctrine
Holland, DeWitte T., 88
Holy Spirit
  inspiration of, 85
  in missions, 45
  presence of, 46
  in Puritan women's preaching, 91
  as source of authority in preaching, 102, 113
homiletical theory, 78
homiletics. See preaching
homily, 54
hooks, bell, 8
Humbert of Romans, 53
Hutchinson, Anne, 91
Hyupsung Yeoja Shinhakkyo (Union Methodist Woman's Bible Training School), 123

Iliff School of Theology, 2
Isaiah, 104, 142
Israel, 17
Isshiki, Yoshiko, 155

Japanese Christianity, 156
Jesus
  attitude towards women, 32
  female disciples of, 33
  incarnation, 19, 21
  kerygma of, 26, 29
  resurrection of, 18, 27–30, 42
  teachings of, 32
  women's view, 41
Johnson, Elizabeth A., 75

Juana Inés de la Cruz, Sor, 67–73
  El Divino Narciso, 68, 71
  Hombres Necios, 70
  La Respuesta, 71
  poetry of, 69
  rhetoric of, 72
Judaism
  Diaspora, 24
  Exile, 23
  postexilic synagogue tradition, 24
  role of synagogue, 23
  women in, 24
Julian of Norwich, 61
  Showings, 61, 63
  theology of, 64
  visions of, 64
Jung, Choon Soo, 122
Jung, Hester, 123
Junia, 34

Kienzle, Beverly M., 57
Kim, Chai Choon, 133
Kim, Maria, 127
Kim, Pil Rye, 131
Kim, Soon Ai, 127
Kim, Sung Mu, 131
Kingdom of God. See Christian theology
Kinukawa, Hisako, 155
Koenig, Elisabeth K., 64
Korea
  colonization of, 124
  feminist movement in, 134
  history of, 124–33
  nationalist movement, 125
Korean Christianity
  Great Revivals, 122
  history of, 120–31
  ordination of women, 135
  persecution, 129, 140
  role of women in, 142
Korean evangelicalism, 130

Korean Japanese University Church, 134
Korean liberation theology. *See* minjung theology
Korean Methodist Church, 123
　history of, 130
　ordination of women in, 123
Korean politics, women in, 132
Korean preaching, political, 133, 135, 148
Korean Presbyterian Church, 130
Korean War, 143
Kyohoe Yeosung Yeonhaphoe (United Association of Church Women), 134

Lee, Jarena, 96, 99–104
　call to preach, 102–3
　visions of, 100
Lee, Luther, 114
Lee, Young Sook, 131
Livermore, Mary A., 106
Ludmer, Josefina, 69
Luther, Martin
　theology of, 81
　on women preachers, 83–84
Lydia in Philippi, 33

March First Independence Movement, 127, 136
Mary Magdalene, 28–37
McKenzie, F. A., 124
medieval church
　Cathars, 52
　Waldensians, 52
medieval theology, motherhood of God, 66
medieval women preachers, rhetorical strategies of, 74
metaphor, 76–77
Methodist Conference, Manchester, 87–88

Methodist Episcopal Church, 100, 107
Methodist movement, women as leaders in, 87
Methodist Protestant Church, 107
Mettleton, Asahel, 94
Min, Prince-General Yong-Ik, 120
minjung theology, 133
missionary theology, in Korea, 121
Modestus, 37
Moltmann, Jürgen, 45
monasticism, 56
Moody, Joycelyn K., 101
Moon, Ik Hwan, 133
Mott, Lucretia, 97, 108
Mulier in silentio discat, 72
Mulieres in Ecclesia taceant, 72
Mumford Booth, Catherine, 98

National American Woman Suffrage Association, 109
National Presbyterian Women's Missionary Society, 131
Natroshvili, A. I., 38
Neungdong Church, 144
Nihon Kirishto-Kyo Chosen Kyodan (Korean division of the Japanese Christian Church), 130
Nina, St., 35, 37–40
Nineteenth Amendment (Women's Rights Amendment), 109
North Korea, 134

Osborn, Ronald E., 25
Osborn, Sarah, 94

Palmer, Phoebe, 96
papacy, 112
Papyrus Berolinensis, 36
Park, Chung Hee, 132
Park, Hyung Kyu, 133
Park, Soon Kyung, 134, 152
Parsons, Sally, 96

peace
  concept of, 17–20, 118
  of God, 152
  in Hebrew Bible, 16
  theology of, 16, 118, 151
Peters, Brad, 63
Peters, Hugh, 91
Petroff, Elizabeth A., 63
Phoebe, 34
postmodernism, 15
preachers
  ancient Christian women, 22, 28, 30, 34,
  Asian women, 154
  Korean women, 118, 119
preaching
  in ancient Judaism, 25
  authenticity in, 117
  Christian, origins of, 23
  for consensus-building, 14
  contextual, 11, 13
  cross-cultural, 13
  evangelical, 95
  expository, 23
  goals of, 15
  history of, 112
  Holy Spirit in, 46, 113
  kerygmatic view of, 26, 27
  liturgical, 23
  medieval types, 52–55
  as mission, 46
  "new birth," 95
  New England, 89
  partnership in, 159–60
  political, 153
  Puritan, 90
  religious view of, 24
  on resurrection, 42–43, 46–47
  rhetorical view of, 25
  as subversive rhetoric, 74
  testimonial, 43–44
  transforming power of, 41
  university, 55

Presbyterian Board of Foreign Mission, 124
Princeton, 2, 166
Priscilla, 33
prophesy, 56
Prophets, biblical, 33
Puritanism, 88–95

Quakerism, 85–88

racism, 14, 76
Reformation, Protestant, 80
Reformed theology, 82
revivalism, 94
rhetoric, Greco-Roman, 25–26
Ricci, Carla, 32
Rim, Young Shin, 127, 132
Robert of Basevorn, 55
Rose, Lucy, 159
Russell, Letty, 116, 158

Salvation Army, 98
Schaab, Gloria, 20
Schreiter, Robert, 11, 13
Scranton, Mary F., 120
seminaries, 2–3
Serenus Cressy, 61
sermons
  as epiphany, 78
  medieval, genres of, 57
  monastic, 54
  university, 54
Shaw, Anna H., 98–99, 105–11
Shin, Eu Kyung, 132
Shinto, 129
Sino-Japanese War, 124, 129
Smith, Christine, 116
Smith, Robert H., 29
Sor Juana Inés de la Cruz. *See* Juana Inés de la Cruz, Sor
Spirit of God. *See* Holy Spirit
Stanton, Elizabeth Cady, 97, 108
Stevens, Durham White, 125

Sunohara, Suzuko, 156
synagogues, 23

Taehan Yeoja Kukmindang (People's Party of Korean Women), 131
Tennent, Gilbert, 92
Tennent, William, 92
Tertullian, 5
theological schools. *See* seminaries
Thompson, Marianna, 106
Thurston, Bonnie, 24
Tisdale, Leonora, 11
Torjesen, Karen J., 34

Underwood, Horace G., 120
Unitarian Church, 98
Urban Industrial Mission (UIM), 146

Wesley, John, 86–88
Whang, Esther, 127
White, Eugene E., 90
Whitefield, George, 92

Willard, Frances, 98, 108
Wilson, Woodrow, 109
Woman's Foreign Missionary Society, 107
women's rights movement, 97
  in Asia, 155
women's studies. *See* Feminist theory
women's suffrage movement, 108
worship, synagogal, 24
Wren, Brian, 76
Wright Cook, Charity, 94

Yaesukyo Jaekun Kyohoe (Reconstruction Church of Jesus), 141
Yale Divinity School, 2
Yeom, Ai Na, 130
Yi dynasty, 119
Yoo, Kwan Soon, 127

Ziel, Catherine, 116
Zinzendorf, Nikolaus, 86

www.ingramcontent.com/pod-product-compliance
Lightning Source LLC
Chambersburg PA
CBHW070316230426
43663CB00011B/2148